Springer Theses

Recognizing Outstanding Ph.D. Research

Aims and Scope

The series "Springer Theses" brings together a selection of the very best Ph.D. theses from around the world and across the physical sciences. Nominated and endorsed by two recognized specialists, each published volume has been selected for its scientific excellence and the high impact of its contents for the pertinent field of research. For greater accessibility to non-specialists, the published versions include an extended introduction, as well as a foreword by the student's supervisor explaining the special relevance of the work for the field. As a whole, the series will provide a valuable resource both for newcomers to the research fields described, and for other scientists seeking detailed background information on special questions. Finally, it provides an accredited documentation of the valuable contributions made by today's younger generation of scientists.

Theses are accepted into the series by invited nomination only and must fulfill all of the following criteria

- They must be written in good English.
- The topic should fall within the confines of Chemistry, Physics, Earth Sciences, Engineering and related interdisciplinary fields such as Materials, Nanoscience, Chemical Engineering, Complex Systems and Biophysics.
- The work reported in the thesis must represent a significant scientific advance.
- If the thesis includes previously published material, permission to reproduce this must be gained from the respective copyright holder.
- They must have been examined and passed during the 12 months prior to nomination.
- Each thesis should include a foreword by the supervisor outlining the significance of its content.
- The theses should have a clearly defined structure including an introduction accessible to scientists not expert in that particular field.

More information about this series at http://www.springer.com/series/8790

Zechao Li

Understanding-Oriented Multimedia Content Analysis

Doctoral Thesis accepted by
University of Chinese Academy of Sciences, Beijing, China

 Springer

Author
Dr. Zechao Li
Nanjing University of Science
   and Technology
Nanjing
China

Supervisor
Prof. Hanqing Lu
National Laboratory of Pattern Recognition,
   Institute of Automation
Chinese Academy of Sciences
Haidian District, Beijing
China

ISSN 2190-5053   ISSN 2190-5061   (electronic)
Springer Theses
ISBN 978-981-10-9941-0   ISBN 978-981-10-3689-7   (eBook)
DOI 10.1007/978-981-10-3689-7

Printed on acid-free paper

This Springer imprint is published by Springer Nature
The registered company is Springer Nature Singapore Pte Ltd.
The registered company address is: 152 Beach Road, #21-01/04 Gateway East, Singapore 189721, Singapore

This work is dedicated to my parents, and all my friends. Their support and encouragement keep me forward.

Supervisor's Foreword

Multimedia content analysis has attracted extensive attention in the multimedia and social media research communities. Its goal is to reveal the semantic information intelligently. Zechaos' Ph.D. work focuses on understanding-oriented multimedia content analysis from the low-level visual representation to the high-level semantic understanding. As a key member of my group, he made a number of significant contributions in his research work. He investigated advanced multimedia content analysis approaches and proposed understanding-oriented multimedia content analysis approaches, including data representation (feature selection and feature extraction), tag recommendation, and multimedia news services. He directly integrated the visual understanding and learning models into a unified framework. The visual understanding guides the model learning while the learned models improve the visual understanding. The inspiring idea of understanding-oriented multimedia content analysis has been recognized as opening up possibilities to challenging multimedia content and context understanding. The proposed structured subspace learning framework has been successfully generalized to social image understanding, (semi-) supervised classification and clustering. His work has brought in new thoughts and disruptive models in understanding multimedia data. I believe that this book will benefit researchers and students conducting research on multimedia computing and social multimedia analysis.

Beijing, China
January 2017

Prof. Hanqing Lu

Preface

The amount of today's multimedia contents explosively grows due to the popularization and rapid growth of digital mobile devices and social media tools. To efficiently analyze and understand the multimedia content is still a challenging task. Over the past decade, many advanced methods have been proposed in the literature, including a few books on this topic. However, there is no book offering a systematic introduction to multimedia content analysis towards an understanding-oriented approach. Therefore, this book will focus on a novel "understanding" framework for multimedia content interpretation. This book offers a systematic introduction to multimedia content analysis towards an understanding-oriented approach. It integrates the visual understanding and learning models into a unified framework, within which the visual understanding guides the model learning while the learned models improve the visual understanding. More specifically, the book presents multimedia content representations and analysis including feature selection, feature extraction, image tagging, user-oriented tag recommendation, and understanding-oriented multimedia applications. By providing the fundamental technologies and the state-of-the-art methods, this book will be of interest to graduate students and researchers working in the field computer vision and machine learning.

Chapter 1 introduces the background, challenges, and progresses of understanding-oriented multimedia content analysis. Chapters 2 and 3 introduce some works of understanding-oriented data representation. The personalized tag recommendation work is detailed in Chap. 4, followed by understanding-oriented multimedia news services in Chaps. 5 and 6. Chapter 7 concludes the book by summarizing the major points and identifying the future works.

Nanjing, China   Zechao Li
January 2017

Parts of this book have been published in the following articles:

- Zechao Li, Jing Liu, Jinhui Tang, Hanqing Lu. Robust Structured Subspace Learning for Data Representation. IEEE Trans. on Pattern Analysis and Machine Intelligence 37(10): 2085–2098, 2015.
- Zechao Li, Jinhui Tang. Unsupervised Feature Selection via Nonnegative Spectral Analysis and Redundancy Control. IEEE Trans. on Image Processing 24(12): 5343–5355, 2015.
- Zechao Li, Jing Liu, Yi Yang, Xiaofang Zhou, Hanqing Lu. Clustering-Guided Sparse Structural Learning for Unsupervised Feature Selection. IEEE Trans. Knowledge and Data Engineering 26(9): 2138–2150, 2014.
- Jing Liu, Zechao Li, Jinhui Tang, Yu Jiang and Hanqing Lu. Personalized Geo-Specific Tag Recommendation for Photos on Social Websites. IEEE Trans. on Multimedia 16(3): 588–600, 2014.
- Zechao Li, Jinhui Tang, Xueming Wang, Jing Liu, Hanqing Lu. Multimedia News Summarization in Search. ACM Trans. on Intelligent Systems and Technology 7(3): 33 (1–20), 2016.
- Zechao Li, Jing Liu, Meng Wang, Changsheng Xu, Hanqing Lu. Enhancing News Organization for Convenient Retrieval and Browsing. ACM Trans. on Multimedia Computing, Communications and Applications 10(1): 1 (1–20), 2013.
- Zechao Li, Jing Liu, Xiaobin Zhu and Hanqing Lu: Multi-modal Multi-correlation Person-centric News Retrieval. In ACM Conference on Information and Knowledge Management, 2010.

Acknowledgements

First of all, I would like to express my gratitude to my supervisor, Prof. Hanqing Lu, for his long-term support and help. Professor Lu provided a well-equipped and active working environment for me and gave me full freedom to investigate any research problem of interest. His valuable suggestions and criticism play a significant role on my way toward a full-fledged researcher.

I would also thank Prof. Changsheng Xu (IEEE Fellow), for his guidance during my visiting study at China-Singapore Institute of Digital Media (CSIDM). Professor Jing Liu is another guider of my research. She gave me many pieces of advice in my research methodologies and her revision on my papers that I achieved remarkable progress. Her passion for academic research is of great importance to my decision to start my research career. I also thank Prof. Jian Cheng, Jinqiao Wang, Yifan Zhang, Meng Wang, Jinhui Tang, and Richang Hong. They spent a lot of time with me and provided me with a great deal of assistance. Much of my academic inspiration stems from discussions with them.

In addition, thanks are due to my colleagues in Image and Video Analysis (IVA) lab, including Chao Liang, Yang Liu (Male), Chunjie Zhang, Bo Wang, Chuanghua Gui, Xiao Yu Zhang, Si Liu, Tianzhu Zhang, Xiaobin Zhu, Peng Li, Yu Jiang, Yang Liu (Female), Wei Fu, Biao Niu, Yong Li, Cong Leng, Ting Yuan, among others, my colleagues in MultiMedia Computing (MMC) group, including Jitao Sang, Weiqing Min, Lei Yu, Zhaoquan Yuan, Ming Yan, among others. They helped me a lot during these years in many aspects. I will never forget the joyful and rewarding days spent with them. I am also grateful to all my good friends, wherever they are. My thanks go to everyone who contributed to my progress and happiness.

This book was partially supported by the 973 Program of China (Project No. 2014CB347600), and the National Natural Science Foundation of China under Grant No. 61402228.

Contents

Notations

Throughout this book, the lowercase italic letters (i.e., i, j, n, etc.) and the uppercase italic letters (i.e., A, B, M, etc.) denote scalars, while the bold uppercase characters (i.e, $\mathbf{W}, \mathbf{X}$, etc.) and the bold lowercase characters (i.e, $\mathbf{a}, \mathbf{x}$, etc.) are utilized to denote matrices and vectors, respectively. For any matrix $\mathbf{A}$, $\mathbf{a}^i$ means the i-th column vector of $\mathbf{A}$, $\mathbf{a}_i$ means the i-th row vector of $\mathbf{A}$, A_{ij} denotes the (i, j)-element of $\mathbf{A}$ and $\text{Tr}[\mathbf{A}]$ is the trace of $\mathbf{A}$ if $\mathbf{A}$ is square. $\mathbf{A}^T$ denotes the transposed matrix of $\mathbf{A}$. The Frobenius norm of a matrix $\mathbf{A} \in \mathbb{R}^{m \times n}$ is defined as $\|\mathbf{A}\|_F^2 = \sum_{i=1}^m \sum_{j=1}^n A_{ij}^2 = \text{Tr}[\mathbf{A}^T\mathbf{A}]$. The $\ell_{2,p}$-norm ($p \in (0, 1]$) of $\mathbf{A}$ is defined as

$$\|\mathbf{A}\|_{2,p} = \left(\sum_{i=1}^r \left(\sqrt{\sum_{j=1}^t A_{ij}^2} \right)^p \right)^{\frac{1}{p}} = \left(\sum_{i=1}^r \|\mathbf{a}_i\|_2^p \right)^{\frac{1}{p}}. \tag{1}$$

Note that in practice, $\|\mathbf{a}^i\|_2$ could be close to zero. For this case, we can follow the traditional regularization way and define $D_{ii} = \frac{1}{\|\mathbf{a}^i\|_2 + \varepsilon}$, where ε is very small constant. When $\varepsilon \to 0$, it is easy to verify that $\frac{1}{\|\mathbf{a}^i\|_2 + \varepsilon}$ approximates $\frac{1}{\|\mathbf{a}^i\|_2}$. Furthermore, let $\mathbf{I}_m$ denote the identity matrix in $\mathbb{R}^{m \times m}$.

Chapter 1
Introduction

Abstract Multimedia content analysis is to understand the semantic information of multimedia data (such as text, image, audio, video, etc.). It is reasonable and necessary to develop understanding-oriented multimedia content analysis and incorporate model learning and understanding into a unified framework. In this chapter, we will first present an overview of multimedia content analysis and understanding, introduce the challenges and progresses in this field, and then describe the specifications of understanding-oriented multimedia content analysis. Finally, we give the organization of this book.

1.1 Multimedia Analysis and Understanding

With the popularity of intelligent devices (e.g., smart phones) and social media websites (e.g., flickr.com, youTube.com, etc.), multimedia data, especially images and videos, have been explosively increasing and playing an important role in our daily work and life. Taking facebook.com as an example, it reported in November 2013 that there are about 350 million images uploaded daily. There are 100 h of video uploaded to YouTube every minute, resulting in an estimate of more than 2 billion videos totally by the end of 2013. This significantly extends the scope and application areas of multimedia. For example, Tencents free messaging and calling tool, Wechat, has attracted more than 300 million users in less than 2 years, which is tending to replace the traditional short message service (SMS). To say the least, we are really now living in a media world. Thereupon, it is necessary to develop approaches to intelligently analyze and understand the massive multimedia data.

Multimedia content analysis and understanding is to analyze and understand multimedia data (such as image, video, audio, graphic, etc.) using approaches from machine learning, artificial intelligence, and pattern recognition communities [7, 13]. In literatures, multimedia content analysis and understanding is deemed as a cross-disciplinary research area concerning with the intersection of image processing, computer vision, machine learning, artificial intelligence, pattern recognition, data mining, etc. It involves with techniques in visual/auditory physiology, signal processing, computer vision, information retrieval, etc. [43]. As shown in Fig. 1.1,

© Springer Nature Singapore Pte Ltd. 2017
Z. Li, *Understanding-Oriented Multimedia Content Analysis*, Springer Theses,
DOI 10.1007/978-981-10-3689-7_1

Fig. 1.1 Illustration of
multimedia content analysis
and understanding

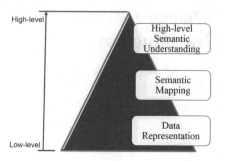

there are usually three steps for multimedia content analysis and understanding, i.e., data representation, semantic mapping, and semantic applications. To better implement these three steps, it is necessary to analyze the characters of multimedia data.

- **Big** data. Multimedia is increasingly becoming the "biggest big data" as the most important and valuable source for insights and information. It covers from everyones experiences to everything happening in the world. As such, multimedia big data is spurring on tremendous amounts of research and development of related technologies and applications.
- **Social** data. Currently, multimedia data are mainly created and uploaded by users. Users can tag and commend on the uploaded multimedia data. Besides, there are rich metadata associated with multimedia data in the social sharing websites, such as EXIF, GPS, user, group, etc. That is, there are rich social context information associated with multimedia data.
- **Heterogenous** data. Multimedia data contain multiple types of data, such as text, image, audio, video, etc. The same semantic can be described by data from different modalities. Essentially, data from different modalities have different properties, and they are heterogenous. Besides, social multimedia data have more heterogenous information, such as GPS information, user-provided tags, users' comments, and the group information.

By considering the above characters, researchers have devoted substantial attention to developing methods for multimedia content analysis and understanding, such as data presentation [1, 18, 35, 40, 52, 55], metric learning [15, 21, 25, 39, 49], hashing [5, 30, 47, 48, 54], tag refinement and assignment [2, 22, 28, 50], semantic segmentation [26, 27, 32, 33, 36], and retrieval [6, 23, 45]. Thanks to the wide prevalence of multimedia data and the increasing demands for multimedia services, there has been a growing number of research on multimedia analysis and understanding, evidenced by both the volume of papers produced each year.

In spite of this, it is challenging to intelligently understand the multimedia content. It is well known that multimedia data are usually represented by the low-level features, such as images are described by the low-level visual features. There exists the well-known "Semantic Gap" [8], which is defined as the difference between the information that one can extract from the visual data and the interpretation that the same data have for a user in a given situation. Besides, it is a challenge that how to uncover a better representation for multimedia data.

- Multimedia Data Representation. Multimedia data can be described by a variety of visual features, which are often quite different from each other. The dimension of data feature space is becoming increasingly large. It is inevitable to introduce noisy and/or redundant features. The effectiveness and efficiency of learning methods drop exponentially as the dimensionality increases, which is commonly referred to as the "curse of dimensionality" [16]. Therefore, it is a fundamental problem to find a suitable representation of high-dimensional data [4], which can enhance the performance of numerous tasks, such as multimedia analysis.
- Semantic Mapping. Due to the well-known semantic gap, it is challenging to identify better semantic mappings from the low-level feature space to the high-level semantic space. On the other hand, social multimedia data have rich context information, such as user-provided tags, users' descriptions, users' comments, GPS information, EXIF information, etc. It is beneficial for reducing the semantic gap to explore social context information, which can help to learn better semantic mappings.
- Multimedia Understanding. The ultimate goal is to understand the semantic information of multimedia data according to the corresponding application. With the proliferation of multimedia data, many interesting multimedia applications have been designed, such as mobile product retrieval, clothing retrieval [11, 29], multimedia news retrieval, recommendation [17, 37, 38], etc. Therefore, we should develop understanding-oriented approaches for the applications, which may help to attract more users and bring in bigger gains.

1.2   Challenges and Progresses

Although many previous methods have been proposed to address the problems of multimedia content analysis and understanding, there are some challenges for multimedia understanding and potential applications.

Multimedia Big Data. Multimedia is increasingly becoming the "biggest big dat," which brings in new challenges. First, the traditional methods trained on a small-scale training set may cease to be effective for the multimedia big data. Second, for small data, it takes acceptable time to learn models. Unfortunately, it may take much time to deal with the multimedia big data. Consequently, how to efficiently and effectively deal with multimedia big data is important, and there is also an abysmal lack of new methods adaptively to multimedia big data.

Understanding-oriented Representation. Traditional features of multimedia data are extracted independent from the follow-up understanding tasks. From the perspective of representation, the features of multimedia data are always noisy and/or redundant, and the dimension of features is becoming increasingly high. For the hand-crafted features, people manually design a feature extraction pipeline by the guidance based on the priors. For the deep features, features are extracted using the deep networks pre-trained on the irrelevant data. As a consequence, data representation should be identified by selection or extracting understanding-oriented features for the follow-up multimedia tasks. How to discover the semantic representations and develop understanding-oriented feature learning approaches become critical in multimedia content analysis.

Social Multimedia Data. Nowadays, multimedia data are almost generated and consumed under social media circumstances, which are referred to as social multimedia [43]. The user-generated mechanism gives rise to the issues of low quality, due to their diverse background, users have different preferences. That is to say, the user-provided information is often subjective, noisy, diverse, and incomplete. Many multimedia understanding tasks suffer from these characteristics. How to handle the low-quality data becomes critical in multimedia analysis and understanding. Besides, social multimedia is interconnected. For example, images are uploaded and tagged by users, and may grouped differently by various users. These interconnected information should be considered for effective social multimedia analysis and understanding.

Heterogeneous Data. Multimedia data usually include textual, visual, and audio data. It is very common that the same semantic concept is described by multimodal data, e.g., text, image, and video. Moreover, emerging social media services have also given birth to multimedia data with novel modality, such as location data in check-in services. The heterogeneous data with different modalities bring in challenges to multimedia analysis and understanding. How to design solutions to model the heterogeneous data is also worth studying.

To address the above challenges, many researchers have devoted much effort to new solutions. In the following, we highlight some key tasks to briefly introduce the progresses.

Data representation is the preliminary problem in multimedia content analysis and understanding. Some methods have been proposed to learn understanding-oriented representation, including feature selection and extraction. For unsupervised feature selection, clustering is utilized to explore discriminative information, which is helpful for understanding-oriented feature subset selection [9, 42, 44, 51]. Some feature selection methods have been proposed for multimedia understanding tasks, such as image annotation [40] and video semantic recognition [12, 14]. In addition, data representation learned by exploring social context information has also attracted extensive attentions [1, 10, 43].

Tag refinement and assignment is the fundamental problem in multimedia content analysis and understanding, of which the task is to estimate the relevance between tags and samples. Image annotation is a classic task that trains annotation models depending on a small-scale manually-labeled data [3, 24, 41]. With the proliferation of social multimedia data, multimedia data are often associated with user-provided tags. However, the noisy or incomplete correspondence between multimedia data and tags prohibits them from being leveraged for precise multimedia retrieval and effective management. Thus, social multimedia tag refinement and assignment has attracted increasing attention [20, 22, 28, 31, 46, 53]. Tang et al. [46] proposed a kNN-sparse graph-based approach to remove most of the semantically unrelated links among the data. For social images, user-provided tags are often incomplete, subjective, and noisy. To improve the quality of tags, tag refinement is to fine the original tags of images by complementing relevant tags and removing the irrelevant or noisy tags. For new images, tag assignment is to assign tags according to the estimated relevance between images and tags.

Multimedia applications based on understanding indicate the means of exploiting the collective knowledge for multimedia content understanding and the task-specific knowledge. Many interesting multimedia applications have been developed based on understanding the multimedia data, such as tag recommendation, cloth retrieval, logo retrieval, product recommendation, advertisement recommendation, multimedia news services, and so on. Liu et al. [34] proposed a personal tag recommendation method by incorporating image understanding, and the user preference and geolocation information discovering. Clothing retrieval [29] is proposed to understand the content of clothes images by proposing a hierarchical deep search framework. Multimedia news services try to understand the multimedia news data according to the principle of the Five Ws: Who, Where, When, What, and Why. And multimodal data such as text, images, and videos are jointly explored to provide users vivid and rich results. Thanks to the theoretical progresses to deal with noise, sparsity, and heterogeneity, multimedia technologies have been successfully applied to problems like mobile and wearable computing, disease prevention, and clinical treatment. There will be more novel multimedia applications, which need to understand the multimedia content first.

1.3 Understanding-Oriented Multimedia Content Analysis

Although many researchers have devoted much time and energy to the goal of multimedia understanding and proposed many approaches to promote the development of multimedia computing technology, multimedia content analysis and understanding still remains open. Especially, the emergence of social multimedia has brought new challenges as well as opportunities.

The goal of multimedia content analysis is to uncover the semantic information of multimedia content, i.e., multimedia content understanding. Based on the understanding, we develop new applications to provide convenience in people daily work and life. The property of social multimedia offers a new solution perspective for multimedia content understanding. As a consequence, multimedia content analysis approaches should be proposed centering on the understanding goal. That is to say, understanding-oriented methods are desired for multimedia content analysis: (I) Data representation is learned with the guide of understanding. Understanding-oriented feature learning (including feature selection and) tries to explore the high-level semantic information to guide the learning procedure. (II) Understanding-oriented mapping is to learn a better mapping function that can well and easily predict the semantic labels of data based on the representations.

(III) Understanding-oriented multimedia applications provide convenient manners for users to quickly master the desired information. Social multimedia provides much helpful information for understanding the multimedia data, which should be considered in the understanding-oriented multimedia content analysis. Besides, understanding the personalized demands is critical to most multimedia allocations.

Therefore, in this book, we introduce our recent work on understanding-oriented multimedia content analysis. Note that this is the first understanding-oriented schema for the multimedia content analysis task. Specifically, we address three basic tasks in understanding-oriented multimedia content analysis as follows:

- **Understanding-oriented Data Representation**: understanding-oriented feature selection and feature extraction [19];
- **Personalized Tag Recommendation**: understanding-oriented tag recommendation by uncovering user preference and geo-location information;
- **Understanding-oriented Multimedia News Services**: understanding-oriented multimedia news applications including retrieval and summarization.

1.4   Organization of This Book

The book contains totally seven chapters. This chapter is introduction. Chapters 2 and 3 introduce our work on understanding-oriented data representation. The proposed personalized tag recommendation work is detailed in Chap. 4, followed with understanding-oriented multimedia news services in Chaps. 5 and 6. Chapter 7 concludes the book by summarizing the major points and identifying the future works.

Chapter 2: Understanding-oriented unsupervised feature selection. Many pattern analysis and data mining problems have witnessed high-dimensional data represented by a large number of features. In practice, not all the features are important and discriminative, since most of them are often correlated or redundant to each other, and sometimes noisy. These high-dimensional features may bring some disadvantages, such as over-fitting, low efficiency, and poor performance, to the traditional learning models. Therefore, it is necessary and challenging to select an optimal feature subset from high-dimensional data to remove irrelevant and redundant features, increase learning accuracy, and improve results comprehensibility. Besides, it is worth uncovering the discriminative information in the unsupervised scenario to guide the learning of understanding-oriented feature subsets.

Chapter 3: Understanding-oriented feature learning. It is a fundamental problem to find a suitable representation of high-dimensional data. Different from feature selection, feature learning is to learn an appropriate representation of data by uncovering a latent subspace rather than find a better subset. To learn a understanding-oriented feature representation, we proposed to learn an underlying subspace by integrating image understanding and feature learning into a joint learning framework. The learned subspace is adopted as an intermediate space to reduce the semantic gap between the low-level visual features and the high-level semantics.

Chapter 4: Personalized tag recommendation. Social tagging becomes increasingly important to organize and search large-scale community-contributed photos on social websites. To facilitate generating high-quality social tags, tag recommendation by automatically assigning relevant tags to photos draws particular research interest. In this chapter, we focus on the personalized tag recommendation task and try to identify user-preferred, geo-location-specific as well as semantically relevant tags for a photo by leveraging rich contexts of the freely available community-contributed photos.

Chapter 5: Understanding-oriented multimedia news retrieval. To facilitate users to access news quickly and comprehensively, the news elements of "Where", "Who", "What", and "When" are enhanced. Understanding-oriented multimedia news retrieval system is developed to focus on different news elements. Matrix factorization models are proposed to mine the underlying relationships between news persons and news documents, as well as news geo-locations and news documents. News images are also explored to enhance the relationships among news persons, and enrich news documents.

Chapter 6: Understanding-oriented multimedia news summarization. It is a necessary but challenging task to relieve users from the proliferative news information and allow them to quickly and comprehensively master the information of the whats and hows that are happening in the world every day. A multimedia news summarization system is developed to uncover the underlying topics among query-related news information and threads the news events within each topic to generate a query-related brief overview. One representative image is also selected to visualize each topic as a complement to the text information. Finally, a friendly interface is designed to present users with the hierarchical summarization of their required news information.

References

1. Baecchi, C., Uricchio, T., Bertinia, M., Bimbo, A.D.: A multimodal feature learning approach for sentiment analysis of social network multimedia. Multimed. Tools Appl. **75**(5), 2507–2525 (2016)
2. Ballan, L., Bertinia, M., Serrab, G., Bimbo, A.D.: A data-driven approach for tag refinement and localization in web videos. Comput. Vis. Image Underst. **140**, 58–67 (2015)
3. Barnard, K., Duygulu, P., Forsyth, D., de Freitas, N., Blei, D.M., Jordan, M.I.: Matching words and pictures. J. Mach. Learn. Res. **3**, 1107–1135 (2003)
4. Belhumeur, P.N., Hespanha, J.P., Wu, X., Kriegman, D.J.: Eigenfaces vs. fisherfaces: recognition using class specific linear projection. IEEE Trans. Pattern Anal. Mach. Intell. **19**(7), 711–720 (1997)
5. Cao, L., Li, Z., Mu, Y., Chang, S.F.: Submodular video hashing: a unified framework towards video pooling and indexing. In: Proceedings of ACM International Conference on Multimedia, pp. 299–308 (2012)
6. Datta, R., Joshi, D., Li, J., Wang, J.Z.: Image retrieval: ideas, influences, and trends of the new age. ACM Comput. Surv. **40**(2), 5:1–5:60 (2006)
7. Divakaran, A.: Multimedia Content Analysis-Theory and Applications. Springer, New York (2008)

8. Dorai, C., Venkatesh, S.: Bridging the semantic gap with computational media aesthetics. IEEE MultiMed. **10**(2), 15–17 (2003)
9. Du, L., Shen, Z., Li, X., Zhou, P., Shen, Y.D.: Local and global discriminative learning for unsupervised feature selection. In: Proceedings of IEEE International Conference on Data Mining, pp. 131–140 (2013)
10. Fang, C., Jin, H., Yang, J., Lin, Z.: Collaborative feature learning from social media. In: Proceedings of IEEE Conference on Computer Vision and Pattern Recognition, pp. 577–585 (2015)
11. Fu, J., Wang, J., Li, Z., Xu, M., Lu, H.: Efficient clothing retrieval with semantic-preserving visual phrases. In: Proceedings of Asian Conference on Computer Vision, pp. 420–431 (2012)
12. Fu, W., Wang, J., Li, Z., Lu, H., Ma, S.: Learning semantic motion patterns for dynamic scenes by improved sparse topical coding. In: Proceedings of IEEE International Conference on Multimedia and Expo, pp. 296–301 (2012)
13. Gong, Y., Xu, W.: Machine Learning for Multimedia Content Analysis. Springer, New York (2007)
14. Han, Y., Yang, Y., Ma, Z., Yan, Y., Sebe, N., Zhou, X.: Semisupervised feature selection via spline regression for video semantic recognition. IEEE Trans. Neural Netw. Learn. Syst. **26**(2), 252–264 (2015)
15. Hoi, S.C.H., Liu, W., Chang, S.F.: Semi-supervised distance metric learning for collaborative image retrieval. In: Proceedings of IEEE Conference on Computer Vision and Pattern Recognition (2008)
16. Hughes, G.: On the mean accuracy of statistical pattern recognizers. IEEE Trans. Inf. Theory **14**(1), 55–63 (1968)
17. Jiang, Y., Liu, J., Zhang, X., Li, Z., Lu, H.: TCRec: product recommendation via exploiting social-trust network and product category information. In: Proceedings of International World Wide Web Conference, pp. 233–234 (2013)
18. Jin, L., Gao, S., Li, Z., Tang, J.: Hand-crafted features or machine learnt features? together they improve RGB-D object recognition. In: Proceedings of IEEE International Symposium on Multimedia, pp. 311–319 (2014)
19. Li, Z.: Understanding-oriented visual representation learning. In: Proceedings of International Conference on Internet Multimedia Computing and Service, pp. 80:1–80:3 (2015)
20. Li, Z., Tang, J.: Deep matrix factorization for social image tag refinement and assignment. In: Proceedings of IEEE International Workshop on Multimedia Signal Processing, pp. 1–6 (2015)
21. Li, Z., Tang, J.: Weakly supervised deep metric learning for community-contributed image retrieval. IEEE Trans. Multimed. **17**(11), 1989–1999 (2015)
22. Li, Z., Tang, J.: Weakly supervised deep matrix factorization for social image understanding. IEEE Trans. Image Process. **26**(1), 276–288 (2017)
23. Li, Z., Liu, J., Lu, H.: Sparse constraint nearest neighbour selection in cross-media retrieval. In: Proceedings of IEEE International Conference on Image Processing, pp. 1465–1468 (2010)
24. Li, Z., Liu, J., Zhu, X., Liu, T., Lu, H.: Image annotation using multi-correlation probabilistic matrix factorization. In: Proceedings of ACM Conference on Multimedia, pp. 1187–1190 (2010)
25. Li, Z., Liu, J., Jiang, Y., Tang, J., Lu, H.: Low rank metric learning for social image retrieval. In: Proceedings of ACM International Conference on Multimedia, pp. 853–856 (2012)
26. Li, Y., Liu, J., Li, Z., Liu, Y., Lu, H.: Object co-segmentation via discriminative low rank matrix recovery. In: Proceedings of ACM International Conference on Multimedia, pp. 749–752 (2013)
27. Li, Y., Liu, J., Li, Z., Lu, H., Ma, S.: Object co-segmentation via salient and common regions discovery. Neurocomputing **172**, 225–234 (2016)
28. Li, X., Uricchio, T., Ballan, L., Bertini, M., Snoek, C., Bimbo, A.D.: Socializing the semantic gap: a comparative survey on image tag assignment, refinement, and retrieval. ACM Comput. Surv. **49**(1), 14:1–14:39 (2016)
29. Lin, K., Yang, H.F., Liu, K.H., Hsiao, J.H., Chen, C.S.: Rapid clothing retrieval via deep learning of binary codes and hierarchical search. In: Proceedings of ACM International Conference on Multimedia Retrieval, pp. 499–502 (2015)

30. Liu, W., Zhang, T.: Multimedia hashing and networking. IEEE Multimed. **23**(3), 75–79 (2016)
31. Liu, D., Hua, X.S., Yang, L., Wang, M., Zhang, H.J.: Tag ranking. In: Proceedings of International World Wide Web Conference, pp. 351–360 (2009)
32. Liu, Y., Liu, J., Li, Z., Lu, H.: Noisy tag alignment with image regions. In: Proceedings of IEEE International Conference on Multimedia and Expo, pp. 266–271 (2012)
33. Liu, Y., Liu, J., Li, Z., Tang, J., Lu, H.: Weakly-supervised dual clustering for image semantic segmentation. In: Proceedings of IEEE Conference on Computer Vision and Pattern Recognition, pp. 2075–2082 (2013)
34. Liu, J., Li, Z., Tang, J., Jiang, Y., Lu, H.: Personalized geo-specific tag recommendation for photos on social websites. IEEE Trans. Multimed. **16**(3), 588–600 (2014)
35. Liu, B., Liu, J., Li, Z., Lu, H.: Image representation learning by deep appearance and spatial coding. In: Proceedings of Asian Conference on Computer Vision, pp. 659–672 (2014)
36. Liu, Y., Liu, J., Li, Z., Lu, H.: Boosted miml method for weakly-supervised image semantic segmentation. Multimed. Tools Appl. **74**(2), 543–559 (2015)
37. Liu, J., Jiang, J., Li, Z., Zhang, X., Lu, H.: Domain-sensitive recommendation with user-item subgroup analysis. IEEE Trans. Knowl. Data Eng. **28**(4), 939–950 (2016)
38. Liu, J., Jiang, J., Li, Z., Zhang, X., Lu, H.: Domain-sensitive recommendation with user-item subgroup analysis. In: Proceedings of IEEE International Conference on Data Engineering, pp. 1466–1467 (2016)
39. Lu, J., Wang, G., Deng, W., Moulin, P., Zhou, J.: Multi-manifold deep metric learning for image set classification. In: Proceedings of IEEE Conference on Computer Vision and Pattern Recognition, pp. 1137–1145 (2015)
40. Ma, Z., Nie, F., Yang, Y., Uijlings, J., Sebe, N., Hauptmann, A.: Discriminating joint feature analysis for multimedia data understanding. IEEE Trans. Multimed. **14**(4), 1021–1030 (2012)
41. Makadia, A., Pavlovic, V., Kumar, S.: Baselines for image annotation. Int. J. Comput. Vis. **90**(1), 88–105 (2010)
42. Qian, M., Zhai, C.: Robust unsupervised feature selection. In: Proceedings of International Joint Conference on Artificial Intelligence, pp. 1621–1627 (2014)
43. Sang, J.: User-Centric Social Multimedia Computing. Springer, Berlin (2014)
44. Shi, L., Du, L., Shen, Y.D.: Robust spectral learning for unsupervised feature selection. In: Proceedings of IEEE International Conference on Data Mining, pp. 977–982 (2014)
45. Smeulders, A.W.M., Worring, M., Santini, S., Gupta, A., Jain, R.: Content-based image retrieval at the end of the early years. IEEE Trans. Pattern Anal. Mach. Intell. **22**(12), 1349–1380 (2010)
46. Tang, J., Hong, R., Yan, S., Chua, T.S., Qi, G.J., Jain, R.: Image annotation by KNN-sparse graph-based label propagation over noisily tagged web images. ACM Trans. Intell. Syst. Technol. **2**(2), 14 (2011)
47. Tang, J., Li, Z., Wang, M., Zhao, R.: Neighborhood discriminant hashing for large-scale image retrieval. IEEE Trans. Image Process. **24**(9), 2827–2840 (2015)
48. Tang, J., Li, Z., Zhang, L., Huang, Q.: Semantic-aware hashing for social image retrieval. In: Proceedings of ACM International Conference on Multimedia Retrieval, pp. 483–486 (2015)
49. Wang, F., Jiang, S., Herranz, L., Huang, Q.: Improving image distance metric learning by embedding semantic relations. In: Proceedings of Pacific-Rim Conference on Multimedia, pp. 424–434 (2012)
50. Wang, M., Ni, B., Hua, X.S., Chua, T.S.: Assistive tagging: a survey of multimedia tagging with human-computer joint exploration. ACM Comput. Surv. **44**(4), 25:1–25:24 (2012)
51. Yang, Y., Shen, H.T., Ma, Z., Huang, Z., Zhou, X.: $\ell_{2,1}$-norm regularized discriminative feature selection for unsupervised learning. In: Proceedings of International Joint Conference on Artificial Intelligence, pp. 1589–1594 (2011)
52. Yang, X., Zhang, T., Xu, C.: Cross-domain feature learning in multimedia. IEEE Trans. Multimed. **17**(1), 64–78 (2015)
53. Zhu, G., Yan, S., Ma, Y.: Image tag refinement towards low-rank, content-tag prior and error sparsity. In: Proceedings of ACM Conference on Multimedia, pp. 461–470 (2010)

54. Zhu, X., Huang, Z., Cheng, H., Cui, J., Shen, H.T.: Sparse hashing for fast multimedia search. ACM Trans. Inf. Syst. **31**(2), 9 (2013)
55. Zou, H., Du, J.X., Zhai, C.M., Wang, J.: Deep learning and shared representation space learning based cross-modal multimedia retrieval. In: Proceedings of International Conference on Intelligent Computing, pp. 322–331 (2016)

Chapter 2
Understanding-Oriented Unsupervised Feature Selection

Abstract In many image processing and pattern recognition problems, visual contents of images are currently described by high-dimensional features, which are often redundant and noisy. Toward this end, we propose two novel understanding-oriented unsupervised feature selection schemes. For exploring discriminative information, nonnegative spectral analysis is proposed to learn more accurate cluster labels of the input images. For feature selection, the hidden structure shared by different features and the redundancy among different features are explored, respectively. Row-wise sparse models with the $\ell_{2,p}$-norm ($0 < p \leq 1$) are leveraged to make the proposed models suitable for feature selection and robust to noise.

2.1 Introduction

In many image processing and multimedia problems, images are usually represented by high-dimensional visual features, such as local features (such as SIFT [28]). In practice, it is well known that all features that characterize images are not usually equal important for a given task and most of them are often correlated or redundant to each other, and sometimes noisy [13]. Besides, it is hard to discriminate images of different classes from each other in the high-dimensional space of visual features. That is, these high-dimensional features may bring some disadvantages, such as over-fitting, low efficiency, and poor performance, to the traditional learning models [42]. As a consequence, it is necessary and challenging to select an optimal feature subset from high-dimensional image to remove irrelevant and redundant features, increase learning accuracy, and improve the performance comprehensibility.

The task of selecting the "best" feature subset is known as *feature selection*, which is an important and widely used method. The importance of feature selection in improving both the efficiency and accuracy of image processing is three-hold. First, it can result in computationally efficient algorithms since the dimensionality of selected feature subset is much lower. Second, it enables to provide a better understanding of the underlying structure of the data. Finally, it can improve the

---

© 2017 IEEE. Reprinted, with permission, from Li et al. [25], and Li and Tang [26].

© Springer Nature Singapore Pte Ltd. 2017
Z. Li, *Understanding-Oriented Multimedia Content Analysis*, Springer Theses,
DOI 10.1007/978-981-10-3689-7_2

performance by removing noisy and redundant features. Therefore, many feature selection methods have been proposed and studied [5, 17, 19, 21, 27, 33, 34, 39, 47]. These algorithms can be categorized as supervised algorithms, semi-supervised algorithms and unsupervised algorithms, according to the way of utilizing label information. Since the discriminative information is encoded in the labels, supervised and semi-supervised approaches can generally achieve good performance. However, the labels of data annotated by human experts are typically expensive and time-consuming and there is usually no shortage of unlabeled data in many real-world applications. Consequently, it is quite promising and demanding to develop unsupervised feature selection techniques, which may be more practical.

In unsupervised feature selection, features are selected based on a frequently used criterion which evaluates features by their capability of keeping certain properties of the data, such as the data distribution, the redundancy of features, or local structure. The whole features contain necessary features (which are essential for the task), redundant features (which are useful but dependent on each other. Thus, not all of the redundant features are not necessary.), noisy features (which degrade the performance), and indifferent features (which do not matter for the task). The goal of feature selection is to select necessary features, discard noisy or indifferent features, and control the use of redundant features. The previous methods do not jointly consider these four features. Besides, they fail to exploit discriminative information from data. On the other hand, due to the absence of labels that would guide the search for discriminative features, unsupervised feature selection is considered as a much harder problem [14], which evaluates feature relevance by their capability of keeping certain properties of the data.

In light of all these factors, we propose a novel understanding-oriented unsupervised feature selection framework to explore discriminative information from data and the latent structural analysis, select necessary features, discard noisy or indifferent features and control the use of redundant features simultaneously. Due to the importance of discriminative information, it is necessary and beneficial to exploit discriminative information in unsupervised feature selection. As a consequence, we propose a novel nonnegative spectral analysis scheme to uncover discriminative information by learning more accurate cluster indicators. With nonnegative and orthogonality constraints, the learned cluster indicators are much closer to the ideal ones and can be readily utilized to obtain more accurate cluster labels, which can be utilized to guide feature selection. The joint learning of the cluster labels and feature selection matrix enables to select the most discriminative features. For the sake of feature selection, the predictive matrix is constrained to be sparse in rows, which is formulated as a general $\ell_{2,p}$-norm ($0 < p \leq 1$) minimization term. Furthermore, on one hand, the features are correlated as they jointly reflect the semantic components. It is reasonable to assume that the features share a common structure in a low-dimensional space. The cluster indicators are predicted by the original features together with the features in the low-dimensional subspace. The latent structural analysis can uncover the feature correlations to make the results more reliable. On the other hand, the redundancy between features is explicitly exploited to control the redundancy of the selected features. The proposed problems are formulated

as optimization problems with well-defined objective functions. To solve the proposed problems, simple yet efficient iterative algorithms are proposed. Extensive
experiments are conducted on face data, handwritten digit data, document data, and
biomedical data. The experimental results show that compared with several representative algorithms, the proposed approaches achieve encouraging performance. Most
of the work in this chapter has been published in [25, 26].

2.2 Related Work

According to the availability of label information, feature selection algorithms can be
classified into three broad categories: supervised, semi-supervised, and unsupervised
approaches. More details can be obtained in [19, 48]. In this section, we will elaborate
unsupervised feature selection methods.

From the perspective of selection strategy, the unsupervised feature selection
approaches can be broadly categorized as the *filter*, *wrapper*, and *embedded* ones.
For filter methods [9, 17, 30, 47], a proxy measure is utilized to score a feature subset
instead of the error rate. The simplest measure may be the variance score with the
assumption that larger variance means better representation ability. However, there is
no reason to assume that these features are useful for discriminating data in different
classes. Laplacian Score [17] selects features which can best reflect the underlying
manifold structure. However, the redundancy among features is not exploited, which
may result in redundant features and compromise the performance. Filters are usually
less computationally intensive than wrappers, but produce a feature set which is
not tuned to a specific type of predictive model. Wrapper methods [14, 42, 46]
score feature subsets using use a predictive model. They wrap feature search around
the learning algorithms and utilize the learned results to select features. Clustering
is a commonly utilized learning algorithm [5, 14, 46]. The clusterability of the
input data points is measured by analyzing the spectral properties of the affinity
matrix. MCFS [5] uses a two-step spectral regression approach to unsupervised
feature selection. Embedded methods [10, 23] perform feature selection as a part of
the model construction process, which fall in between filters and wrappers in terms
of computational complexity.

State-of-the-art algorithms exploit discriminative information and feature correlation to select features [12, 27, 35, 38, 43]. Nonnegative Discriminative Feature
Selection (NDFS) [27] proposes nonnegative spectral clustering to guide feature
selection and selects features over the whole feature space. In [12], a global and a
set of locally linear regression model are integrated into a unified learning framework. Qian et al. [35] extended NDFS to handle outliers or noise data. The graph
embedding and sparse spectral regression are improved in [38]. However, the above
methods do not explicitly control the redundancy between features, which may lead
to redundancy existing in the selected features.

Some methods have been designed to consider the dependency between
features. In [45], the redundancy between selected features is removed using a

correlation-based filter. Peng et al. [34] proposed a mutual information-based two-stage feature selection approach to choose features with least redundancy by minimizing the mutual information among the selected features. A multilayer perceptron neural network is designed for feature selection with consideration a measure of linear dependency to control the redundancy in [6]. However, they only focus on considering the dependency between features, and fail to select discriminative features. In this work, we select features by considering the dependency between features and the discriminant information simultaneously. The most discriminant features with controlled redundancy are selected.

Different from previous work, the proposed framework exploits nonnegative spectral analysis, the underlying structure analysis and explicitly controls the redundancy between features in a joint framework for unsupervised feature learning. One general sparse model with $\ell_{2,p}$-norm ($0 < p \leq 1$) is adopted to learn a better sparsity matrix.

2.3 Clustering-Guided Sparse Structural Learning for Unsupervised Feature Selection

Assume that we have n samples $\mathbb{X} = \{\mathbf{x}_i\}_{i=1}^n$. Let $\mathbf{X} = [\mathbf{x}_1, \ldots, \mathbf{x}_n]$ denote the data matrix, in which $\mathbf{x}_i \in \mathbb{R}^d$ is the feature descriptor of the ith sample. Suppose these n samples are sampled from c classes. Denote $\mathbf{Y} = [\mathbf{y}_1, \ldots, \mathbf{y}_n]^T \in \{0, 1\}^{n \times c}$, where $\mathbf{y}_i \in \{0, 1\}^{c \times 1}$ is the cluster indicator vector for $\mathbf{x}_i$. That is, $Y_{ij} = 1$ if the sample $\mathbf{x}_i$ is assigned to the jth cluster, and $Y_{ij} = 0$ otherwise. The scaled cluster indicator matrix $\mathbf{F}$ is defined:

$$\mathbf{F} = [\mathbf{f}_1, \mathbf{f}_2, \ldots, \mathbf{f}_c] = \mathbf{Y}(\mathbf{Y}^T \mathbf{Y})^{-\frac{1}{2}}, \tag{2.1}$$

It turns out that

$$\mathbf{F}^T \mathbf{F} = (\mathbf{Y}^T \mathbf{Y})^{-\frac{1}{2}} \mathbf{Y}^T \mathbf{Y} (\mathbf{Y}^T \mathbf{Y})^{-\frac{1}{2}} = \mathbf{I}_c, \tag{2.2}$$

where $\mathbf{I}_c \in \mathbb{R}^{c \times c}$ is an identity matrix.

To select the discriminative features for unsupervised learning, we propose a Clustering-Guided Sparse Structural Learning (CGSSL) method to jointly exploit the cluster analysis and sparse structural analysis simultaneously. Clustering techniques are adopted to learn the cluster indicators (which can be regarded as pseudo class labels), which are used to guide the process of structural learning. Meanwhile, the pseudo class labels are also predicted by the structural learning with predictive functions, which correlate the samples and the pseudo class labels. To conduct effective feature selection, we impose the sparse feature selection models on the regularization term. Therefore, CGSSL is formulated as

$$\min_{\mathbf{F}, h} J(\mathbf{F}) + \sum_{i=1}^c \left(\alpha \sum_{j=1}^n l(h_i(\mathbf{x}_j), \mathbf{f}_i) + \Omega(h_i) \right)$$

$$\text{s.t.} \quad \mathbf{F} = \mathbf{Y}(\mathbf{Y}^T \mathbf{Y})^{-\frac{1}{2}}, \tag{2.3}$$

where $J(\mathbf{F})$ is a clustering criterion, $l(\cdot, \cdot)$ is the loss function, $h_i(\cdot)$ is a predictive function for the ith cluster, and $\Omega(\cdot)$ is a regularization function with sparsity. α is a trade-off parameter.

2.3.1 Nonnegative Spectral Clustering

In cluster analysis, graph-theoretic methods have been well studied and utilized in many applications. As one of graph-theoretic methods, spectral clustering has been verified to be effective to detect the cluster structure of data and has received significant research attention. Therefore, we adopt spectral clustering as the cluster analysis technique.

Clearly, an effective cluster indicator matrix is more capable to reflect the discriminative information of the input data. The local geometric structure of data plays an important role in data clustering, which has been exploited by many spectral clustering algorithms [32, 37, 40]. Note that there are many different algorithms to uncover local data structure. In this work, we use the strategy proposed in [37] to be the criterion for its simplicity. The local geometric structure can be effectively modeled by a nearest neighbor graph on a scatter of data points. To construct the affinity graph $\mathbf{S}$, we define

$$
S_{ij} = \begin{cases} \exp\left(-\frac{\|\mathbf{x}_i - \mathbf{x}_j\|^2}{\sigma^2}\right) & \mathbf{x}_i \in \mathcal{N}_k(\mathbf{x}_j) \text{ or } \mathbf{x}_j \in \mathcal{N}_k(\mathbf{x}_i) \\ 0 & \text{otherwise,} \end{cases}
$$

where $\mathcal{N}_k(\mathbf{x})$ is the set of k-nearest neighbors of $\mathbf{x}$. The local geometrical structure can be exploited by

$$
\min_{\mathbf{F}} \frac{1}{2} \sum_{i,j=1}^n S_{ij} \|\frac{\mathbf{f}_i}{\sqrt{E_{ii}}} - \frac{\mathbf{f}_j}{\sqrt{E_{jj}}}\|_2^2 = \text{Tr}[\mathbf{F}^T \mathbf{L} \mathbf{F}], \tag{2.5}
$$

where $\mathbf{E}$ is a diagonal matrix with $E_{ii} = \sum_{j=1}^n S_{ij}$ and $\mathbf{L} = \mathbf{E}^{-1/2}(\mathbf{E} - \mathbf{S})\mathbf{E}^{-1/2}$ is the normalized graph Laplacian matrix. Therefore $J(\mathbf{F})$ is defined as

$$
J(\mathbf{F}) = \text{Tr}[\mathbf{F}^T \mathbf{L} \mathbf{F}]. \tag{2.6}
$$

According to the definition of $\mathbf{F}$, its elements are constrained to be discrete values, making the problem (2.3) an NP-hard problem [37]. A well-known solution is to relax it from discrete values to continuous ones while keeping the property of Eq. (2.2) [37], i.e., the objective function (2.3) is relaxed to

$$
\min_{\mathbf{F},h} \text{Tr}[\mathbf{F}^T \mathbf{L} \mathbf{F}] + \sum_{i=1}^c \left(\alpha \sum_{j=1}^n l(h_i(\mathbf{x}_j), \mathbf{f}_i) + \Omega(h_i) \right)
$$

$$
\text{s.t.} \quad \mathbf{F}^T \mathbf{F} = \mathbf{I}_c. \tag{2.7}
$$

Note that according to the definition of the cluster indicator matrix $\mathbf{F}$, each element F_{ij} indicates the relationship between the ith sample and the jth cluster, which is nonnegative by nature. Unfortunately, the optimal $\mathbf{F}$ of the problem (2.7) has mixed signs, which violates its definition. Moreover, the mixed signs make it difficult to get the cluster labels. Discrete process, such as spectral rotation or Kmeans, is performed in previous works to obtain the cluster labels. However, our work is a one-step model and contains no discrete process, which makes the learned $\mathbf{F}$ severely deviate from the ideal cluster indicators. To address this problem, it is natural and reasonable to impose nonnegative constraints on $\mathbf{F}$. When both nonnegative and orthogonal constraints are satisfied, only one element in each row of $\mathbf{F}$ is greater than zero and all of the others are zeros, which makes the results more appropriate for clustering. Note that if there exists one row with at least two positive elements, $\mathbf{F}$ cannot satisfy the orthogonality constraint because it results in positive nondiagonal elements in $\mathbf{F}^T\mathbf{F}$. Let us assume that there are m ($m \geq 2$) positive elements in the ith row of $\mathbf{F}$: $\{F_{ik_1}, \ldots, F_{ik_m}\}$. When j and l are within $\{k_1, \ldots, k_m\}$, and $j \neq l$, we obtain:

$$(\mathbf{F}^T\mathbf{F})_{jl} = \sum_{q=1}^{n} F_{qj} F_{ql} \geq F_{ij} F_{il} > 0, \qquad (2.8)$$

which conflicts the orthogonality condition. Because of this characteristic, the learned $\mathbf{F}$ is more accurate, and more capable to provide discriminative information. Therefore, we rewrite (2.7) as

$$\min_{\mathbf{F},h} \mathrm{Tr}[\mathbf{F}^T\mathbf{L}\mathbf{F}] + \sum_{i=1}^{c} \left(\alpha \sum_{j=1}^{n} l(h_i(\mathbf{x}_j), \mathbf{f}_i) + \Omega(h_i) \right)$$

$$\text{s.t.} \quad \mathbf{F}^T\mathbf{F} = \mathbf{I}_c, \quad \mathbf{F} \geq 0. \qquad (2.9)$$

It is worth noting that we adopt $\mathbf{L}$ defined in (2.5) for simplicity while other sophisticated Laplacian matrices can be used as well.

2.3.2 Sparse Structural Analysis

In CGSSL, the features which are most discriminative to the pseudo class labels are selected. To this end, we adopt a linear model to predict the pseudo labels. Since the features are correlated to jointly reflect the semantic components that can represent some semantic meaning, we propose to exploit feature combinations as well as the original features for the pseudo label prediction. Motivated by [4, 20], the semantic components are uncovered by a shared structure learning model, which enables to learn a more discriminative predictors to make the learned results more reliable. For simplicity, we assume that the shared structure is a hidden low-dimensional subspace in this work. Therefore, the original data features together with the features in the low-dimensional subspace are both used to predict the pseudo labels of samples:

$$h_i(\mathbf{x_j}) = \mathbf{v}_i^T \mathbf{x}_j + \mathbf{p}_i^T \mathbf{Q}^T \mathbf{x}_j, \tag{2.10}$$

where $\mathbf{v}_i \in \mathbb{R}^d$ and $\mathbf{p}_i \in \mathbb{R}^r$ are the weight vectors, and $\mathbf{Q} \in \mathbb{R}^{d \times r}$ is the linear transformation to parameterize the shared r-dimensional subspace. To make the problem tractable, the orthogonal constraint $\mathbf{Q}^T \mathbf{Q} = \mathbf{I}_r$ is imposed. Denote $\mathbf{V} = [\mathbf{v}_1, \ldots, \mathbf{v}_c] \in \mathbb{R}^{d \times c}$ and $\mathbf{P} = [\mathbf{p}_1, \ldots, \mathbf{p}_c] \in \mathbb{R}^{r \times c}$. Thus, we have

$$\sum_{i=1}^{c} \left(\sum_{j=1}^{n} l(h_i(\mathbf{x}_j), \mathbf{f}_i) + \Omega(h_i) \right)$$
$$= l((\mathbf{V} + \mathbf{Q}\mathbf{P})^T \mathbf{X}, \mathbf{F}) + \Omega(\mathbf{V}, \mathbf{P}). \tag{2.11}$$

By defining $\mathbf{W} = \mathbf{V} + \mathbf{Q}\mathbf{P}$ and combining (2.9) and (2.11), our formulation becomes

$$\min_{\mathbf{V}, \mathbf{W}, \mathbf{Q}, \mathbf{F}} \mathrm{Tr}[\mathbf{F}^T \mathbf{L} \mathbf{F}] + \alpha l(\mathbf{W}^T \mathbf{X}, \mathbf{F}) + \Omega(\mathbf{V}, \mathbf{W})$$
$$\text{s.t.} \quad \mathbf{F}^T \mathbf{F} = \mathbf{I}_c, \ \mathbf{F} \geq 0; \ \mathbf{Q}^T \mathbf{Q} = \mathbf{I}_r. \tag{2.12}$$

To solve the optimization problem in (2.12), we first decide which loss function is chosen for $l(\cdot, \cdot)$ and which regularization functions used for Ω. In this work, we utilize the least square loss $l(x, y) = (x - y)^2$ for simplicity. For $\mathbf{V}$, the quadratic regularization is used, that is, $\|\mathbf{V}\|_F^2 = \|\mathbf{W} - \mathbf{Q}\mathbf{P}\|_F^2$. To achieve feature selection across all samples, $\ell_{2,1}$-norm regularization is adopted for $\mathbf{W}$ to guarantee that $\mathbf{W}$ is sparse in rows. So we have

$$\min_{\mathbf{P}, \mathbf{W}, \mathbf{Q}, \mathbf{F}} \mathcal{O} = \mathrm{Tr}[\mathbf{F}^T \mathbf{L} \mathbf{F}] + \alpha \|\mathbf{F} - \mathbf{X}^T \mathbf{W}\|_F^2 + \beta \|\mathbf{W}\|_{2,1} + \gamma \|\mathbf{W} - \mathbf{Q}\mathbf{P}\|_F^2$$
$$\text{s.t.} \quad \mathbf{F}^T \mathbf{F} = \mathbf{I}_c, \ \mathbf{F} \geq 0; \ \mathbf{Q}^T \mathbf{Q} = \mathbf{I}_r. \tag{2.13}$$

β and γ are two regularization parameters. The joint minimization of the regression model and $\ell_{2,1}$-norm regularization term enables $\mathbf{W}$ to evaluate the correlation between pseudo labels and features, making it particularly suitable for feature selection. More specifically, $\mathbf{w}_i$, the ith row of $\mathbf{W}$, shrinks to zero if the ith feature is less discriminative to the pseudo labels $\mathbf{F}$. Once $\mathbf{W}$ is learned, we can select the top p ranked features by sorting all d features according to $\|\mathbf{w}_i\|_2$ ($i = 1, \ldots, d$) in descending order. Therefore, the features corresponding to zero rows of $\mathbf{W}$ will be discarded when performing feature selection.

2.3.3 Optimization

The optimization problem (2.13) involves the $\ell_{2,1}$-norm which is nonsmooth and cannot have a closed form solution. Consequently, we propose an iterative optimization algorithm.

We can see that the optimal $\mathbf{P}$ in the optimization problem (2.13) can be expressed in terms of $\mathbf{W}$ and $\mathbf{Q}$. By setting the derivative $\partial\mathcal{O}/\partial\mathbf{P} = 0$, we obtain

$$2\gamma(\mathbf{Q}^T\mathbf{QP} - \mathbf{Q}^T\mathbf{W}) = 0 \Rightarrow \mathbf{P} = \mathbf{Q}^T\mathbf{W}. \tag{2.14}$$

Because we have the property that $\mathbf{Q}^T\mathbf{Q} = \mathbf{I}_r$.

Now, by substituting $\mathbf{P}$ in $\mathcal{O}$ with Eq. (2.14), the objective function $\mathcal{O}$ is written as follows:

$$\begin{aligned}
\mathcal{O} &= \mathrm{Tr}[\mathbf{F}^T\mathbf{LF}] + \alpha\|\mathbf{F} - \mathbf{X}^T\mathbf{W}\|_F^2 + \beta\|\mathbf{W}\|_{2,1} \\
&\quad + \gamma\mathrm{Tr}[(\mathbf{W} - \mathbf{QQ}^T\mathbf{W})^T(\mathbf{W} - \mathbf{QQ}^T\mathbf{W})] \\
&= \mathrm{Tr}[\mathbf{F}^T\mathbf{LF}] + \alpha\|\mathbf{F} - \mathbf{X}^T\mathbf{W}\|_F^2 + \beta\|\mathbf{W}\|_{2,1} \\
&\quad + \gamma\mathrm{Tr}[\mathbf{W}^T(\mathbf{I}_d - \mathbf{QQ}^T)(\mathbf{I}_d - \mathbf{QQ}^T)\mathbf{W}]
\end{aligned} \tag{2.15}$$

Since $(\mathbf{I}_d - \mathbf{QQ}^T)(\mathbf{I}_d - \mathbf{QQ}^T) = \mathbf{I}_d - \mathbf{QQ}^T$, by setting the derivative $\partial\mathcal{O}/\partial\mathbf{W} = 0$, we get

$$\begin{aligned}
&\alpha\mathbf{X}(\mathbf{X}^T\mathbf{W} - \mathbf{F}) + \beta\mathbf{DW} + \gamma(\mathbf{I}_d - \mathbf{QQ}^T)\mathbf{W} = 0 \\
\Leftrightarrow\quad &(\alpha\mathbf{XX}^T + \beta\mathbf{D} + \gamma(\mathbf{I}_d - \mathbf{QQ}^T))\mathbf{W} = \alpha\mathbf{XF} \\
\Leftrightarrow\quad &\mathbf{W} = \alpha(\mathbf{G} - \gamma\mathbf{QQ}^T))^{-1}\mathbf{XF} \\
\Leftrightarrow\quad &\mathbf{W} = \alpha\mathbf{H}^{-1}\mathbf{XF}
\end{aligned} \tag{2.16}$$

Here $\mathbf{D}$ is a diagonal matrix with $D_{ii} = \frac{1}{2\|\mathbf{w}_i\|_2}$.[1] $\mathbf{G} = \alpha\mathbf{XX}^T + \beta\mathbf{D} + \gamma\mathbf{I}_d$ and $\mathbf{H} = \mathbf{G} - \gamma\mathbf{QQ}^T$.

Owing to $\|\mathbf{A}\|_F^2 = \mathrm{Tr}(\mathbf{A}^T\mathbf{A})$ for any arbitrary matrix $\mathbf{A}$, we can rewrite Eq. (2.15) as follows:

$$\begin{aligned}
\mathcal{O} &= \mathrm{Tr}[\mathbf{F}^T\mathbf{LF}] + \alpha\mathrm{Tr}[(\mathbf{X}^T\mathbf{W} - \mathbf{F})^T(\mathbf{X}^T\mathbf{W} - \mathbf{F})] \\
&\quad + \beta\|\mathbf{W}\|_{2,1} + \gamma\mathrm{Tr}[\mathbf{W}^T(\mathbf{I}_d - \mathbf{QQ}^T)\mathbf{W}] \\
&= \mathrm{Tr}[\mathbf{W}^T(\alpha\mathbf{XX}^T + \beta\mathbf{D} + \gamma\mathbf{I}_d - \gamma\mathbf{QQ}^T)\mathbf{W}] \\
&\quad - 2\alpha\mathrm{Tr}[\mathbf{W}^T\mathbf{XF}] + \alpha\mathrm{Tr}[\mathbf{F}^T\mathbf{F}] + \mathrm{Tr}[\mathbf{F}^T\mathbf{LF}] \\
&= \mathrm{Tr}[\mathbf{W}^T(\mathbf{HW} - 2\alpha\mathbf{XF})] + \mathrm{Tr}[\mathbf{F}^T(\alpha\mathbf{I}_n + \mathbf{L})\mathbf{F}]
\end{aligned} \tag{2.17}$$

By substituting the expression for $\mathbf{W}$ in Eq. (2.16) into Eq. (2.17), since $\mathbf{H} = \mathbf{H}^T$, we obtain the following equation:

---

[1] In practice, $\|\mathbf{w}_i\|_2$ could be close to zero but not zero. Theoretically, it could be zeros. For this case, we can regularize $D_{ii} = \frac{1}{2\sqrt{(\mathbf{w}_i^T\mathbf{w}_i + \varepsilon)}}$, where ε is very small constant. When $\varepsilon \to 0$, we can see that $\frac{1}{2\sqrt{(\mathbf{w}_i^T\mathbf{w}_i + \varepsilon)}}$ approximates $\frac{1}{2\sqrt{\mathbf{w}_i^T\mathbf{w}_i}}$.

$$\mathcal{O} = \mathrm{Tr}[\alpha^2 \mathbf{F}^T \mathbf{X}^T (\mathbf{H}^{-1}\mathbf{H}\mathbf{H}^{-1} - 2\mathbf{H}^{-1})\mathbf{X}\mathbf{F}] + \mathrm{Tr}[\mathbf{F}^T (\alpha \mathbf{I}_n + \mathbf{L})\mathbf{F}]$$

$$= \mathrm{Tr}[\mathbf{F}^T (\alpha \mathbf{I}_n + \mathbf{L})\mathbf{F}] - \alpha^2 \mathrm{Tr}[\mathbf{F}^T \mathbf{X}^T \mathbf{H}^{-1} \mathbf{X}\mathbf{F}] \qquad (2.18)$$

By substituting Eq. (2.18) into the problem (2.13), we have the following optimization problem w.r.t. $\mathbf{Q}$:

$$\max_{\mathbf{Q}^T \mathbf{Q} = \mathbf{I}_r} \mathrm{Tr}[\mathbf{F}^T \mathbf{X}^T \mathbf{H}^{-1} \mathbf{X}\mathbf{F}] \qquad (2.19)$$

To compute the matrix inverse, using the Sherman–Morrison–Woodbury formula [18]: $(\mathbf{A} + \mathbf{UCV})^{-1} = \mathbf{A}^{-1} - \mathbf{A}^{-1}\mathbf{U} (\mathbf{C}^{-1} + \mathbf{VA}^{-1}\mathbf{U})^{-1} \mathbf{VA}^{-1}$, we have

$$\mathbf{H}^{-1} = (\mathbf{G} - \gamma \mathbf{Q}\mathbf{Q}^T)^{-1}$$

$$= \mathbf{G}^{-1} + \gamma \mathbf{G}^{-1}\mathbf{Q}(\mathbf{I}_r - \gamma \mathbf{Q}^T \mathbf{G}^{-1}\mathbf{Q})^{-1}\mathbf{Q}^T \mathbf{G}^{-1}. \qquad (2.20)$$

Thus, by using the property that $\mathrm{Tr}[\mathbf{A}\mathbf{B}] = \mathrm{Tr}[\mathbf{B}\mathbf{A}]$ for any arbitrary matrices $\mathbf{A}$ and $\mathbf{B}$, the optimization problem (2.19) is equivalent to

$$\max \mathrm{Tr}[\mathbf{F}^T \mathbf{X}^T \mathbf{G}^{-1}\mathbf{Q}(\mathbf{I}_r - \gamma \mathbf{Q}^T \mathbf{G}^{-1}\mathbf{Q})^{-1}\mathbf{Q}^T \mathbf{G}^{-1}\mathbf{X}\mathbf{F}]$$

$$\Leftrightarrow \max \mathrm{Tr}[(\mathbf{I}_r - \gamma \mathbf{Q}^T \mathbf{G}^{-1}\mathbf{Q})^{-1}\mathbf{Q}^T \mathbf{G}^{-1}\mathbf{X}\mathbf{F}\mathbf{F}^T \mathbf{X}^T \mathbf{G}^{-1}\mathbf{Q}]$$

$$\Leftrightarrow \qquad \max \mathrm{Tr}[(\mathbf{Q}^T (\mathbf{I}_d - \gamma \mathbf{G}^{-1})\mathbf{Q})^{-1}\mathbf{Q}^T \mathbf{T}\mathbf{Q}]$$

$$\Leftrightarrow \qquad \max \mathrm{Tr}[\mathbf{Q}^T \mathbf{N}^{-1}\mathbf{T}\mathbf{Q}]$$

$$\text{s.t.} \quad \mathbf{Q}^T \mathbf{Q} = \mathbf{I}_r, \qquad (2.21)$$

where $\mathbf{T} = \mathbf{G}^{-1}\mathbf{X}\mathbf{F}\mathbf{F}^T \mathbf{X}^T \mathbf{G}^{-1}$ and $\mathbf{N} = \mathbf{I}_d - \gamma \mathbf{G}^{-1}$. Note that $\mathbf{N}$ is positive definite [20], thus $\mathbf{Q}$ can be easily obtained by the eigen-decomposition of $\mathbf{N}^{-1}\mathbf{T}$.

Substituting the expression for $\mathcal{O}$ in Eq. (2.18) into Eq. (2.13), we obtain the following optimization problem w.s.t. $\mathbf{F}$.

$$\min_{\mathbf{F}} \mathrm{Tr}[\mathbf{F}^T (\mathbf{L} + \alpha \mathbf{I}_n - \alpha^2 \mathbf{X}^T \mathbf{H}^{-1}\mathbf{X})\mathbf{F}]$$

$$\text{s.t.} \quad \mathbf{F}^T \mathbf{F} = \mathbf{I}_c; \; \mathbf{F} \geq 0 \qquad (2.22)$$

Then we relax the orthogonal constraint and rewrite the above optimization problem as follows:

$$\min_{\mathbf{F} \geq 0} \mathrm{Tr}[\mathbf{F}^T \mathbf{M}\mathbf{F}] + \frac{\lambda}{2} \|\mathbf{F}^T \mathbf{F} - \mathbf{I}_c\|_F^2. \qquad (2.23)$$

Here $\mathbf{M} = \mathbf{L} + \alpha \mathbf{I}_n - \alpha^2 \mathbf{X}^T \mathbf{H}^{-1}\mathbf{X}$ and $\lambda > 0$ is a parameter to control the orthogonality condition. In practice, λ should be large enough to insure the orthogonality satisfied. Let ϕ_{ij} be the Lagrange multiplier for constraint $F_{ij} \geq 0$ and $\Phi = [\phi_{ij}]$. Since $\|\mathbf{A}\|_F^2 = \mathrm{Tr}(\mathbf{A}^T \mathbf{A})$, the Lagrange function is

---

Algorithm 1 CGSSL for Feature Selection

Input:

　Data matrix $\mathbf{X} \in \mathbb{R}^{d \times n}$; Parameters $\alpha, \beta, \gamma, \lambda, k, c, r$ and p

1: Construct the k-nearest neighbor graph and calculate $\mathbf{L}$;

2: The iteration step $t = 0$; Initialize $\mathbf{F}_0 \in \mathbb{R}^{n \times c}$ and set $\mathbf{D}_0 \in \mathbb{R}^{d \times d}$ as an identity matrix;

3: **repeat**

4:　　$\mathbf{G}_t = \alpha \mathbf{X}\mathbf{X}^T + \beta \mathbf{D}_t + \gamma \mathbf{I}_d$;

5:　　$\mathbf{N}_t = \mathbf{I}_d - \gamma \mathbf{G}_t^{-1}$;

6:　　$\mathbf{T}_t = \mathbf{G}_t^{-1} \mathbf{X}\mathbf{F}_t \mathbf{F}_t^T \mathbf{X}^T \mathbf{G}_t^{-1}$;

7:　　Obtain $\mathbf{Q}_{t+1}$ by the eigen-decomposition of $\mathbf{N}_t^{-1}\mathbf{T}_t$;

8:　　$\mathbf{H}_t = \mathbf{G}_t - \gamma \mathbf{Q}_{t+1}\mathbf{Q}_{t+1}^T$;

9:　　$\mathbf{M}_t = \mathbf{L} + \alpha \mathbf{I}_n - \alpha^2 \mathbf{X}^T \mathbf{H}_t^{-1}\mathbf{X}$;

10:　　$(F_{t+1})_{ij} = (F_t)_{ij} \frac{(\lambda F_t)_{ij}}{(\mathbf{M}_t F_t + \lambda F_t F_t^T F_t)_{ij}}$;

11:　　$\mathbf{W}_{t+1} = \mathbf{H}_t^{-1}\mathbf{X}\mathbf{F}_{t+1}$;

12:　　Update the diagonal matrix $\mathbf{D}$ as

$$\mathbf{D}_{t+1} = \begin{bmatrix} \frac{1}{2\|(\mathbf{w}_{t+1})_1\|_2} & & \\ & \cdots & \\ & & \frac{1}{2\|(\mathbf{w}_{t+1})_d\|_2} \end{bmatrix};$$

13:　　t=t+1;

14: **until** Convergence criterion satisfied

Output:

　Sort all d features according to $\|(\mathbf{w}_t)_i\|_2$ in descending order and select the top p ranked features.

$$\text{Tr}[\mathbf{F}^T \mathbf{M}\mathbf{F}] + \frac{\lambda}{2}\text{Tr}[(\mathbf{F}^T \mathbf{F} - \mathbf{I}_c)^T (\mathbf{F}^T \mathbf{F} - \mathbf{I}_c)] + \text{Tr}[\Phi \mathbf{F}^T]. \tag{2.24}$$

Setting its derivative with respect to $\mathbf{F}$ to 0, we have

$$2\mathbf{M}\mathbf{F} + 2\lambda \mathbf{F}(\mathbf{F}^T \mathbf{F} - \mathbf{I}_c) + \Phi = 0. \tag{2.25}$$

Using the Karush–Kuhn–Tuckre (KKT) condition [22] $\phi_{ij}F_{ij} = 0$, we obtain the updating rules:

$$2[\mathbf{M}\mathbf{F} + \lambda \mathbf{F}(\mathbf{F}^T \mathbf{F} - \mathbf{I}_c)]_{ij}F_{ij} + \Phi_{ij}F_{ij} = 0$$

$$\Rightarrow F_{ij} \leftarrow F_{ij} \frac{(\lambda \mathbf{F})_{ij}}{(\mathbf{M}\mathbf{F} + \lambda \mathbf{F}\mathbf{F}^T \mathbf{F})_{ij}}. \tag{2.26}$$

Then we normalize $\mathbf{F}$ with $(\mathbf{F}^T \mathbf{F})_{ii} = 1, i = 1, \ldots, c$.

From the above analysis, we can see that $\mathbf{D}$ related to $\mathbf{W}$ is required to solve $\mathbf{Q}$ and $\mathbf{F}$ and it is still not straightforward to obtain $\mathbf{W}, \mathbf{Q}$, and $\mathbf{F}$. To this end, we design an iterative algorithm to solve the proposed formulation, which is summarized in Algorithm 1.

Now, we briefly analyze the computational complexity. In our case, $c \ll n, c \ll d$ and $r < d$. The complexity of calculating the inverse of a few matrices is $O(d^3)$ and the eigen-decomposition of $\mathbf{N}^{-1}\mathbf{T}$ also needs $O(d^3)$ in complexity. In each iteration step, the cost for updating $\mathbf{Q}$ is $O(d^3 + nd^2)$. It takes $O(d^3 + nd^2 + dn^2)$ to update $\mathbf{F}$ and $O(d^3)$ to update $\mathbf{W}$, respectively. Thus the overall cost for CGSSL is $O(t(d^3 + nd^2 + dn^2))$, where t is the number of iterations.

2.3.4 Convergence Analysis

The proposed iterative procedure in Algorithm 1 can be verified to converge to the optimal solutions by the following theorem.

Theorem 2.1 *The alternative updating rules in Algorithm 1 monotonically decrease the objective function value of (2.13) in each iteration.*

Proof For convenience, let us denote

$$\mathcal{L}(\mathbf{Q}, \mathbf{F}, \mathbf{W}) = \text{Tr}[\mathbf{F}^T \mathbf{L} \mathbf{F}] + \alpha \|\mathbf{F} - \mathbf{X}^T \mathbf{W}\|_F^2 + \beta \|\mathbf{W}\|_{2,1}$$
$$+ \gamma \|\mathbf{W} - \mathbf{Q}\mathbf{Q}^T \mathbf{W}\|_F^2 + \frac{\lambda}{2} \|\mathbf{F}^T \mathbf{F} - \mathbf{I}_c\|_F^2 \qquad (2.27)$$

From the above analysis, the problem (2.13) can be relaxed into the following problem:

$$\min_{\mathbf{Q}^T\mathbf{Q} = \mathbf{I}_r, \mathbf{F} \geq 0, \mathbf{W}} \mathcal{L}(\mathbf{Q}, \mathbf{F}, \mathbf{W}) \qquad (2.28)$$

With $\mathbf{F}_t$ and $\mathbf{W}_t$ fixed, we can see that

$$\mathbf{Q}_{t+1} = \arg \max_{\mathbf{Q}^T\mathbf{Q}=\mathbf{I}_r} \text{Tr}[\mathbf{Q}^T \mathbf{N}_t^{-1} \mathbf{T}_t \mathbf{Q}]$$
$$\Rightarrow \text{Tr}[\mathbf{Q}_{t+1}^T \mathbf{N}_t^{-1} \mathbf{T}_t \mathbf{Q}_{t+1}] \geq \text{Tr}[\mathbf{Q}_t^T \mathbf{N}_t^{-1} \mathbf{T}_t \mathbf{Q}_t]. \qquad (2.29)$$

Thus we obtain

$$\mathcal{L}(\mathbf{Q}_{t+1}, \mathbf{F}_t, \mathbf{W}_t) \leq \mathcal{L}(\mathbf{Q}_t, \mathbf{F}_t, \mathbf{W}_t). \qquad (2.30)$$

With $\mathbf{W}_t$ and $\mathbf{Q}_{t+1}$ fixed, by introducing an auxiliary function of $\mathcal{L}(\mathbf{Q}_{t+1}, \mathbf{F}_t, \mathbf{W})$ as in [24], it is easy to prove

$$\mathcal{L}(\mathbf{Q}_{t+1}, \mathbf{F}_{t+1}, \mathbf{W}_t) \leq \mathcal{L}(\mathbf{Q}_{t+1}, \mathbf{F}_t, \mathbf{W}_t). \qquad (2.31)$$

It can easily verified that Eq. (2.16) is the solution to the following problem with $\mathbf{Q}_{t+1}$ and $\mathbf{F}_{t+1}$ fixed.

$$\min_{\mathbf{W}} \alpha \|\mathbf{X}^T \mathbf{W} - \mathbf{F}_{t+1}\|_F^2 + \beta \text{Tr}[\mathbf{W}^T \mathbf{D}_t \mathbf{W}]$$
$$+ \gamma \|\mathbf{W} - \mathbf{Q}_{t+1}\mathbf{Q}_{t+1}^T \mathbf{W}\|_F^2 \qquad (2.32)$$

For the ease of representation, let us define $g(\mathbf{W}) = \alpha\|\mathbf{X}^T\mathbf{W} - \mathbf{F}_{t+1}\|_F^2 + \gamma\|\mathbf{W} - \mathbf{Q}_{t+1}\mathbf{P}_{t+1}\|_F^2$. Accordingly, in the tth iteration, we have

$$\mathbf{W}^{t+1} = \arg\min_{\mathbf{W}} g(\mathbf{W}) + \beta\mathrm{Tr}[\mathbf{W}^T\mathbf{D}_t\mathbf{W}]$$

$$\Rightarrow g(\mathbf{W}_{t+1}) + \beta\mathrm{Tr}[\mathbf{W}_{t+1}^T\mathbf{D}_t\mathbf{W}_{t+1}] \le g(\mathbf{W}_t) + \beta\mathrm{Tr}[\mathbf{W}_t^T\mathbf{D}_t\mathbf{W}_t]$$

$$\Rightarrow g(\mathbf{W}_{t+1}) + \beta\sum_i \frac{\|(\mathbf{w}_{t+1})_i\|_2^2}{2\|(\mathbf{w}_t)_i\|_2} \le g(\mathbf{W}_t) + \beta\sum_i \frac{\|(\mathbf{w}_t)_i\|_2^2}{2\|(\mathbf{w}_t)_i\|_2}$$

$$\Rightarrow g(\mathbf{W}_{t+1}) + \beta\|\mathbf{W}_{t+1}\|_{2,1} - \beta(\|\mathbf{W}_{t+1}\|_{2,1} - \sum_i \frac{\|(\mathbf{w}_{t+1})_i\|_2^2}{2\|(\mathbf{w}_t)_i\|_2})$$

$$\le g(\mathbf{W}_t) + \beta\|\mathbf{W}_t\|_{2,1} - \beta(\|\mathbf{W}_t\|_{2,1} - \sum_i \frac{\|(\mathbf{w}_t)_i\|_2^2}{2\|(\mathbf{w}_t)_i\|_2}). \tag{2.33}$$

According to the Lemmas in [33], $\|\mathbf{W}_{t+1}\|_{2,1} - \sum_i \frac{\|(\mathbf{w}_{t+1})_i\|_2^2}{2\|(\mathbf{w}_t)_i\|_2} \le \|\mathbf{W}^t\|_{2,1} - \sum_i \frac{\|(\mathbf{w}_t)_i\|_2^2}{2\|(\mathbf{w}_t)_i\|_2}$. Thus,

$$g(\mathbf{W}_{t+1}) + \beta\|\mathbf{W}^{t+1}\|_{2,1} \le g(\mathbf{W}_t) + \beta\|\mathbf{W}^t\|_{2,1}. \tag{2.34}$$

Therefore, we arrive at

$$\mathscr{L}(\mathbf{Q}_{t+1}, \mathbf{F}_{t+1}, \mathbf{W}_{t+1}) \le \mathscr{L}(\mathbf{Q}_{t+1}, \mathbf{F}_{t+1}, \mathbf{W}_t). \tag{2.35}$$

Based on Eqs. (2.30), (2.31) and (2.35), we obtain

$$\mathscr{L}(\mathbf{Q}_{t+1}, \mathbf{F}_{t+1}, \mathbf{W}_{t+1}) \le \mathscr{L}(\mathbf{Q}_{t+1}, \mathbf{F}_{t+1}, \mathbf{W}_t)$$
$$\le \mathscr{L}(\mathbf{Q}_{t+1}, \mathbf{F}_t, \mathbf{W}_t) \le \mathscr{L}(\mathbf{Q}_t, \mathbf{F}_t, \mathbf{W}_t). \tag{2.36}$$

Thus, the objective function monotonically decreases using the updating rules in Algorithm 1 and Theorem 2.1 is proved.

According to Theorem 2.1, we can see that the iterative approach in Algorithm 1 converges to local optimal solutions. The proposed optimization algorithm is efficient. In the experiment, we observe that our algorithm usually converges around only 20 iterations.

2.3.5   Discussions

In this section, we discuss the relationships between the proposed method and several algorithms, including SPFS [48], MCFS [5], UDFS [43], and NDFS [27].

Connection with SPFS: SPFS [48] performs feature selection by preserving sample similarity, which can handle feature redundancy. It is formulated as:

$$\min_{\|\mathbf{W}\|_{2,1}\leq\tau} \sum_{i,j=1}^{n} (\mathbf{x}_i^T \mathbf{W}\mathbf{W}^T \mathbf{x}_j - S_{ij})^2. \tag{2.37}$$

Here $\tau(\tau > 0)$ is a hyper-parameter. The connection between SPFS and CGSSL is discovered as follows.

Proposition 2.1 *SPFS has the similar fashion with the proposed CGSSL when $\alpha \to +\infty$, $\gamma = 0$ and the orthogonal and nonnegative constraints are removed.*

Proof When $\alpha \to +\infty$, and the orthogonal and nonnegative constraints are removed, we have $\mathbf{F} = \mathbf{X}^T \mathbf{W}$. Then, with $\gamma = 0$ CGSSL becomes

$$\min_{\mathbf{W}} \text{Tr}[\mathbf{W}^T \mathbf{XLX}^T \mathbf{W}] + \beta\|\mathbf{W}\|_{2,1}$$

$$= \frac{1}{2} \sum_{i,j=1}^{n} S_{ij} \|\mathbf{x}_i^T \mathbf{W} - \mathbf{x}_j^T \mathbf{W}\|^2 + \beta\|\mathbf{W}\|_{2,1}. \tag{2.38}$$

Compared the problems (2.37) with (2.38), they both try to keep data similarity with different criteria. That is, Proposition 2.1 is proved.

Connection with MCFS: MCFS [5] uses a two-step strategy to select features according to spectral analysis and is formulated as the following form.

$$\min_{\mathbf{F}^T \mathbf{F}=\mathbf{I}_c} \text{Tr}[\mathbf{F}^T \mathbf{LF}] \tag{2.39}$$

$$\min_{\mathbf{w}_i} \|\mathbf{f}_i - \mathbf{X}^T \mathbf{w}_i\| + \beta\|\mathbf{w}_i\|_1 \tag{2.40}$$

$\|\mathbf{w}_i\|_1$ is the ℓ_1-norm of $\mathbf{w}_i$.

Proposition 2.2 *MCFS and CGSSL have similar fashions with different regularization forms on $\mathbf{W}$, when $\gamma = 0$ and the nonnegative constraint is removed.*

Proof When $\gamma = 0$ and the nonnegative constraint removed, the proposed formulation becomes

$$\min_{\mathbf{W},\mathbf{F}^T \mathbf{F}=\mathbf{I}_c} \text{Tr}[\mathbf{F}^T \mathbf{LF}] + \alpha\|\mathbf{F} - \mathbf{X}^T \mathbf{W}\| + \beta\|\mathbf{W}\|_{2,1}. \tag{2.41}$$

If we set $\alpha \to 0$ and $\beta \to 0$, the above problem leads to a two-step algorithm. That is,

$$\min_{\mathbf{F}^T\mathbf{F}=\mathbf{I}_c} \text{Tr}[\mathbf{F}^T\mathbf{L}\mathbf{F}] \tag{2.42}$$

$$\min_{\mathbf{W}} \sum_{i=1}^{c} \|\mathbf{f}_i - \mathbf{X}^T\mathbf{w}_i\| + \frac{\beta}{\alpha}\|\mathbf{w}_i\|_2. \tag{2.43}$$

We can see that the regularization function for $\mathbf{w}_i$ is different. Thus, Proposition 2.2 is proved.

Different from MCFS, CGSSL is an one-step algorithm. Thus, CGSSL is more general. Second, $\mathbf{F}$ is constrained to be nonnegative. When both nonnegative and orthogonal constraints are satisfied, the learned $\mathbf{F}$ is much closer to the ideal result, and the solution can be directly obtained without discretization. Finally, we perform clustering and feature selection simultaneously, which explicitly enforces that $\mathbf{F}$ can be linearly approximated by the selected features, making the results more accurate.

Connection with UDFS: UDFS [43] was proposed to select discriminative features by optimizing the following objective function

$$\min_{\mathbf{W}^T\mathbf{W}=\mathbf{I}_c} \text{Tr}[\mathbf{W}^T\mathbf{X}\mathbf{L}\mathbf{X}^T\mathbf{W}] + \beta\|\mathbf{W}\|_{2,1}. \tag{2.44}$$

Proposition 2.3 *UDFS and CGSSL have similar fashions when $\alpha \to +\infty$, $\gamma = 0$ and the nonnegative constraint is removed.*

Proof With $\alpha \to +\infty$ and the nonnegative constraint removed, we have $\mathbf{F} = \mathbf{X}^T\mathbf{W}$. Then when $\gamma = 0$, the proposed CGSSL formulation becomes

$$\min_{\mathbf{W}^T\mathbf{X}\mathbf{X}^T\mathbf{W}=\mathbf{I}_c} \text{Tr}[\mathbf{W}^T\mathbf{X}\mathbf{L}\mathbf{X}^T\mathbf{W}] + \beta\|\mathbf{W}\|_{2,1}. \tag{2.45}$$

Therefore, UDFS and CGSSL have similar fashions with different orthogonal constraints.

In this extreme case, $\mathbf{F}$ is enforced to be linear, i.e., $\mathbf{F} = \mathbf{X}^T\mathbf{W}$. However, as indicated in [37], it is likely that $\mathbf{F}$ is nonlinear in many applications. Hence, CGSSL is superior to UDFS due to its flexibility of linearity. Additionally, $\mathbf{F}$ is constrained to be nonnegative, making it more accurate than the one with mixed signs. Therefore, CGSSL is more capable to select discriminative features, verified by our experiments.

Connection with NDFS: NDFS [27] is our preliminary version, which does not exploit the underlying structure. Its formulation is presented as follows

$$\min_{\mathbf{W},\mathbf{F}} \text{Tr}[\mathbf{F}^T\mathbf{L}\mathbf{F}] + \alpha\|\mathbf{X}^T\mathbf{W} - \mathbf{F}\|_F^2 + \beta\|\mathbf{W}\|_{2,1}$$

$$\text{s.t.} \quad \mathbf{F}^T\mathbf{F} = \mathbf{I}, \ \mathbf{F} \geq 0. \tag{2.46}$$

By setting $\gamma = 0$, the problem (2.13) leads to the above problem. Thus we have the following proposition.

Proposition 2.4 *NDFS is a special case of the proposed CGSSL algorithm, when* $\lambda = 0$.

2.3.6 Experiments

In this section, we evaluate the performance of the proposed formulation, which can be applied to many applications, such as clustering and classification. Following previous unsupervised feature selection work [5, 43], we only evaluate the performance of CGSSL for feature selection and compared with representative algorithms in terms of clustering. In our experiments, we first select the top p features and then utilize Kmeans algorithm to cluster samples based on the selected features.

2.3.6.1 Data Sets

The experiments are conducted on 12 publicly available datasets, including three face image data sets (i.e., UMIST [1], JAFFE [29], and Pointing4 [16]), three handwritten digit image data sets [i.e., a subset of MNIST used in [44], Binary Alphabet (BA) [1] and a subset of USPS with 40 samples randomly selected for each class [1]], three text data sets (i.e., WebKB collected by the University of Texas [11], tr11 [2], and oh15 [2]), and three biomedical data sets (i.e., Tox-171 [3], Tumors9 [3], and Leukemia1 [3]). Data sets from different areas serve as a good test bed for a comprehensive evaluation. Table 2.1 summarizes the details of these 12 data sets used in experiments.

Table 2.1 Dataset description

Domain	Dataset	n	d	c
Face images	UMIST	575	644	20
	JAFFE	213	676	10
	Poingting4	2790	1120	15
Handwritten digits images	MNIST	5000	784	10
	BA	1404	320	36
	USPS	400	256	10
Text data	WebKB	814	4029	7
	tr11	414	6429	9
	oh15	913	3100	10
Biomedical data	TOX-171	171	5748	4
	Tumors9	60	5726	9
	Leukemia1	72	5327	3

2.3.6.2 Compared Scheme

To validate the effectiveness of CGSSL for feature selection, we compare it with one baseline and several unsupervised feature selection methods. The compared algorithms are enumerated as follows:

1. **Baseline**: All original features are adopted;
2. **MaxVar**: Features corresponding to the maximum variance are selected to obtain the best expressive features;
3. **LS** [17]: Features consistent with Gaussian Laplacian matrix are selected to best preserve the local manifold structure [17];
4. **SPEC** [47]: Features are selected using spectral regression;
5. **SPFS-SFS** [48]: The traditional forward search strategy is utilized for similarity preserving feature selection in the SPFS framework.
6. **MCFS** [5]: Features are selected based on spectral analysis and sparse regression problem;
7. **UDFS** [43]: Features are selected by a joint framework of discriminative analysis and $\ell_{2,1}$-norm minimization.
8. **CGSSL**: The proposed Cluster-Guided Sparse Structural Learning method.

2.3.6.3 Parameter Setting

There are some parameters to be set in advance. For LS, SPEC, MCFS, UDFS and CGSSL, we set $k = 5$ for all the datasets to specify the size of neighborhoods. For CGSSL, to guarantee the orthogonality satisfied, we fix $\lambda = 10^8$ in our experiments. To fairly compare different unsupervised feature selection algorithms, we tune the parameters for all methods by a "grid-search" strategy from $\{10^{-8}, 10^{-6}, \ldots, 10^8\}$. The dimensionality of the low-dimensional space is set $r = \min(5 \times \max(\lfloor \frac{c-1}{5} \rfloor, 1), c - 1)$ in the experiments since the performance is not very sensitive to it. The numbers of selected features are set as $\{50, 100, 150, 200, 250, 300\}$ for all the datasets except USPS. Because the total feature number of USPS is 256, we set the number of selected features as $\{50, 80, 110, 140, 170, 200\}$. For all the algorithms, we report the the best clustering results from the optimal parameters. Different parameters may be used for different databases. In our experiments, we adopt Kmeans algorithm to cluster samples based on the selected features. The performance of Kmeans clustering depends on initialization. Following [5, 43], we repeat the clustering 20 times with random initialization for each setup. The average results with standard deviation (std) are reported. In real applications, it is impossible to tune parameters using the "grid-search" strategy. But it is an acceptable method to tune parameters for experimental comparisons since all the compared methods are with the well-chosen parameter values. The parameter sensitivity study and convergence study for CGSSL will be shown in the following subsection.

2.3.6.4 Evaluation Metrics

With the selected features, we evaluate the performance in terms of clustering by two widely used evaluation metrics, i.e., Accuracy (ACC) and Normalized Mutual Information (NMI). The larger ACC and NMI are, the better performance is. ACC is defined by

$$\text{ACC} = \frac{1}{n} \sum_{i=1}^{n} \delta(c_i, \text{map}(g_i)), \tag{2.47}$$

where c_i is the clustering label and g_i is the ground truth label of $\mathbf{x}_i$. $\text{map}(g_i)$ is the optimal mapping function that permutes clustering labels and the ground truth labels. The optimal mapping can be obtained by using the Kuhn–Munkres algorithm. $\delta(c_i, g_i)$ is an indicator function that equals to 1 if $c_i = g_i$ and equals to 0 otherwise. NMI is defined as

$$\text{NMI} = \frac{\sum_{l,h=1}^{c} t_{l,h} \log(\frac{n \times t_{l,h}}{t_l \hat{t}_h})}{\sqrt{\left(\sum_{l=1}^{c} t_l \log \frac{t_l}{n}\right)\left(\sum_{h=1}^{c} \hat{t}_h \log \frac{\hat{t}_h}{n}\right)}}, \tag{2.48}$$

where t_l is the number of samples in the lth cluster $\mathscr{C}_l$ according to clustering results and $\hat{t}_h$ is the number of samples in the hth ground truth class $\mathscr{G}_h$. $t_{l,h}$ is the number of overlap between $\mathscr{C}_l$ and $\mathscr{G}_h$.

2.3.6.5 Performance Comparison

We now empirically evaluate the performance of these nine feature selection algorithms in terms of ACC and NMI. The detailed results on the face, handwritten digit, text, and biomedical data sets are summarized in Tables 2.2, 2.3, 2.4, and 2.5, respectively. The results demonstrate that compared to the compared algorithms, CGSSL achieves the best performance on all the 12 data sets, which validates its effectiveness.

From the above four tables, we have the following observations. (1) Compared with the baseline, it can be observed that feature selection is necessary and effective by removing the noise and redundancy. It can not only reduce the number of features and make the algorithms more efficient, but also enhance the performance. (2) It is better to perform feature selection jointly. The joint feature selection algorithms, such as MCFS, UDFS, and CGSSL are always superior to the methods selecting features one after another, such as MaxVar and SPEC. (3) By utilizing the local geometric structure of data distribution, LS, SPEC, MCFS, UDFS, and CGSSL usually yield superior performance. (4) MCFS, UDFS, and CGSSL achieve more accurate clustering performance by exploiting discriminative information, which demonstrates that it is crucial to uncover the discriminative information in the unsupervised case. (5) CGSSL outperforms SPEC and MCFS. SPEC and MCFS adopt a two-step approach to introduce spectral analysis into feature selection while CGSSL is an one-step

Table 2.2 Clustering results comparison on the face data sets. The best results are highlighted in bold

Dataset	Baseline	MaxVar	LS	SPFS-SFS	SPEC	MCFS	UDFS	CGSSL
ACC ± std (%)								
UMIST	41.8 ± 2.7	45.8 ± 2.8	45.9 ± 2.9	44.8 ± 3.5	47.9 ± 3.0	46.3 ± 3.6	48.6 ± 3.7	**53.4 ± 3.1**
JAFFE	72.5 ± 9.2	67.3 ± 5.8	74.0 ± 7.6	74.6 ± 9.4	76.9 ± 7.2	78.8 ± 9.1	76.7 ± 7.1	**82.3 ± 7.5**
Pointing4	35.9 ± 2.2	44.0 ± 2.8	37.1 ± 1.6	37.4 ± 1.3	38.6 ± 2.2	46.2 ± 2.9	45.1 ± 2.4	**51.1 ± 2.6**
NMI ± std (%)								
UMIST	62.3 ± 2.3	63.5 ± 1.5	63.9 ± 1.8	63.2 ± 3.3	65.2 ± 2.0	66.7 ± 1.9	67.3 ± 3.0	**70.9 ± 2.2**
JAFFE	80.0 ± 5.7	70.3 ± 4.2	79.4 ± 7.0	82.1 ± 4.9	82.8 ± 3.8	83.4 ± 5.0	82.3 ± 6.5	**87.5 ± 5.1**
Pointing4	41.7 ± 1.4	50.8 ± 1.8	42.7 ± 1.2	43.4 ± 1.4	40.5 ± 1.0	53.1 ± 1.1	52.4 ± 1.7	**57.7 ± 1.3**

Table 2.3 Clustering results comparison on the handwritten digit data sets. The best results are highlighted in bold

Dataset	Baseline	MaxVar	LS	SPFS-SFS	SPEC	MCFS	UDFS	CGSSL
ACC ± std (%)								
MNIST	52.2 ± 5.0	53.3 ± 2.7	54.3 ± 4.8	54.6 ± 3.2	55.6 ± 5.2	56.5 ± 4.1	56.6 ± 4.2	**59.3 ± 3.6**
BA	40.3 ± 2.0	40.7 ± 1.7	42.1 ± 1.7	41.6 ± 1.7	42.2 ± 2.2	41.5 ± 1.8	42.7 ± 1.8	**45.1 ± 1.8**
USPS	62.6 ± 5.3	63.8 ± 4.3	64.9 ± 5.1	65.1 ± 2.9	65.5 ± 3.8	64.4 ± 3.1	66.2 ± 4.7	**68.3 ± 4.5**
NMI ± std (%)								
MNIST	47.8 ± 2.3	48.6 ± 1.1	48.6 ± 2.0	49.1 ± 1.8	49.7 ± 2.0	50.0 ± 1.8	50.8 ± 1.6	**52.8 ± 1.8**
BA	56.5 ± 1.3	56.9 ± 1.3	57.3 ± 0.8	57.2 ± 1.2	57.9 ± 1.1	57.5 ± 0.8	58.1 ± 1.0	**60.0 ± 1.1**
USPS	56.9 ± 3.1	58.1 ± 2.7	58.7 ± 3.0	58.1 ± 1.9	59.5 ± 2.1	59.3 ± 2.9	60.1 ± 4.3	**62.0 ± 2.8**

Table 2.4 Clustering results comparison on the text data sets. The best results are highlighted in bold

Dataset	Baseline	MaxVar	LS	SPFS-SFS	SPEC	MCFS	UDFS	CGSSL
ACC ± std (%)								
WebKB	56.7 ± 2.7	54.6 ± 2.8	56.8 ± 2.9	60.7 ± 0.1	61.1 ± 2.8	61.3 ± 2.3	61.7 ± 3.2	**63.1 ± 3.0**
tr11	30.9 ± 2.0	30.5 ± 1.0	31.6 ± 1.6	30.6 ± 1.1	35.1 ± 1.8	36.3 ± 4.1	35.9 ± 2.5	**41.1 ± 4.1**
oh15	30.4 ± 3.0	32.9 ± 3.2	33.8 ± 2.7	34.0 ± 3.4	33.8 ± 2.1	33.8 ± 2.8	32.9 ± 2.3	**37.2 ± 2.5**
NMI ± std (%)								
WebKB	11.4 ± 5.0	17.1 ± 1.4	10.6 ± 4.0	11.4 ± 3.7	17.2 ± 3.1	17.6 ± 0.8	18.1 ± 3.3	**19.0 ± 1.7**
tr11	7.0 ± 1.4	7.6 ± 1.1	8.0 ± 2.0	6.2 ± 0.6	11.5 ± 2.9	13.5 ± 3.3	13.7 ± 1.9	**19.5 ± 3.9**
oh15	17.7 ± 3.0	22.1 ± 2.7	23.2 ± 2.8	23.2 ± 3.0	23.6 ± 2.2	23.1 ± 3.0	21.8 ± 2.0	**24.9 ± 1.8**

Table 2.5 Clustering results comparison on the biomedical data sets. The best results are highlighted in bold

Dataset	Baseline	MaxVar	LS	SPFS-SFS	SPEC	MCFS	UDFS	CGSSL
ACC ± std (%)								
TOX-171	40.9 ± 3.6	41.0 ± 2.7	41.8 ± 1.5	41.7 ± 5.0	44.9 ± 2.7	42.7 ± 2.1	45.7 ± 2.0	**48.6 ± 1.4**
Tumors9	40.2 ± 5.3	41.0 ± 5.2	42.3 ± 3.6	42.8 ± 4.6	41.0 ± 3.4	41.8 ± 4.9	42.9 ± 4.5	**46.8 ± 4.6**
Leukemia1	56.7 ± 9.2	58.5 ± 11.6	70.2 ± 7.2	70.3±6.4	60.2 ± 4.7	70.8 ± 10.1	71.2 ± 10.6	**74.7 ± 8.7**
NMI ± std (%)								
TOX-171	12.7 ± 4.0	12.4 ± 2.6	13.5 ± 0.8	12.2 ± 5.4	18.1 ± 1.0	13.4 ± 2.6	19.2 ± 2.2	**25.7 ± 2.8**
Tumors9	38.2 ± 4.9	40.2 ± 2.8	41.9 ± 3.3	42.0 ± 3.4	38.7 ± 2.5	40.3 ± 6.0	42.2 ± 4.2	**44.4 ± 3.4**
Leukemia1	23.4 ± 1.4	27.2 ± 19.3	34.0 ± 11.1	34.0 ± 11.7	31.1 ± 3.3	39.0 ± 11.8	40.8 ± 12.0	**48.5 ± 8.9**

framework and performs spectral analysis and feature selection simultaneously. (6) CGSSL achieves higher ACC and NMI than MCFS by imposing the nonnegative constraint, which makes the scaled cluster indicators more accurate. In summary, CGSSL achieves best performance on all data sets by exploiting nonnegative spectral analysis and structural learning with $\ell_{2,1}$-norm regularization simultaneously for feature selection.

2.4 Nonnegative Spectral Analysis and Redundancy Control for Unsupervised Feature Selection

The proposed CGSSL method ignores the redundancy among the features. The select subset may be not compact. To select the discriminative features with controlled redundancy, we propose a new Nonnegative Spectral analysis with Constrained Redundancy (NSCR) method to exploit clustering analysis and explicitly consider the redundancy between features simultaneously. NSCR is formulated as

$$\min_{\mathbf{F},\mathbf{W}} J(\mathbf{F}) + \alpha l(h(\mathbf{W};\mathbf{X}),\mathbf{F}) + \beta \Omega(\mathbf{W}) + \lambda g(\mathbf{W})$$

$$\text{s.t.}\quad \mathbf{F} = \mathbf{Y}(\mathbf{Y}^T\mathbf{Y})^{-\frac{1}{2}}, \tag{2.49}$$

where $J(\mathbf{F})$ is a clustering criterion, $l(\cdot,\cdot)$ is the loss function, $h(\cdot)$ is a predictive function, $\Omega(\cdot)$ is a regularization function with row sparsity, and $g(\cdot)$ is a function to control the redundancy. α, β, and λ are three nonnegative trade-off parameter.

2.4.1 The Objective Function

For the clustering criterion $J(\mathbf{F})$, following the above section, we utilize the proposed nonnegative spectral analysis.

$$J(\mathbf{F}) = \text{Tr}[\mathbf{F}^T\mathbf{L}\mathbf{F}], \quad \text{s.t.}\quad \mathbf{F}^T\mathbf{F} = \mathbf{I}_c, \ \mathbf{F} \geq 0. \tag{2.50}$$

In NSCR, the features which are most discriminative to the cluster indicators are selected. To this end, we assume that there is a linear transformation between features and the cluster indicators and adopt a linear model to predict the cluster indicators. Therefore, we have the following function:

$$h(\mathbf{W};\mathbf{X}) = \mathbf{X}^T\mathbf{W} \tag{2.51}$$

where $\mathbf{W} = [\mathbf{w}^1,\ldots,\mathbf{w}^c] \in \mathbb{R}^{d \times c}$ is the linear transformation matrix to predict the cluster indicators. To learn a more discriminative predictors for more reliable results and make our method robust to noisy features, we impose a more general and better sparse model on $\mathbf{W}$. It has been verified by extensive computational studies that ℓ_p-norm $(0 < p < 1)$ can lead to sparser solution than using ℓ_1-norm [7, 8], and $\ell_{2,p}$-norm based minimization can also achieve a better sparsity solution than $\ell_{2,1}$-norm [41]. Thus, we introduce a $\ell_{2,p}$-norm based regularization for Ω to guarantee that $\mathbf{W}$ is sparse in rows. It can discard noisy or indifferent features

$$\Omega(\mathbf{W}) = \sum_{i=1}^{d} \|\mathbf{w}_i\|_2^p = \|\mathbf{W}\|_{2,p}^p. \tag{2.52}$$

The proposed problem in (2.49) can be rewritten as

$$\min_{\mathbf{F},\mathbf{W}} J(\mathbf{F}) + \alpha l(\mathbf{X}^T\mathbf{W}, \mathbf{F}) + \beta \|\mathbf{W}\|_{2,p}^p + \lambda g(\mathbf{W}) \text{ s.t. } \mathbf{F}^T\mathbf{F} = \mathbf{I}_c, \mathbf{F} \geq 0. \tag{2.53}$$

Under the guide of nonnegative spectral clustering, the feature selection matrix with $\ell_{2,p}$-norm regularization can select necessary features and discard noisy or indifferent features. However, correlated features may be selected simultaneously since currently we do not penalize the proposed method for redundant features. For example, if the ith feature is highly correlated to the jth feature, we do not need to select both of them simultaneously. Toward this end, we introduce a penalty factor $g(\mathbf{W})$ into our feature selection scheme to control the redundancy while selecting features. Many strategies can be used to define the penalty for using redundant features. In this work, we adopt the correlation between features to define $g(\mathbf{W})$.

$$g(\mathbf{W}) = \frac{1}{d(d-1)} \sum_{i=1}^{d} \|\mathbf{w}_i\|_2 \sum_{j=1, j\neq i}^{d} \|\mathbf{w}_j\|_2 C_{ij} \tag{2.54}$$

$C_{ij} \geq 0$ is a measure of correlation between the ith feature and the jth feature. $\|\mathbf{w}_i\|_2$ is a weight to measure the importance of the ith feature. The correlation can be measured linearly or nonlinearly. For a linear measure, the Pearsons correlation coefficient between the ith feature and the jth feature can be used. The mutual information between the ith feature and the jth feature can be used to measure the nonlinear correlation. In this work, the mutual information is adopted. If we set $C_{ii} = 0$, we have

$$g(\mathbf{W}) = \frac{1}{d(d-1)} \sum_{i,j=1}^{d} \|\mathbf{w}_i\|_2 \|\mathbf{w}_j\|_2 C_{ij}. \tag{2.55}$$

The normalized factor $\frac{1}{d(d-1)}$ is used just to make the regularization term independent of the number of features. By taking the redundancy into account, our method can avoid selected many members of a redundant set of features.

By incorporating the nonnegative spectral clustering, sparse prediction model and the redundancy control into a unified framework, we obtain the following optimization problem:

$$
\min_{\mathbf{F},\mathbf{W}} \mathrm{Tr}[\mathbf{F}^T \mathbf{L}\mathbf{F}] + \alpha l(\mathbf{X}^T\mathbf{W}, \mathbf{F}) + \beta \|\mathbf{W}\|_{2,p}^p + \frac{\lambda}{d(d-1)} \sum_{i,j=1}^{d} \|\mathbf{w}_i\|_2 \|\mathbf{w}_j\|_2 C_{ij}
$$

$$
\text{s.t.} \quad \mathbf{F}^T\mathbf{F} = \mathbf{I}_c, \ \mathbf{F} \geq 0. \tag{2.56}
$$

To solve the optimization problem in (2.56), we first decide which loss function is chosen for $l(\cdot, \cdot)$. In this work, we utilize the least square loss $l(x, y) = \frac{1}{2}(x - y)^2$ for simplicity and set $\gamma = \frac{\lambda}{d(d-1)}$. Hence we have

$$
\min_{\mathbf{F},\mathbf{W}} \mathrm{Tr}[\mathbf{F}^T \mathbf{L}\mathbf{F}] + \frac{\alpha}{2}\|\mathbf{F} - \mathbf{X}^T\mathbf{W}\|_F^2 + \beta \|\mathbf{W}\|_{2,p}^p + \gamma \sum_{i,j=1}^{d} \|\mathbf{w}_i\|_2 \|\mathbf{w}_j\|_2 C_{ij}
$$

$$
\text{s.t.} \quad \mathbf{F}^T\mathbf{F} = \mathbf{I}_c, \ \mathbf{F} \geq 0. \tag{2.57}
$$

The joint minimization of the regression model and $\ell_{2,p}$-norm regularization term enables $\mathbf{W}$ to evaluate the correlation between pseudo labels and features, making it particularly suitable for feature selection. More specifically, $\mathbf{w}_i$, the ith row of $\mathbf{W}$, shrinks to zero if the ith feature is less discriminative to the pseudo labels $\mathbf{F}$. It can guarantee that the necessary features are selected and the noisy or indifferent features are discarded. The consideration of the redundancy can explicitly control the redundancy between the selected features. Once $\mathbf{W}$ is learned, we can select the top r ranked features by sorting all d features according to $\|\mathbf{w}_i\|_2$ ($i = 1, \ldots, d$) in descending order. Therefore, the features corresponding to zero rows of $\mathbf{W}$ will be discarded when performing feature selection.

2.4.2 Optimization

Since ℓ_p ($0 < p < 1$) vector norm is neither convex nor Lipschitz continuous, $\ell_{2,p}$ matrix pseudo norm is not convex or Lipschitz continuous yet. The optimization problem (2.57) involves the $\ell_{2,p}$-norm which is not convex and nonsmooth. Consequently, we propose an iterative optimization algorithm to solve the optimization problem (2.57). For the ease of representation, let us define

$$
\mathscr{L}(\mathbf{F}, \mathbf{W}) = \mathrm{Tr}[\mathbf{F}^T \mathbf{L}\mathbf{F}] + \frac{\alpha}{2}\|\mathbf{F} - \mathbf{X}^T\mathbf{W}\|_F^2 + \beta \|\mathbf{W}\|_{2,p}^p + \gamma \sum_{i,j=1}^{d} \|\mathbf{w}_i\|_2 \|\mathbf{w}_j\|_2 C_{ij}.
$$

$$
\tag{2.58}
$$

By computing the derivative of $\mathscr{L}$ with respect to $\mathbf{w}_i$,[2] we obtain:

$$\frac{\partial \mathscr{L}}{\partial \mathbf{w_i}} = \alpha \mathbf{X}(\mathbf{X}^T \mathbf{w}_i - \mathbf{f}_i) + \beta \frac{\mathbf{w}_i}{\|\mathbf{w}_i\|_2} + \gamma \frac{\sum_j \|\mathbf{w}_j\|_2 C_{ij}}{\|\mathbf{w}_i\|_2} \mathbf{w}_i. \tag{2.59}$$

The following equation can be easily induced

$$\frac{\partial \mathscr{L}}{\partial \mathbf{W}} = \alpha \mathbf{X}(\mathbf{X}^T \mathbf{W} - \mathbf{F}) + \beta \mathbf{D}\mathbf{W} + \gamma \mathbf{H}\mathbf{W}, \tag{2.60}$$

where $\mathbf{D}$ is a diagonal matrix with $D_{ii} = \frac{p}{2\|\mathbf{w}_i\|_2^{2-p}}$ and $\mathbf{H}$ is another diagonal matrix with $H_{ii} = \frac{\sum_j \|\mathbf{w}_j\|_2 C_{ij}}{2\|\mathbf{w}_i\|_2}$. Setting $\frac{\partial \mathscr{L}(\mathbf{F},\mathbf{W})}{\partial \mathbf{W}} = 0$, we have

$$\alpha \mathbf{X}(\mathbf{X}^T \mathbf{W} - \mathbf{F}) + \beta \mathbf{D}\mathbf{W} + \gamma \mathbf{H}\mathbf{W} = 0$$
$$\Rightarrow \mathbf{W} = \alpha(\alpha \mathbf{X}\mathbf{X}^T + \beta \mathbf{D} + \gamma \mathbf{H})^{-1}\mathbf{X}\mathbf{F}$$
$$= \mathbf{G}^{-1}\mathbf{X}\mathbf{F} \tag{2.61}$$

Here $\mathbf{G} = \mathbf{X}\mathbf{X}^T + \frac{\beta}{\alpha}\mathbf{D} + \frac{\gamma}{\alpha}\mathbf{H}$.

Owing to $\|\mathbf{A}\|_F^2 = \text{Tr}(\mathbf{A}^T\mathbf{A})$ for any arbitrary matrix $\mathbf{A}$, we can rewrite Eq. (2.58) as follows:

$$\mathscr{L} = \text{Tr}[\mathbf{F}^T \mathbf{L}\mathbf{F}] + \alpha \text{Tr}[(\mathbf{X}^T \mathbf{W} - \mathbf{F})^T (\mathbf{X}^T \mathbf{W} - \mathbf{F})] + \beta \text{Tr}[\mathbf{W}^T \mathbf{D}\mathbf{W}] + \gamma \text{Tr}[\mathbf{W}^T \mathbf{H}\mathbf{W}]$$
$$= \text{Tr}[\mathbf{F}^T \mathbf{L}\mathbf{F}] + \alpha \text{Tr}[\mathbf{F}^T \mathbf{F}] - 2\alpha \text{Tr}[\mathbf{W}^T \mathbf{X}\mathbf{F}] + \text{Tr}[\mathbf{W}^T (\alpha \mathbf{X}\mathbf{X}^T + \beta \mathbf{D} + \gamma \mathbf{H})\mathbf{W}]. \tag{2.62}$$

By substituting the expression for $\mathbf{W}$ in Eq. (2.61) into the above equation, we have

$$\mathscr{L}(\mathbf{F}) = \text{Tr}[\mathbf{F}^T (\mathbf{L} + \alpha \mathbf{I}_n - \alpha \mathbf{X}^T \mathbf{G}^{-1}\mathbf{X})\mathbf{F}]. \tag{2.63}$$

Thus, we obtain the following optimization problem *w.s.r.* $\mathbf{F}$

$$\min_{\mathbf{F}} \text{Tr}[\mathbf{F}^T \mathbf{M}\mathbf{F}] \quad \text{s.t.} \quad \mathbf{F}^T \mathbf{F} = \mathbf{I}_c; \; \mathbf{F} \geq 0. \tag{2.64}$$

Here $\mathbf{M} = \mathbf{L} + \alpha \mathbf{I}_n - \alpha \mathbf{X}^T \mathbf{G}^{-1}\mathbf{X}$. Then we relax the orthogonal constraint by incorporating the orthogonal constraint of $\mathbf{F}$ into the objective function via Langrange multiplier and obtain the optimization problem as follows:

$$\min_{\mathbf{F} \geq 0} \text{Tr}[\mathbf{F}^T \mathbf{M}\mathbf{F}] + \frac{\mu}{2}\|\mathbf{F}^T \mathbf{F} - \mathbf{I}_c\|_F^2 \tag{2.65}$$

---

[2] In practice, $\|\mathbf{w}_i\|_2$ could be close to zero but not zero. Theoretically, it could be zeros. For this case, we can regularize $\|\mathbf{w}_i\|_2 \leftarrow \|\mathbf{w}_i\|_2 + \varepsilon$, where ε is a very small constant. When $\varepsilon \to 0$, we can see that $\|\mathbf{w}_i\|_2 + \varepsilon$ approximates $\|\mathbf{w}_i\|_2$.

$\mu > 0$ is a parameter to control the orthogonality condition. In practice, λ should be large enough to insure the orthogonality satisfied. Let ϕ_{ij} be the Lagrange multiplier for constraint $F_{ij} \geq 0$ and $\Phi = [\phi_{ij}]$. The Lagrange function is

$$\text{Tr}[\mathbf{F}^T \mathbf{M} \mathbf{F}] + \frac{\mu}{2}\text{Tr}[(\mathbf{F}^T \mathbf{F} - \mathbf{I}_c)^T (\mathbf{F}^T \mathbf{F} - \mathbf{I}_c)] + \text{Tr}[\Phi \mathbf{F}^T]. \qquad (2.66)$$

Setting its derivative with respect to $\mathbf{F}$ to 0, we have

$$2\mathbf{M}\mathbf{F} + 2\mu\mathbf{F}(\mathbf{F}^T \mathbf{F} - \mathbf{I}_c) + \Phi = 0. \qquad (2.67)$$

Using the Karush–Kuhn–Tuckre (KKT) condition [22] $\phi_{ij} F_{ij} = 0$, we obtain the updating rules:

$$2[\mathbf{M}\mathbf{F} + \lambda\mathbf{F}(\mathbf{F}^T \mathbf{F} - \mathbf{I}_c)]_{ij} F_{ij} + \Phi_{ij} F_{ij} = 0$$
$$\Rightarrow \quad [\mathbf{M}\mathbf{F} + \lambda\mathbf{F}(\mathbf{F}^T \mathbf{F} - \mathbf{I}_c)]_{ij} F_{ij} = 0. \qquad (2.68)$$

There may exist mix-signed elements in $\mathbf{M}$. To guarantee the nonnegative property of $\mathbf{F}$, by introducing $\mathbf{M} = \mathbf{M}^+ - \mathbf{M}^-$, where $M_{ij}^+ = (|M_{ij}| + M_{ij})/2$ and $M_{ij}^- = (|M_{ij}| - M_{ij})/2$, the above equation is equivalent to

$$[(\mathbf{M}^+ - \mathbf{M}^-)\mathbf{F} + \mu\mathbf{F}(\mathbf{F}^T \mathbf{F} - \mathbf{I}_c)]_{ij} F_{ij} = 0. \qquad (2.69)$$

Here $| \cdot |$ denotes the absolute value function. Thus, we have

$$F_{ij} \leftarrow F_{ij} \frac{(\mathbf{M}^- \mathbf{F} + \mu\mathbf{F})_{ij}}{(\mathbf{M}^+ \mathbf{F} + \mu\mathbf{F}\mathbf{F}^T \mathbf{F})_{ij}}. \qquad (2.70)$$

Then we normalize $\mathbf{F}$ with $(\mathbf{F}^T \mathbf{F})_{ii} = 1, i = 1, \ldots, c$.

From the above analysis, we can see that $\mathbf{D}$ and $\mathbf{H}$ related to $\mathbf{W}$ is required to solve $\mathbf{F}$ and it is still not straightforward to obtain $\mathbf{W}$ and $\mathbf{F}$. To this end, we design an iterative algorithm to solve the proposed formulation, which is summarized in Algorithm 2.

The alternative updating rules in Algorithm 2 monotonically decrease the objective function value of (2.57) in each iteration. That is, the proposed iterative procedure in Algorithm 2 can be verified to be convergent. The convergence is also experimentally verified in our experiments. Besides, the proposed optimization algorithm is efficient. In the experiments, we observe that our algorithm usually converges around only 20 iterations.

Now, we briefly analyze the computational complexity. In our case, $c \ll n$ and $c \ll d$. It takes $O(nd^2)$ to obtain $\mathbf{C}$. The complexity of calculating the inverse of a matrix is $O(d^3)$. In each iteration step, the cost for updating $\mathbf{G}$ based on $\mathbf{W}$ and $\mathbf{C}$ is

---

Algorithm 2 The Proposed NSCR Method

Input:

  Data matrix $\mathbf{X} \in \mathscr{R}^{d \times n}$;

  Parameters $\alpha, \beta, \gamma, \mu, k, c$ and p

1: Construct the k-nearest neighbor graph and calculate $\mathbf{L}$;

2: Construct the correlation matrix between features $\mathbf{C}$;

3: The iteration step $t = 1$; Initialize $\mathbf{F}_t \in \mathscr{R}^{n \times c}$, set $\mathbf{D}_t \in \mathscr{R}^{d \times d}$ as an identity matrix and $\mathbf{H}_t \in \mathscr{R}^{d \times d}$ as a zero matrix;

4: **repeat**

5:   $\mathbf{G}_t = \mathbf{X}\mathbf{X}^T + \frac{\beta}{\alpha}\mathbf{D}_t + \frac{\gamma}{\alpha}\mathbf{H}_t$;

6:   $\mathbf{M}_t = \mathbf{L} + \alpha\mathbf{I}_n - \alpha\mathbf{X}^T\mathbf{G}_t^{-1}\mathbf{X}$;

7:   $\mathbf{M}_t^+ = (|\mathbf{M}_t| + \mathbf{M}_t)/2$ and $\mathbf{M}_t^- = (|\mathbf{M}_t| - \mathbf{M}_t)/2$;

8:   $(F_{t+1})_{ij} = (F_t)_{ij} \frac{(\mathbf{M}_t^- \mathbf{F}_t + \mu \mathbf{F}_t)_{ij}}{(\mathbf{M}_t^+ \mathbf{F}_t + \mu \mathbf{F}_t \mathbf{F}_t^T \mathbf{F}_t)_{ij}}$;

9:   $\mathbf{W}_{t+1} = \mathbf{G}_t^{-1}\mathbf{X}\mathbf{F}_{t+1}$;

10:   Update the diagonal matrix $\mathbf{D}$ as

  $$\mathbf{D}_{t+1} = \begin{bmatrix} \frac{p}{2\|(\mathbf{w}_{t+1})_1\|_2^{2-p}} & & \\ & \cdots & \\ & & \frac{p}{2\|(\mathbf{w}_{t+1})_d\|_2^{2-p}} \end{bmatrix};$$

11:   Update the diagonal matrix $\mathbf{H}$ as

  $$\mathbf{H}_{t+1} = \begin{bmatrix} \frac{\sum_j \|(\mathbf{w}_{t+1})_j\|_2 C_{1j}}{2\|(\mathbf{w}_{t+1})_1\|_2} & & \\ & \cdots & \\ & & \frac{\sum_j \|(\mathbf{w}_{t+1})_j\|_2 C_{dj}}{2\|(\mathbf{w}_{t+1})_d\|_2} \end{bmatrix};$$

12:   t=t+1;

13: **until** Convergence criterion satisfied

Output:

  Sort all d features according to $\|(\mathbf{w}_t)_i\|_2$ in descending order and select the top r ranked features.

$O(cd + d^2)$. It needs $O(d^3)$ to obtain $\mathbf{G}^{-1}$. The cost for updating $\mathbf{M}$ is $O(nd^2 + n^2 d)$. It takes $O(cn^2)$ to update $\mathbf{F}$ and $O(nd^2)$ to update $\mathbf{W}$, respectively. Thus the overall cost for the proposed NSCR is $O(T(d^3 + nd^2 + dn^2))$, where T is the number of iterations.

2.4.3 Experiments

In this section, we experimentally evaluate the performance of the proposed NSCR method for unsupervised feature selection, which can be applied to many applications, such as clustering and classification. We only evaluate the performance of NSCR and compared with representative algorithms in terms of clustering. In our experiments, we first select the top r features and then utilize Kmeans algorithm to cluster images based on the selected features.

2.4.3.1   Data Sets

The experiments are conducted on nine publicly available image datasets, including four face image data sets, i.e., UMIST [1], AT&T [36], JAFFE [29], and Pointing4 [44], three handwritten digit data sets, i.e., MNIST used in [44], Binary Alphabet (BA) [1] and a subset of USPS with 40 samples randomly selected for each class [1], and two object image databases, i.e., COIL20 [31] and Caltech101 [15]. Data sets from different areas serve as a good test bed for a comprehensive evaluation.

Some datasets have been introduced in Sect. 2.3. In the AT&T face image dataset [36], there are 10 gray scale images for each of the 40 human objects. There were taken at different times, varying the lighting, facial expressions and facial details. The image size is 32 × 32. The COIL20 [31] database contains 32 × 32 gray scale images of 20 objects viewed from varying angles and each object has 72 images. The Caltech101 dataset [15] contains 9144 images of 101 classes and an additional class of background images. In our experiments, we select the 10 largest categories, except the BACKGROUND_GOOGLE category. The SIFT descriptor is extracted and then 1000-dimensional bag of visual word is generated to represent each image. Table 2.6 summarizes the details of these nine benchmark data sets used in the experiments in terms of the total number n of images, the total number c of clusters and the feature dimension d.

2.4.3.2   Compared Scheme

To validate the effectiveness of the proposed NSCR for feature selection, we compare it with one baseline and several unsupervised feature selection methods. The compared algorithms are enumerated as follows:

- **Baseline**: All original visual features are adopted.

Table 2.6 Image dataset description. n is the number of images; d denotes the dimension of features; c is the number of clusters.

Domain	Dataset	n	d	c
Face image	UMIST	575	644	20
	AT&T	400	1024	40
	JAFFE	213	676	10
	Poingting4	2790	1120	15
Handwritten digits image	MNIST	5000	784	10
	BA	1404	320	36
	USPS	400	256	10
Object image	Coil20	1440	1024	20
	Caltech101	3379	1000	10

- **MaxVar**: Features corresponding to the maximum variance are selected to obtain the expressive features.
- **LS** [17]: Features consistent with Gaussian Laplacian matrix are selected to preserve the local manifold structure.
- **SPEC** [47]: Features are selected using spectral regression based on pairwise image similarity.
- **SPFS-SFS** [48]: The traditional forward search strategy is utilized for similarity preserving feature selection in the SPFS framework.
- **MCFS** [5]: Features are selected based on spectral analysis and sparse regression in a two-step scheme;
- **UDFS** [43]: Features are selected by exploiting the local structure for local discriminative information and row-sparse models for feature correlations simultaneously.
- **SCR**: A special case of the proposed method without considering the redundancy constraint for unsupervised feature selection, i.e., $\gamma = 0$.
- **NSCR**: The proposed method with Nonnegative Spectral analysis and Controlled Redundancy for unsupervised feature selection.

In the compared methods, there are some hyper-parameters to be set in advance. The same strategy used in Sect. 2.3 is adopted.

2.4.3.3 Results on Synthetic Data

To well evaluate the effectiveness of the proposed NSCR method on the feature selection task, we conduct experiments on one widely used synthetic dataset, i.e., Corral [45]. It contains six Boolen features $(A0, A1, B0, B1, I, R)$, in which the relevant features, irrelevant features, and redundant features are provided. Specifically, the class labels of data points are defined by $(A0 \wedge A1) \vee (B0 \wedge B1)$ while $A0, A1, B0$, and $B1$ are independent to each other. Feature R is redundant by matching the class label 75% of the time, while feature I is uniformly random. That is, features $A0, A1$, $B0$, and $B1$ are necessary features, feature R is the redundant feature while feature I is the noisy feature. The results of features ranked by different methods are presented in Table 2.7. For each method, features are selected from left to right, top to bottom. It can be seen that if the top four features are selected, only the proposed method can remove the noisy feature and the redundant feature simultaneously while other methods fail to filter out the redundant feature, which demonstrates the effectiveness of the proposed method for feature selection.

Table 2.7 The rank of features by different methods on the Corral data. Features are selected from left to right, top to bottom.

	MaxVar	LS	SPEC	SPFS-SFS	MCFS	UDFS	SCR	NSCR
Rank	$R, A0, A1,$ $B0, B1, I$	$R, A0, B0,$ $A1, B1, I$	$R, A0, A1,$ $B0, B1, I$	$R, B1, A0,$ $B0, A1, I$	$R, A0, B0,$ $A1, B1, I$	$A1, R, B0,$ $A0, B1, I$	$B0, B1, A1,$ $R, A0, I$	$B1, B0, A1,$ $A0, R, I$

2.4.3.4   Performance Comparison on Real-world Data

We now empirically evaluate the performance of these nine feature selection algorithms for clustering in terms of ACC and NMI. The detailed results on the face, handwritten digit and object data sets are summarized in Tables 2.8, 2.9, and 2.10, respectively. The results demonstrate that NSCR achieves the best performance on all the nine image sets compared to other eight feature selection algorithms, which validates its effectiveness.

From the above experimental results, we have the following observations. First, it is observed that NSCR achieves better performance than SCR by considering the nonnegative constraint. It demonstrates that it is necessary and effective to introduce the nonnegative constraint. The improved NSCR enables to remove the redundant features while preserving the necessary features. Second, NSCR is both superior to MCFS by introducing the nonnegative constraint, which makes the scaled cluster indicators more accurate. They can select more necessary features. Third, NSCR, UDFS, and MCFS achieve larger values of ACC and NMI by exploiting discriminative information from data. It demonstrates that it is crucial to uncover the discriminative information in the unsupervised case, which can remove noisy features and indifferent features. Fourth, NSCR achieves more accurate clustering performance than SPEC and MCFS. SPEC and MCFS adopt a two-step approach to introduce spectral analysis into feature selection while NSCR is an one-step framework and perform spectral analysis and feature selection simultaneously. Fifth, by exploiting the local geometric structure of data distribution, LS, SPEC, MCFS, UDFS, and NSCR usually yield superior performance. Besides, it can be seen that it is necessary to select features jointly rather than one by one. The joint feature selection algorithms, such as MCFS, UDFS, and NSCR are always superior to the methods selecting features one after another, such as MaxVar and SPEC. Finally, compared with the baseline, it can be observed that feature selection is necessary and effective by removing the noise. It can not only reduce the number of features and make the algorithms more efficient, but also improve the performance. In conclusion, NSCR achieves the best performance on all data sets by exploiting nonnegative spectral analysis and redundancy between features simultaneously for feature selection, which can select necessary features, control the use of redundant features and discard noisy or indifferent features.

2.5   Discussions

In this chapter, we propose a novel understanding-oriented unsupervised feature selection framework, which exploits nonnegative spectral analysis, the latent structure analysis, and explicitly control the redundancy between features while a parse model with the $\ell_{2,p}$-norm is introduced. The proposed framework can select necessary features, remove noisy, or indifferent features while control the redundancy between the selected features. The cluster indicators learned by nonnegative spectral

Table 2.8 Clustering results comparison on the face image data sets. The best results are highlighted in bold

Dataset	Baseline	MaxVar	LS	SPEC	SPFS-SFS	MCFS	UDFS	SCR	NSCR
ACC ± std (%)									
UMIST	41.3 ± 2.9	45.6 ± 4.9	46.1 ± 1.9	48.5 ± 4.4	47.7 ± 2.9	47.5 ± 3.6	49.5 ± 3.2	54.6 ± 1.1	**56.7 ± 2.6**
AT&T	50.8 ± 3.1	46.5 ± 3.2	47.6 ± 2.2	50.7 ± 3.2	51.9 ± 2.5	52.9 ± 2.9	52.3 ± 2.1	53.7 ± 1.9	**56.2 ± 1.3**
JAFFE	73.6 ± 9.2	72.2 ± 5.1	74.9 ± 6.4	75.6 ± 5.8	76.6 ± 6.3	77.4 ± 6.1	77.9 ± 4.9	82.2 ± 4.2	**82.9 ± 4.0**
Pointing4	35.6 ± 1.7	44.8 ± 2.0	38.0 ± 1.7	38.9 ± 2.5	39.3 ± 1.1	47.2 ± 1.9	45.4 ± 3.0	50.1 ± 1.8	**52.3 ± 1.1**
NMI ± std (%)									
UMIST	62.7 ± 1.8	63.7 ± 3.7	64.1 ± 1.2	67.6 ± 1.9	62.7 ± 2.2	67.1 ± 2.3	69.3 ± 3.5	71.6 ± 1.5	**73.4 ± 2.5**
AT&T	71.2 ± 1.8	68.9 ± 2.4	69.5 ± 1.4	71.4 ± 1.6	72.6 ± 1.5	73.5 ± 1.5	72.0 ± 1.9	71.3 ± 0.6	**74.5 ± 1.7**
JAFFE	80.8 ± 5.9	74.7 ± 4.1	81.2 ± 4.4	82.3 ± 4.4	83.1 ± 3.8	81.7 ± 4.5	82.1 ± 3.8	86.2 ± 2.2	**87.7 ± 3.1**
Pointing4	41.4 ± 1.0	51.6 ± 1.6	55.3 ± 1.5	56.3 ± 1.4	42.7 ± 1.2	55.8 ± 1.6	52.4 ± 1.6	57.0 ± 1.5	**57.9 ± 1.0**

Table 2.9 Clustering results comparison on the handwritten digit data sets. The best results are highlighted in bold

Dataset	Baseline	MaxVar	LS	SPEC	SPFS-SFS	MCFS	UDFS	SCR	NSCR
ACC ± std (%)									
MNIST	50.1 ± 5.3	54.2 ± 3.1	52.9 ± 3.4	53.3 ± 4.7	54.9 ± 4.7	55.8 ± 3.7	57.3 ± 2.5	58.7 ± 1.9	**60.8 ± 2.7**
BA	40.7 ± 1.7	41.7 ± 1.1	42.6 ± 2.3	41.8 ± 1.4	42.5 ± 2.1	42.3 ± 1.7	42.8 ± 1.9	42.1 ± 1.0	**45.7 ± 1.6**
USPS	62.8 ± 5.1	64.1 ± 1.3	64.5 ± 5.0	65.9 ± 4.0	63.4 ± 3.3	65.9 ± 2.8	65.2 ± 3.6	68.1 ± 1.5	**72.0 ± 2.6**
NMI ± std (%)									
MNIST	47.2 ± 2.4	48.1 ± 1.8	48.2 ± 1.5	49.1 ± 2.2	49.6 ± 2.1	50.4 ± 1.6	51.1 ± 1.4	50.9 ± 1.3	**53.9 ± 2.4**
BA	56.4 ± 0.9	57.3 ± 0.6	58.1 ± 0.6	57.4 ± 0.8	57.6 ± 1.2	57.9 ± 1.0	58.1 ± 1.0	57.3 ± 0.5	**60.0 ± 1.3**
USPS	58.5 ± 3.1	60.2 ± 0.8	58.9 ± 2.8	59.2 ± 1.8	56.5 ± 1.7	59.4 ± 2.4	60.1 ± 3.4	61.8 ± 1.1	**63.9 ± 1.1**

Table 2.10 Clustering results comparison on the object image data sets. The best results are highlighted in bold

Dataset	Baseline	MaxVar	LS	SPEC	SPFS-SFS	MCFS	UDFS	SCR	NSCR
ACC ± std (%)									
COIL20	59.0 ± 5.7	58.4 ± 4.0	57.3 ± 3.0	61.0 ± 2.1	62.5 ± 2.6	61.7 ± 4.3	62.9 ± 2.6	65.3 ± 3.6	**67.2 ± 1.5**
Caltech101	47.7 ± 3.8	40.1 ± 1.9	47.6 ± 2.3	48.6 ± 3.2	49.2 ± 2.7	50.2 ± 5.0	50.8 ± 2.9	52.3 ± 1.8	**54.3 ± 2.4**
NMI ± std (%)									
COIL20	72.9 ± 2.8	70.5 ± 0.9	70.4 ± 1.1	74.1 ± 2.4	76.2 ± 1.6	74.7 ± 2.3	75.9 ± 1.1	77.3 ± 1.7	**78.9 ± 1.2**
Caltech101	34.5 ± 4.5	35.0 ± 2.0	37.5 ± 2.7	36.3 ± 2.2	33.4 ± 2.3	38.0 ± 5.3	38.4 ± 2.5	50.9 ± 1.3	**42.2 ± 1.4**

clustering are used to provide label information for unsupervised feature selection. To facilitate feature selection, the predictive matrix is constrained to be sparse in rows. By imposing the $\ell_{2,p}$-norm regularization, the proposed methods jointly selects the most discriminative features across the entire feature space. For future work, we will focus on extending our methods in the kernel learning framework and the local learning framework. Besides, how to select the adaptive hyper-parameters and the number of selected features are also our directions for future research.

By the proposed understanding-oriented feature selection framework, better feature subsets can be chosen to represent the contents of images. However, the contents of images are still described by the low-level visual features. The semantic gap between low-level features and high-level semantic still exist, although it may be reduced to a certain degree by the understanding-oriented feature selection methods. The better way may be to learn a good representation for data, i.e., feature extraction. The understanding-oriented feature representation is desired to be studied.

On the other hand, we known that social images are associated with user-provided tags. Although these tags are imperfect, they can reflect the semantic information of images to a certain degree. It is believed that users express their individual understanding through tags. Thus, the user-provided tags enable to help us to select better feature subsets or learn better data representation. Meanwhile, the imperfect problem of the user-provided tags should be handled during the learning procedure. Better data representations can be found by exploring the user-provided tags.

References

1. http://cs.nyu.edu/~roweis/data.html
2. http://tunedit.org/repo/Data/Text-wc
3. http://featureselection.asu.edu/datasets.php
4. Ando, R.K., Zhang, T.: A framework for learning predictive structures from multiple tasks and unlabeld data. J. Mach. Learn. Res. **6**, 1817–1853 (2005)
5. Cai, D., Zhang, C., He, X.: Unsupervised feature selection for multi-cluster data. In: Proceedings of ACM SIGKDD International Conference Knowledge Discovery and Data Mining, pp. 333–342 (2010)
6. Chakraborty, R., Pal, N.: Feature selection using a neural framework with controlled redundancy. IEEE Trans. Neural Netw. Learn. Syst. **26**(1), 35–50 (2015)
7. Chartrand, R.: Exact reconstructions of sparse signals via nonconvex minimization. IEEE Signal Process Lett. **14**(10), 2832–2852 (2007)
8. Chen, X., Xu, F., Ye, Y.: Lower bound theory of nonzero entries in solutions of ℓ_2-ℓ_p minimization. SIAM J. Sci. Comput. **32**(5), 2832–2852 (2010)
9. Cheung, Y.M., Zeng, H.: Local kernel regression score for selecting features of high-dimensional data. IEEE Trans. Knowl. Data Eng. **21**(12), 1798–1802 (2009)
10. Constantinopoulos, C., Titsia, M.K., Likas, A.: Bayesian feature and model selection for gaussian mixture models. IEEE Trans. Pattern Anal. Mach. Intell. **28**(6), 1013–1018 (2006)
11. Craven, M., DiPasquo, D., Freitag, D., McCallum, A., Mitchell, T.M., Nigam, K., Slattery, S.: Learning to extract symbolic knowledge from the world wide web. In: Proceedings of AAAI Conference on Artificial Intelligence (1998)

12. Du, L., Shen, Z., Li, X., Zhou, P., Shen, Y.D.: Local and global discriminative learning for unsupervised feature selection. In: Proceedings of IEEE International Conference on Data Mining, pp. 131–140 (2013)
13. Duda, R., Hart, P., Stork, D.: Pattern Recognition, 2nd edn. Wiley, New York (2001)
14. Dy, J.G., Brodley, C.E.: Feature selection for unsupervised learning. J. Mach. Learn. Res. **5**, 845–889 (2004)
15. Fei-Fei, L., Fergus, R., Perona, P.: Learning generative visual models from few training examples: an incremental bayesian approach tested on 101 object categories. In: Proceedings of IEEE Computer Vision and Pattern Recognition Workshop on Generative-Model Based Vision, pp. 178–186 (2004)
16. Gourier, N., Hall, D., Crowley, J.: Estimating face orientation from robust detection of salient facial features. In: Proceedings of ICPR Workshop on Visual Observation of Deictic Gestures, pp. 1–9 (2004)
17. He, X., Cai, D., Niyogi, P.: Laplacian score for feature selection. In: Advances in Neural Information Processing Systems, pp. 507–514 (2005)
18. Higham, N.J.: Accuracy and Stability of Numerical Algorithms, 2nd edn. Society for Industrial and Applied Mathematics, Manchester (2002)
19. Jain, A., Zongker, D.: Feature selection: evaluation, application, and small sample performance. IEEE Trans. Pattern Anal. Mach. Intell. **19**(2), 153–158 (1997)
20. Ji, S., Zhang, L., Yu, S., Ye, J.: A shared-subspace learning framework for multi-label classification. ACM Trans. Knowl. Discov. Data **4**(2), 1817–1853 (2010)
21. Jiang, W., Er, G., Dai, Q., Gu, J.: Similarity-based online feature selection in content-based image retrieval. IEEE Trans. Image Process. **15**(3), 702–712 (2006)
22. Kuhn, H., Tucker, A.: Nonlinear programming. In: Berkeley Symposium on Mathematical Statistics and Probabilistics (1951)
23. Law, M.H., Figueirdo, M.A., Jain, A.K.: Simultaneous feature selection and clustering using mixture models. IEEE Trans. Pattern Anal. Mach. Intell. **26**(9), 1154–1166 (2004)
24. Lee, D., Seung, H.: Learning the parts of objects by nonnegative matrix factorization. Nature **401**, 788–791 (1999)
25. Li, Z., Liu, J., Yang, Y., Zhou, X., Lu, H.: Clustering-guided sparse structural learning for unsupervised feature selection. IEEE Trans. Knowl. Data Eng. **9**(26), 2138–2150 (2014)
26. Li, Z., Tang, J.: Unsupervised feature selection via nonnegative spectral analysis and redundancy control. IEEE Trans. Image Process. **24**(12), 5343–5355 (2015)
27. Li, Z., Yang, Y., Liu, J., Zhou, X., Lu, H.: Unsupervised feature selection using nonnegative spectral analysis. In: Proceedings of National Conference on Artificial Intelligence (AAAI), pp. 1026–1032 (2012)
28. Lowe, D.G.: Distinctive image features from scale-invariant keypoints. Int. J. Comput. Vis. **60**(2), 91–110 (2004)
29. Lyons, M.J., Budynek, J., Akamatsu, S.: Automatic classification of single facial images. IEEE Trans. Pattern Anal. Mach. Intell. **21**(12), 1357–1362 (1999)
30. Mitra, P., Murthy, C.A., Pal, S.K.: Unsupervised feature selection using feature similarity. IEEE Trans. Pattern Anal. Mach. Intell. **24**(3), 301–312 (2002)
31. Nene, S., Nayar, S., Murase, H.: Columbia object image library. Tech. Rep. Tech. Rep. CUCS-005-96, Columbia University (1996)
32. Ng, A.Y., Jordan, M., Weiss, Y.: On spectral clustering: analysis and an algorithm. In: Advances in Neural Information Processing Systems (2001)
33. Nie, F., Huang, H., Cai, X., Ding, C.: Efficient and robust feature selection via joint $\ell_{2,1}$-norms minimization. In: Advances in Neural Information Processing Systems, pp. 1813–1821 (2010)
34. Peng, H.C., Long, F.H., Ding, C.: Feature selection based on mutual information: criteria of max-dependency, max-relevance, and min-redundanct. IEEE Trans. Pattern Anal. Mach. Intell. **27**(8), 1226–1238 (2005)
35. Qian, M., Zhai, C.: Robust unsupervised feature selection. In: Proceedings of International Joint Conference on Artificial Intelligence, pp. 1621–1627 (2014)

36. Samaria, F., Harter, A.: Parameterisation of a stochastic model for human face identification. In: Proceedings of IEEE Workshop on Applications of Computer Vision, pp. 1–9 (1994)
37. Shi, J., Malik, J.: Normalized cuts and image segmentation. IEEE Trans. Pattern Anal. Mach. Intell. **22**, 888–905 (2000)
38. Shi, L., Du, L., Shen, Y.D.: Robust spectral learning for unsupervised feature selection. In: Proceedings of IEEE International Conference on Data Mining, pp. 131–140 (2014)
39. Song, L., Smola, A., Gretton, A., Bedo, J., Borgwardt, K.: Feature selection via dependence maximization. J. Mach. Learn. Res. **13**, 1393–1434 (2012)
40. Tang, Z., Zhang, Y., Li, Z., Lu, H.: Face clustering in videos with proportion prior. In: Proceedings of International Joint Conference on Artificial Intelligence, pp. 2191–2197 (2015)
41. Wang, L., Chen, S., Wang, Y.: A unified algorithm for mixed $\ell_{2,p}$-minimizations and its application in feature selection. Comput. Optim. Appl. **58**(2), 409–421 (2014)
42. Wolf, L., Shashua, A.: Feature selection for unsupervised and supervised inference: the emergence of sparsity in a weight-based approach. J. Mach. Learn. Res. **6**, 1855–1887 (2005)
43. Yang, Y., Shen, H.T., Ma, Z., Huang, Z., Zhou, X.: $\ell_{2,1}$-norm regularized discriminative feature selection for unsupervised learning. In: Proceedings of International Joint Conference on Artificial Intelligence (2011)
44. Yang, Y., Xu, D., Nie, F., Yan, S., Zhuang, Y.: Image clustering using local discriminant models and global integration. IEEE Trans. Image Process. **19**(10), 2761–2773 (2010)
45. Yu, L., Liu, H.: Efficient feature selection via analysis of relevance and redundancy. J. Mach. Learn. Res. **5**(10), 1205–1224 (2004)
46. Zeng, H., Cheung, Y.M.: Feature selection and kernel learning for local learning-based clustering. IEEE Trans. Pattern Anal. Mach. Intell. **33**(8), 1532–1547 (2011)
47. Zhao, Z., Liu, H.: Spectral feature selection for supervised and unsupervised learning. In: Proceedings of International Conference on Machine Learning, pp. 1151–1157 (2007)
48. Zhao, Z., Wang, L., Liu, H., Ye, J.: On similarity preserving feature selection. IEEE Trans. Knowl. Data Eng. **25**(3), 619–632 (2013)

Chapter 3
Understanding-Oriented Feature Learning

Abstract Different from feature selection, feature learning is to learn a new representation for data. To uncover an appropriate latent subspace for data representation, in this chapter we propose a novel Robust Structured Subspace Learning (RSSL) algorithm by integrating image understanding and feature learning into a joint learning framework. The learned subspace is adopted as an intermediate space to reduce the semantic gap between the low-level visual features and the high-level semantics. The proposed method can address multiple image understanding tasks, i.e., image tagging, clustering, and classification.

3.1 Introduction

For many pattern recognition and computer vision problems, images are always represented by a variety of visual features, which are often quite different from each other. The dimension of data feature space is becoming increasingly large. It is inevitable to introduce noisy and/or redundant features. The effectiveness and efficiency of learning methods drop exponentially as the dimensionality increases, which is commonly referred to as the "curse of dimensionality". Therefore, it is a fundamental problem to find a suitable representation of high-dimensional data [4], which can enhance the performance of numerous tasks, such as classification and multimedia analysis. To address these problems, a number of different methods have been developed, such as feature selection (i.e., select a subset of most discriminative features from the original features) [21] and subspace learning (i.e., transform the original features to a lower dimensional subspace) [4, 28]. In this chapter, we focus on learning an appropriate representation of data by uncovering a latent subspace for the purposes of image understanding, which is referred to assigning proper high-level semantic meaning (labels or tags) to given images (normally represented by low-level visual features), including image tagging, clustering[1] and classification.

---

[1]For clustering, the cluster indicators of samples can be deemed as the pseudo-labels of samples.

© Springer Nature Singapore Pte Ltd. 2017   47
Z. Li, *Understanding-Oriented Multimedia Content Analysis*, Springer Theses,
DOI 10.1007/978-981-10-3689-7_3

Recent years have witnessed a widespread interest in subspace learning. A variety of subspace learning models and techniques have been widely used for the representation of high-dimensional data, such as Principal Component Analysis (PCA) [4], Linear Discriminant Analysis (LDA) [4], and Locality Preserving Projection (LPP) [18]. Despite the different motivations of these algorithms, they can be interpreted in a general graph embedding framework [47]. Some manifold learning algorithms such as ISOMAP [44], Laplacian Eigenmap (LE) [5], and Locally Linear Embedding (LLE) [40] are designed to find a low-dimensional subspace in a nonlinear manner.

Nonetheless, these methods only focus on low-level features of data, which are independent of the follow-up tasks and ignore the high-level semantic information. As is known to all, there exists the so-called semantic gap between the low-level features and the high-level semantics, which often degrades the performance [41]. To alleviate the semantic gap, we try to uncover proper representations of data by integrating image understanding and feature learning into a joint learning framework. For this purpose, we propose a novel Robust Structured Subspace Learning (RSSL) framework to discover a compact and more informative feature representation and build a bridge between the low-level features and high-level semantics with the learned subspace by exploiting image understanding, feature learning, and feature correlation simultaneously. Specifically, unlike previous subspace learning models, the proposed framework learns a latent discriminative representation of images by considering the image understanding task in the procedure of feature learning, which makes the uncovered representations well predict the labels. To guarantee that the latent subspace is more compact and discriminative, the intrinsic geometric structure of data, and the local and global structural consistencies over labels are exploited simultaneously and incorporated into the proposed framework. To make our algorithm robust to the outliers and noise, we introduce the $\ell_{2,1}$-norm into the loss function and regularization. To solve the proposed problem, an effective and efficient iterative algorithm is proposed. Finally, we apply the proposed method to the tasks of social image tagging, unsupervised learning (i.e., clustering), semi-supervised and supervised learning (i.e., classification). Most of the work in this chapter has been published in [31].

3.2 Related Work

In this section, we briefly review the related research on feature learning including feature selection [21, 38] and subspace learning [4, 29, 45].

3.2.1 Feature Selection

Feature selection is a process of obtaining a subset of relevant features for model construction and removing redundant or irrelevant features. According to the availability of label information, there are three broad categories: supervised [14, 38, 51], semi-supervised [11], and unsupervised feature selection methods [9, 16]. Traditional feature selection usually ignores the correlations among features, such as Fisher Score [14] and Laplacian Score [16]. To this end, some sparsity-based approaches have been studied to exploit the feature correlation [33]. $\ell_{2,1}$-norm has been shown effective for sparse feature selection [38] and gains increasing interest. In [33], clustering and feature selection are incorporated into a joint framework to select a feature subset having strong discriminative power. Different from them, the proposed algorithm is an integrated framework which leverages feature learning and image understanding. In addition, several feature selection algorithms can be deemed as special cases of our framework.

3.2.2 Subspace Learning

Subspace learning sheds light on various tasks in computer vision and multimedia. It projects the original high-dimensional feature space to a low-dimensional subspace, wherein specific statistical properties can be well preserved. The most popular methods include PCA [4], LDA [4], LPP [18], and Neighborhood Preserving Embedding (NPE) [17]. These approaches with different motivations can be interpreted in a general graph embedding framework [47]. The learned projections of these methods are linear combinations of all the original features. Recently, sparse subspace learning has attracted considerable interests. Sparse PCA [52] was proposed based on "Elastic Net" regularization. Cai et al. [8] proposed a unified sparse subspace learning framework based on ℓ_1-norm regularization spectral regression. Some manifold learning approaches are studied to uncover the underlying nonlinear subspace, such as ISOMAP [44], LE [5], and LLE [40]. Factor analysis is another type subspace learning algorithm, such as Singular Value Decomposition (SVD). However, these methods only explore the visual features of images to mine the underlying subspace, whereas the low-level features and the high-level semantics are not linked. Due to the semantic gap, the learned data representations cannot be ensured to well predict labels. In [39], a latent semantic space is uncovered by learning a transformation to link the visual features and tags directly based on low-rank approximation. Some multi-view subspace learning methods are proposed [23–26, 34, 43]. Different from previous work, the proposed method learns a discriminative representation by incorporating image understanding and feature learning into a unified framework. A hidden subspace, which is an intermediate space between the low-level visual space and high-level semantic space, is uncovered to well predict labels. Besides, by introducing the row sparse model, our method is robust to outliers and noise.

3.3   The Proposed RSSL Framework

In this section, we introduce a novel subspace learning method for image understanding, called Robust Structured Subspace Learning (RSSL), which can find a suitable representation of data.

3.3.1   Formulation

Consider a data set consisting of n data points $\{\mathbf{x}_i\}_{i=1}^n$ assigned with c-dimensional binary-valued label vectors $\{\mathbf{y}_i\}_{i=1}^n$, $\mathbf{y}_i \in \{0, 1\}^c$. Here c is the cardinality of the label set $\mathscr{C} = \{t_1, t_2, \ldots, t_c\}$. Let $\mathbf{X} = [\mathbf{x}_1, \ldots, \mathbf{x}_n]$ denote the data matrix, in which $\mathbf{x}_i \in \mathbb{R}^d$ is the feature descriptor of the ith sample, and $\mathbf{Y} = [\mathbf{y}_1, \ldots, \mathbf{y}_n]^T$ be the label matrix of size $n \times c$. The jth column vector of $\mathbf{Y}$ corresponds to a labeling configuration with respect to the tag j and $Y_{ij} = 1$ indicates that $\mathbf{x}_i$ is associated with the label j, and $Y_{ij} = 0$ otherwise. We also introduce a predicted label matrix $\mathbf{F} \in \mathbb{R}^{n \times c}$, where each row $\mathbf{f}^i \in \mathbb{R}^c$ is the predicted label vector of the ith data $\mathbf{x}_i$. The local structure graph $\mathbf{S}$ is defined as follows:

$$
S_{ij} = \begin{cases} \exp\left(-\frac{\|\mathbf{x}_i - \mathbf{x}_j\|^2}{\sigma^2}\right) & \mathbf{x}_i \in \mathscr{N}_k(\mathbf{x}_j) \text{ or } \mathbf{x}_j \in \mathscr{N}_k(\mathbf{x}_i) \\ 0 & \text{otherwise,} \end{cases} \tag{3.1}
$$

where $\mathscr{N}_k(\mathbf{x})$ is the set of k-nearest neighbors of $\mathbf{x}$.

Obtaining a good performance in image understanding tasks always requires to find a good data representation. Features are correlated to represent the semantic information and combinations of features are more discriminative than individual features. We present a formulation to learn appropriate representations of images embedding in a latent subspace. In this work, the underlying subspace is expected to satisfy the two following properties.

1. It should be locally smooth, i.e., the local intrinsic geometric structure should be consistent with that in the original visual space.
2. It should be discriminative to well predict the proper labels.

In light of these properties, it is reasonable to assume that the latent subspace and the original space are linked by a linear transformation $\mathbf{Q} \in \mathbb{R}^{d \times r}$, where r is the dimensionality of the latent subspace. For each data point $\mathbf{x}_i$, the corresponding representation in the latent subspace is $\mathbf{Q}^T \mathbf{x}_i$. To satisfy the first property, we assume that the neighboring data in the original feature space ought to be close to each other in the latent subspace, which is analogous to the Laplace–Beltrami operator on manifolds [13]. This introduces a smooth regularization on the underlying geometric structure between samples in the latent subspace, which is formulated as

$$\min_{\mathbf{Q}^T\mathbf{Q}=\mathbf{I}_r} \frac{1}{2} \sum_{i,j=1}^{n} S_{ij} \left\| \frac{\mathbf{Q}^T\mathbf{x}_i}{\sqrt{E_{ii}}} - \frac{\mathbf{Q}^T\mathbf{x}_j}{\sqrt{E_{jj}}} \right\|_2^2 = \text{Tr}[\mathbf{Q}^T\mathbf{X}\mathbf{L}\mathbf{X}^T\mathbf{Q}], \tag{3.2}$$

where $\mathbf{E}$ is a diagonal matrix with $E_{ii} = \sum_{j=1}^{n} S_{ij}$ and $\mathbf{L} = \mathbf{E}^{-1/2}(\mathbf{E}-\mathbf{S})\mathbf{E}^{-1/2}$ is the normalized graph Laplacian matrix. Note that the orthogonal constraint $\mathbf{Q}^T\mathbf{Q} = \mathbf{I}_r$ is imposed to make the problem tractable.

To fulfill the second property, we introduce predictive functions to find a proper predicted label matrix $\mathbf{F} \in \mathbb{R}^{n \times c}$ with the following attributes.

(i) The predicted labels are supposed to be locally consistent. That is, the labeling information should be consistent among the nearby points.
(ii) The predicted labels should be globally consistent, i.e., they should be consistent with the ground-truth labels.
(iii) The predictive functions should be robust to the outliers and noise.

For simplicity, the linear function is adopted to predict the mapping relationship between the latent space and the label space, i.e.,

$$h_j(\mathbf{x}_i) = \mathbf{p}_j^T \mathbf{Q}^T \mathbf{x}_i. \tag{3.3}$$

Denoting $\mathbf{P} = [\mathbf{p}_1, \ldots, \mathbf{p}_c]$, we obtain

$$h(\mathbf{X}) = \mathbf{P}^T\mathbf{Q}^T\mathbf{X}. \tag{3.4}$$

The least-squares loss function is always used to learn the predictive functions. However, it is very sensitive to outliers and noise. $\ell_{2,1}$-norm has been confirmed to be robust to outliers and noise [38]. Therefore, we propose the following objective function to learn the predictive functions:

$$\min_{\mathbf{P}} \|\mathbf{F} - \mathbf{X}^T\mathbf{Q}\mathbf{P}\|_{2,1} + \lambda \|\mathbf{P}\|_{2,1} \tag{3.5}$$

λ is a nonnegative regularization parameter. In the above objective function, the loss function $\|\mathbf{F}-\mathbf{X}^T\mathbf{Q}\mathbf{P}\|_{2,1}$ is robust to outliers and noise. Meanwhile, the regularization term $\|\mathbf{P}\|_{2,1}$ guarantees that $\mathbf{P}$ is sparse in rows, which requires to select discriminative features in the latent subspace to predict $\mathbf{F}$.

The idea of local and global consistency, i.e., the attributes (i) and (ii), can be generalized as follows:

$$\min_{\mathbf{F}} \frac{1}{2} \sum_{i,j=1}^{n} S_{ij} \left\| \frac{\mathbf{f}^i}{\sqrt{E_{ii}}} - \frac{\mathbf{f}^j}{\sqrt{E_{jj}}} \right\|^2 + \sum_{i=1}^{n} U_{ii} \sum_{l=1}^{c} (F_{il} - Y_{il})^2$$

$$\Leftrightarrow \min_{\mathbf{F}} \text{Tr}[\mathbf{F}^T\mathbf{L}\mathbf{F}] + \text{Tr}[(\mathbf{F} - \mathbf{Y})^T\mathbf{U}(\mathbf{F} - \mathbf{Y})]. \tag{3.6}$$

Here $\mathbf{U}$ is a diagonal matrix defined as

$$U_{ii} = \begin{cases} \zeta & \text{if } \mathbf{x}_i \text{ is tagged;} \\ 0 & \text{otherwise.} \end{cases} \tag{3.7}$$

ζ is a large constant. The first term and the second term in the optimization problem (3.6) guarantee the local and global structural consistency, respectively. Note that $\mathbf{F}$ is the predicted label matrix. It is natural and reasonable to impose a nonnegative constraint on $\mathbf{F}$, i.e., all the elements of $\mathbf{F}$ are required to be nonnegative. Consequently, the optimization problem (3.6) becomes

$$\min_{\mathbf{F} \geq 0} \text{Tr}[\mathbf{F}^T \mathbf{L} \mathbf{F}] + \text{Tr}[(\mathbf{F} - \mathbf{Y})^T \mathbf{U}(\mathbf{F} - \mathbf{Y})] \tag{3.8}$$

By jointly modeling (3.2), (3.5), and (3.8), we obtain

$$\min_{\mathbf{P},\mathbf{Q},\mathbf{F}} \|\mathbf{F} - \mathbf{X}^T \mathbf{Q} \mathbf{P}\|_{2,1} + \alpha(\text{Tr}[\mathbf{F}^T \mathbf{L} \mathbf{F}] + \text{Tr}[(\mathbf{F} - \mathbf{Y})^T \mathbf{U}(\mathbf{F} - \mathbf{Y})])$$
$$+ \beta \text{Tr}[\mathbf{Q}^T \mathbf{X} \mathbf{L} \mathbf{X}^T \mathbf{Q}] + \lambda \|\mathbf{P}\|_{2,1}$$
$$\text{s.t. } \mathbf{Q}^T \mathbf{Q} = \mathbf{I}_r, \mathbf{F} \geq 0, \tag{3.9}$$

where α and β are two trade-off parameters. From the above objective function, we can see that the predictive functions are robust to outliers and noise and can preserve the local and global structural consistency. The third term can avoid the overfitting problem induced by sparse context links $\mathbf{Y}$, and also incorporate the content links into modeling the latent space geometry [39]. By jointly learning the predictive functions and the latent subspace with $\ell_{2,1}$-norm regularization, the proposed formulation ensures that features in the underlying subspace are combinations of original features and reflect semantic information. Thus, they are discriminative to predict labels.

3.3.2   Optimization

The optimization problem (3.9) involves the $\ell_{2,1}$-norm which is non-smooth and cannot have a close-form solution. Consequently, we propose an iterative algorithm. To facilitate the optimization, by defining $\mathbf{W} = \mathbf{Q} \mathbf{P} \in \mathbb{R}^{d \times c}$, we rewrite the problem (3.9) as minimizing the following equation:

$$\mathcal{O} = \|\mathbf{F} - \mathbf{X}^T \mathbf{W}\|_{2,1} + \alpha(\text{Tr}[\mathbf{F}^T \mathbf{L} \mathbf{F}] + \text{Tr}[(\mathbf{F} - \mathbf{Y})^T \mathbf{U}(\mathbf{F} - \mathbf{Y})])$$
$$+ \beta \text{Tr}[\mathbf{Q}^T \mathbf{X} \mathbf{L} \mathbf{X}^T \mathbf{Q}] + \gamma \|\mathbf{W} - \mathbf{Q} \mathbf{P}\|_F^2 + \lambda \|\mathbf{P}\|_{2,1}$$
$$\text{s.t. } \mathbf{Q}^T \mathbf{Q} = \mathbf{I}_r, \mathbf{F} \geq 0 \tag{3.10}$$

In the following, we introduce the proposed update rules in brief and the elaborated inference procedure please refer to the supplemental material.

3.3.2.1 Update P as Given W and Q

By setting the derivative $\partial \mathscr{O} / \partial \mathbf{P} = 0$ and using the property that $\mathbf{Q}^T \mathbf{Q} = \mathbf{I}_r$, we obtain

$$\gamma(\mathbf{Q}^T \mathbf{Q} \mathbf{P} - \mathbf{Q}^T \mathbf{W}) + \lambda \mathbf{D} \mathbf{P} = 0$$
$$\Rightarrow \mathbf{P} = \gamma(\gamma \mathbf{I} + \lambda \mathbf{D})^{-1} \mathbf{Q}^T \mathbf{W} = \gamma \mathbf{V}^{-1} \mathbf{Q}^T \mathbf{W}, \tag{3.11}$$

where $\mathbf{V} = \gamma \mathbf{I}_r + \lambda \mathbf{D}$ and $\mathbf{D}$ is a diagonal matrix with $D_{ii} = \frac{1}{2\|\mathbf{p}^i\|_2}, i = 1, \ldots, r$.

3.3.2.2 Update W as Given P, Q, and F

Now, by substituting $\mathbf{P}$ in $\mathscr{O}$ with Eq. 3.11, the objective function $\mathscr{O}$ is written as follows:

$$\mathscr{O} = \|\mathbf{Z}\|_{2,1} + f(\mathbf{F}) + g(\mathbf{Q}) + \gamma \|\mathbf{W} - \gamma \mathbf{Q} \mathbf{V}^{-1} \mathbf{Q}^T \mathbf{W}\|_F^2 + \lambda \mathrm{Tr}[\gamma^2 \mathbf{W}^T \mathbf{Q} \mathbf{V}^{-1} \mathbf{D} \mathbf{V}^{-1} \mathbf{Q}^T \mathbf{W}]$$
$$= f(\mathbf{F}) + g(\mathbf{Q}) + \mathrm{Tr}[(\mathbf{F} - \mathbf{X}^T \mathbf{W})^T \bar{\mathbf{D}} (\mathbf{F} - \mathbf{X}^T \mathbf{W})] + \gamma \mathrm{Tr}[\mathbf{W}^T (\mathbf{I}_d - \gamma \mathbf{Q} \mathbf{V}^{-1} \mathbf{Q}^T) \mathbf{W}] \tag{3.12}$$

where $\mathbf{Z} = \mathbf{F} - \mathbf{X}^T \mathbf{W}$, $f(\mathbf{F}) = \alpha(\mathrm{Tr}[\mathbf{F}^T \mathbf{L} \mathbf{F}] + \mathrm{Tr}[(\mathbf{F} - \mathbf{Y})^T \mathbf{U}(\mathbf{F} - \mathbf{Y})])$ and $g(\mathbf{Q}) = \beta \mathrm{Tr}[\mathbf{Q}^T \mathbf{X} \mathbf{L} \mathbf{X}^T \mathbf{Q}]$. $\bar{\mathbf{D}}$ is a diagonal matrix with $\bar{D}_{ii} = \frac{1}{2\|\mathbf{z}^i\|_2}$ and we use the property that $\|\mathbf{A}\|_F^2 = \mathrm{Tr}(\mathbf{A}^T \mathbf{A})$ for any arbitrary matrix $\mathbf{A}$. By setting the derivative $\partial \mathscr{O} / \partial \mathbf{W} = 0$, we get

$$\mathbf{X} \bar{\mathbf{D}} (\mathbf{X}^T \mathbf{W} - \mathbf{F}) + \gamma(\mathbf{I}_d - \mathbf{Q} \mathbf{V}^{-1} \mathbf{Q}^T) \mathbf{W} = 0$$
$$\Leftrightarrow (\mathbf{X} \bar{\mathbf{D}} \mathbf{X}^T + \gamma(\mathbf{I}_d - \mathbf{Q} \mathbf{V}^{-1} \mathbf{Q}^T)) \mathbf{W} = \mathbf{X} \bar{\mathbf{D}} \mathbf{F}$$
$$\Leftrightarrow \mathbf{W} = (\mathbf{G} - \gamma^2 \mathbf{Q} \mathbf{V}^{-1} \mathbf{Q}^T)^{-1} \mathbf{X} \bar{\mathbf{D}} \mathbf{F} = \mathbf{H}^{-1} \mathbf{X} \bar{\mathbf{D}} \mathbf{F} \tag{3.13}$$

Here $\mathbf{G} = \mathbf{X} \bar{\mathbf{D}} \mathbf{X}^T + \gamma \mathbf{I}_d$ and $\mathbf{H} = \mathbf{G} - \gamma^2 \mathbf{Q} \mathbf{V}^{-1} \mathbf{Q}^T$.

3.3.2.3 Update Q as Given P, W, and F

First, we rewrite Eq. 3.12 as follows:

$$\mathscr{O} = \mathrm{Tr}[(\mathbf{X}^T \mathbf{W} - \mathbf{F})^T \bar{\mathbf{D}} (\mathbf{X}^T \mathbf{W} - \mathbf{F})] + f(\mathbf{F}) + g(\mathbf{Q}) + \gamma \mathrm{Tr}[\mathbf{W}^T (\mathbf{I}_d - \gamma \mathbf{Q} \mathbf{V}^{-1} \mathbf{Q}^T) \mathbf{W}]$$
$$= \mathrm{Tr}[\mathbf{W}^T \mathbf{H} \mathbf{W}] - 2\mathrm{Tr}[\mathbf{W}^T \mathbf{X} \bar{\mathbf{D}} \mathbf{F}] + \mathrm{Tr}[\mathbf{F}^T \bar{\mathbf{D}} \mathbf{F}] + f(\mathbf{F}) + g(\mathbf{Q}). \tag{3.14}$$

By substituting the expression for $\mathbf{W}$ in Eq. 3.13 into 3.14, since $\mathbf{H} = \mathbf{H}^T$, we obtain the following equation:

$$\mathcal{O} = \text{Tr}[\mathbf{F}^T \bar{\mathbf{D}} \mathbf{X}^T (\mathbf{H}^{-1} \mathbf{H} \mathbf{H}^{-1} - 2\mathbf{H}^{-1}) \mathbf{X} \bar{\mathbf{D}} \mathbf{F}] + \text{Tr}[\mathbf{F}^T \bar{\mathbf{D}} \mathbf{F}] + f(\mathbf{F}) + g(\mathbf{Q})$$
$$= - \text{Tr}[\mathbf{F}^T \bar{\mathbf{D}} \mathbf{X}^T \mathbf{H}^{-1} \mathbf{X} \bar{\mathbf{D}} \mathbf{F}] + \text{Tr}[\mathbf{F}^T \bar{\mathbf{D}} \mathbf{F}] + f(\mathbf{F}) + g(\mathbf{Q}). \tag{3.15}$$

By substituting Eq. 3.15 into the problem (3.10), we have the following optimization problem w.r.t. $\mathbf{Q}$:

$$\max_{\mathbf{Q}^T \mathbf{Q} = \mathbf{I}_r} \text{Tr}[\mathbf{F}^T \bar{\mathbf{D}} \mathbf{X}^T \mathbf{H}^{-1} \mathbf{X} \bar{\mathbf{D}} \mathbf{F}] - g(\mathbf{Q}). \tag{3.16}$$

To compute the matrix inverse, using the Sherman–Morrison–Woodbury formula [19]: $(\mathbf{A} + \mathbf{U}\mathbf{C}\mathbf{V})^{-1} = \mathbf{A}^{-1} - \mathbf{A}^{-1}\mathbf{U}\left(\mathbf{C}^{-1} + \mathbf{V}\mathbf{A}^{-1}\mathbf{U}\right)^{-1}\mathbf{V}\mathbf{A}^{-1}$, we have

$$\mathbf{H}^{-1} = (\mathbf{G} - \gamma^2 \mathbf{Q} \mathbf{V}^{-1} \mathbf{Q}^T)^{-1}$$
$$= \mathbf{G}^{-1} + \gamma^2 \mathbf{G}^{-1} \mathbf{Q} (\mathbf{V} - \gamma^2 \mathbf{Q}^T \mathbf{G}^{-1} \mathbf{Q})^{-1} \mathbf{Q}^T \mathbf{G}^{-1}. \tag{3.17}$$

Thus, using the property that $\text{Tr}[\mathbf{A}\mathbf{B}] = \text{Tr}[\mathbf{B}\mathbf{A}]$, the optimization problem (3.16) is equivalent to

$$\max_{\mathbf{Q}^T \mathbf{Q} = \mathbf{I}_r} \text{Tr}[\mathbf{F}^T \bar{\mathbf{D}} \mathbf{X}^T \mathbf{H}^{-1} \mathbf{X} \bar{\mathbf{D}} \mathbf{F}] - \beta \text{Tr}[\mathbf{Q}^T \mathbf{X} \mathbf{L} \mathbf{X}^T \mathbf{Q}]$$
$$\Leftrightarrow \max_{\mathbf{Q}^T \mathbf{Q} = \mathbf{I}_r} \gamma^2 \text{Tr}[(\gamma \mathbf{I}_r + \lambda \mathbf{D} - \gamma^2 \mathbf{Q}^T \mathbf{G}^{-1} \mathbf{Q})^{-1} \mathbf{Q}^T \mathbf{T} \mathbf{Q}] - \beta \text{Tr}[\mathbf{Q}^T \mathbf{X} \mathbf{L} \mathbf{X}^T \mathbf{Q}]$$
$$\Leftrightarrow \max_{\mathbf{Q}^T \mathbf{Q} = \mathbf{I}_r} \gamma^2 \text{Tr}[\mathbf{Q}^T (\gamma \mathbf{I}_d + \lambda \mathbf{Q} \mathbf{D} \mathbf{Q}^T - \gamma^2 \mathbf{G}^{-1})^{-1} \mathbf{T} \mathbf{Q}] - \beta \text{Tr}[\mathbf{Q}^T \mathbf{X} \mathbf{L} \mathbf{X}^T \mathbf{Q}]$$
$$\Leftrightarrow \max_{\mathbf{Q}^T \mathbf{Q} = \mathbf{I}_r} \text{Tr}[\mathbf{Q}^T \mathbf{N}^{-1} \mathbf{Q}], \tag{3.18}$$

where $\mathbf{T} = \mathbf{G}^{-1} \mathbf{X} \bar{\mathbf{D}} \mathbf{F} \mathbf{F}^T \bar{\mathbf{D}} \mathbf{X}^T \mathbf{G}^{-1}$ and $\mathbf{N} = (\frac{1}{\gamma} \mathbf{I}_d + \frac{\lambda}{\gamma^2} \mathbf{Q} \mathbf{D} \mathbf{Q}^T - \mathbf{G}^{-1})^{-1} \mathbf{T} - \beta \mathbf{X} \mathbf{L} \mathbf{X}^T$. $\mathbf{Q}$ can be relaxedly obtained by the eigen decomposition of $\mathbf{N}^{-1}$. Note that although $\mathbf{N}$ needs $\mathbf{Q}$ as input, the above solution is effective and empirically validated since our algorithm converges very quickly to make $\mathbf{Q}$ stable.

3.3.2.4   Update F as Given P, W, and Q

We substitute the expression in Eq. 3.15 into 3.10 and get the following optimization problem *w.s.t.* $\mathbf{F}$:

$$\min_{\mathbf{F} \geq 0} \text{Tr}[\mathbf{F}^T (\bar{\mathbf{D}} + \alpha \mathbf{L} - \bar{\mathbf{D}} \mathbf{X}^T \mathbf{H}^{-1} \mathbf{X} \bar{\mathbf{D}}) \mathbf{F}] + \alpha \text{Tr}[(\mathbf{F} - \mathbf{Y})^T \mathbf{U} (\mathbf{F} - \mathbf{Y})]. \tag{3.19}$$

Algorithm 3 The Proposed RSSL Algorithm

Input:

    Data matrix $\mathbf{X} \in \mathbb{R}^{d \times n}$ and Tag matrix $\mathbf{Y} \in \mathbb{R}^{n \times c}$; Parameters α, β, γ, λ, k and r

Output:

    Converged $\mathbf{F}$, $\mathbf{P}$, $\mathbf{Q}$ and $\mathbf{W}$.

1: Construct the k-nn graph and calculate $\mathbf{L}$;

2: Compute the selection matrix $\mathbf{U} \in \mathbb{R}^{n \times n}$;

3: Set $t = 0$; Initialize $\mathbf{F}_0 \in \mathbb{R}^{n \times c}$ and $\mathbf{Q}_0 \in \mathbb{R}^{d \times r}$, and set $\bar{\mathbf{D}}_0 \in \mathbb{R}^{n \times n}$ and $\mathbf{D}_0 \in \mathbb{R}^{r \times r}$ as identity matrices;

4: **repeat**

5:    $\mathbf{G}_t = \mathbf{X}\bar{\mathbf{D}}_t\mathbf{X}^T + \gamma\mathbf{I}_d$;

6:    $\mathbf{T}_t = \mathbf{G}_t^{-1}\mathbf{X}\bar{\mathbf{D}}_t\mathbf{F}_t\mathbf{F}_t^T\bar{\mathbf{D}}_t\mathbf{X}^T\mathbf{G}_t^{-1}$;

7:    $\mathbf{N}_t = (\frac{1}{\gamma}\mathbf{I}_d + \frac{\lambda}{\gamma^2}\mathbf{Q}_t\mathbf{D}_t\mathbf{Q}_t^T - \mathbf{G}_t^{-1})^{-1}\mathbf{T}_t - \beta\mathbf{X}\mathbf{L}\mathbf{X}^T$;

8:    Get $\mathbf{Q}_{t+1}$ by the eigen-decomposition of $\mathbf{N}_t^{-1}$;

9:    $\mathbf{H}_t = \mathbf{G}_t - \gamma^2\mathbf{Q}_{t+1}(\gamma\mathbf{I}_r + \lambda\mathbf{D}_t)^{-1}\mathbf{Q}_{t+1}^T$;

10:   $\mathbf{M}_t = \bar{\mathbf{D}}_t + \alpha\mathbf{L} - \bar{\mathbf{D}}_t\mathbf{X}^T\mathbf{H}_t^{-1}\mathbf{X}\bar{\mathbf{D}}_t$;

11:   $(\mathbf{F}_{t+1})_{ij} = (\mathbf{F}_t)_{ij}\frac{(\alpha\mathbf{U}\mathbf{Y}_t)_{ij}}{(\mathbf{M}_t\mathbf{F}_t + \alpha\mathbf{U}\mathbf{F}_t)_{ij}}$;

12:   $\mathbf{W}_{t+1} = \mathbf{H}_t^{-1}\mathbf{X}\bar{\mathbf{D}}_t\mathbf{F}_{t+1}$;

13:   $\mathbf{Z}_{t+1} = \mathbf{F}_{t+1} - \mathbf{X}^T\mathbf{W}_{t+1}$;

14:   $\bar{\mathbf{D}}_{t+1} = \begin{bmatrix} \frac{1}{2\|\mathbf{z}_{t+1}^1\|_2} & & \\ & \cdots & \\ & & \frac{1}{2\|\mathbf{z}_{t+1}^n\|_2} \end{bmatrix}$;

15:   $\mathbf{P}_{t+1} = \gamma(\gamma\mathbf{I}_r + \lambda\mathbf{D}_t)^{-1}\mathbf{Q}_{t+1}^T\mathbf{W}_{t+1}$;

16:   $\mathbf{D}_{t+1} = \begin{bmatrix} \frac{1}{2\|\mathbf{p}_{t+1}^1\|_2} & & \\ & \cdots & \\ & & \frac{1}{2\|\mathbf{p}_{t+1}^r\|_2} \end{bmatrix}$;

17:   t=t+1;

18: **until** Convergence criterion satisfied

Letting $\mathbf{M} = \bar{\mathbf{D}} + \alpha\mathbf{L} - \bar{\mathbf{D}}\mathbf{X}^T\mathbf{H}^{-1}\mathbf{X}\bar{\mathbf{D}}$, ϕ_{ij} be the Lagrange multiplier for constraint $F_{ij} \geq 0$ and $\Phi = [\phi_{ij}]$, the Lagrange function is

$$\text{Tr}[\mathbf{F}^T\mathbf{M}\mathbf{F}] + \alpha\text{Tr}[(\mathbf{F} - \mathbf{Y})^T\mathbf{U}(\mathbf{F} - \mathbf{Y})] + \text{Tr}(\Phi\mathbf{F}^T). \tag{3.20}$$

Setting its derivative with respect to F_{ij} to 0 and using the Karush–Kuhn–Tuckre (KKT) condition [27] $\phi_{ij}F_{ij} = 0$, we obtain the updating rules:

$$\mathbf{M}\mathbf{F} + \alpha\mathbf{U}(\mathbf{F} - \mathbf{Y}) + \Phi = 0$$

$$\Rightarrow F_{ij} \leftarrow F_{ij}\frac{(\alpha\mathbf{U}\mathbf{Y})_{ij}}{(\mathbf{M}\mathbf{F} + \alpha\mathbf{U}\mathbf{F})_{ij}}. \tag{3.21}$$

From the above analysis, we can see that $\mathbf{D}$ and $\bar{\mathbf{D}}$ related to $\mathbf{W}$ is required to solve $\mathbf{Q}$ and $\mathbf{F}$ and it is still not straightforward to obtain $\mathbf{W}$, $\mathbf{Q}$, and $\mathbf{F}$. To this end, we design an iterative algorithm to solve the proposed formulation, which is summarized in Algorithm 3. The convergence criterion used in our experiments is that the number of iterations is more than 20 or $|\mathscr{O}_{t-1} - \mathscr{O}_t|/\mathscr{O}_{t-1} < 0.001$, where $\mathscr{O}_t$ is the value of the objective function in the tth iteration. Once $\mathbf{Q}$ and $\mathbf{W}$ are obtained, given a testing image $\mathbf{x}$, its latent representation and label prediction vector are computed by $\mathbf{b} = \mathbf{Q}^T\mathbf{x}$ and $\mathbf{f} = [f_1, \ldots, f_c]^T = \mathbf{W}^T\mathbf{x}$, respectively. Besides, $\mathbf{P}$ can be deemed as a feature selection matrix in the latent subspace.

3.3.3 Computational Complexity Analysis

In this subsection, we discuss the computational cost of the proposed method. The common way to express the complexity of one algorithm is using big O notation

As stated in Algorithm 3, the k-nn graph is first constructed based on the Euclidean distance in the original space. The corresponding cost is $O(dn^2)$, where n is the number of images and d is the dimension of features. Then, the proposed optimization problem is solved iteratively. In each iteration, $\mathbf{G}$ is computed with the cost of $O(dn^2 + d^2n)$ while the complexity to obtain $\mathbf{G}^{-1}$ is $O(d^3)$. The cost for computing $\mathbf{Q}$ is $O(d^3 + d^2n + dn^2 + dnc)$, in which the time complexities to compute $\mathbf{T}, \mathbf{N}$ and the eigen decomposition are $O(d^2n + dn^2 + dnc + d^3)$, $O(d^3 + d^2n + dn^2)$, and $O(d^3)$, respectively, where c is the number of tags. Since $\gamma\mathbf{I}_r + \lambda\mathbf{D}_t$ is a diagonal matrix and its inversion cost $O(r)$, it needs $O(dr^2 + d^2r)$ to obtain $\mathbf{H}$, where r is the dimension of the subspace. Then $\mathbf{H}^{-1}$ is computed with the cost of $O(d^3)$. With $\mathbf{H}^{-1}$ obtained, it costs $O(d^2n + dn^2)$, $O(n^2c)$, and $O(d^2n + dn + dnc)$ to calculate $\mathbf{M}$, $\mathbf{F}$, and $\mathbf{W}$, respectively. Finally, $\mathbf{Z}, \bar{\mathbf{D}}, \mathbf{P}$, and $\mathbf{D}$ are got with the time complexity of $O(dnc)$, $O(nc + n)$, $O(r + dr^2 + drc)$, and $O(rc + r)$, respectively. Thus the total cost of our method is $O(T(d^2n + dn^2 + d^3 + dnc + dr^2 + d^2r + n^2c + drc) + n^2d)$, where T is the number of iterations in our algorithm. Since $r \ll n$ and $r \ll d$, the whole cost of the proposed method is $O(T(dn^2 + d^2n + d^3 + dnc + n^2c) + dn^2)$.

3.3.4 Image Understanding Tasks

We now elaborate how to apply the proposed learning framework to different image understanding tasks, i.e., social image tagging, clustering, and classification.

Social Image Tagging. For social image tagging, the raw correspondences between social images and their associated tags are available to define $\mathbf{Y}$, but it is possibly imprecise since the community contributed tags annotated by web users could be noisy, irrelevant, and often incomplete for describing the image contents [30, 32]. As a consequence, the goal of social image tagging is to remove noisy and irrelevant tags, complement relevant tags, and add tags to untagged images. It is observed from the aforementioned analysis that the proposed formulation is adaptive to the social image tagging task in nature. The $\ell_{2,1}$ norm in the loss function makes it enable to refine the raw tags. That is, for the learning data, i.e., in-sample, the learned $\mathbf{F}$ is used to refine the raw tags. For the new image $\mathbf{x}$, i.e., out-of-sample, its tag vector is computed by $\mathbf{f} = \mathbf{W}^T \mathbf{x}$.

Clustering. The proposed formulation can be applied to clustering. It enables to find an appropriate representation of data to improve the performance of clustering.

For unsupervised learning, all the diagonal elements of the selection matrix $\mathbf{U}$ are all zeros since there exists no labeled data. The term $\text{Tr}[(\mathbf{F} - \mathbf{Y})^T \mathbf{U}(\mathbf{F} - \mathbf{Y})]$ in the problem (3.10) is equal to 0. In the clustering task, each sample is assigned to one cluster. The matrix $\mathbf{F}$ is deemed to be the scaled cluster indicator matrix and required to be orthogonal. Consequently, the problem (3.10) becomes

$$\min \|\mathbf{Z}\|_{2,1} + \alpha \text{Tr}[\mathbf{F}^T \mathbf{L} \mathbf{F}] + \beta \text{Tr}[\mathbf{Q}^T \mathbf{X} \mathbf{L} \mathbf{X}^T \mathbf{Q}] + \gamma \|\mathbf{W} - \mathbf{Q}\mathbf{P}\|_F^2 + \lambda \|\mathbf{P}\|_{2,1}$$
$$\text{s.t.} \quad \mathbf{Q}^T \mathbf{Q} = \mathbf{I}_r, \, \mathbf{F}^T \mathbf{F} = \mathbf{I}_c, \, \mathbf{F} \geq 0. \tag{3.22}$$

We can see that it is nature and reasonable to impose orthogonal constraint on $\mathbf{F}$ for clustering, which makes the learned $\mathbf{F}$ more accurate. When both nonnegative and orthogonal constraints are satisfied, there is only one element in each row of $\mathbf{F}$ is greater than zero and all of the others are zeros. The solutions of $\mathbf{P}$, $\mathbf{Q}$, and $\mathbf{W}$ are consistent with those in Sect. 3.3.2. To obtain the solution of $\mathbf{F}$, we relax the orthogonal constraint and the Lagrange function (3.20) becomes

$$\min_{\mathbf{F} \geq 0} \text{Tr}[\mathbf{F}^T \mathbf{M} \mathbf{F}] + \frac{\eta}{2} \|\mathbf{F}^T \mathbf{F} - \mathbf{I}_c\|_F^2 + \text{Tr}(\mathbf{\Phi} \mathbf{F}^T). \tag{3.23}$$

$\eta > 0$ is a parameter to control the orthogonality condition. In practice, η should be large enough to insure the orthogonality satisfied. Setting its derivative with respect to F_{ij} to 0 and using the KKT condition [27] $\phi_{ij} F_{ij} = 0$, we obtain the updating rules:

$$\mathbf{M} \mathbf{F} + \eta \mathbf{F}(\mathbf{F}^T \mathbf{F} - \mathbf{I}_c) + \mathbf{\Phi} = 0$$
$$\Rightarrow F_{ij} \leftarrow F_{ij} \frac{(\eta \mathbf{F})_{ij}}{(\mathbf{M} \mathbf{F} + \eta \mathbf{F} \mathbf{F}^T \mathbf{F})_{ij}}. \tag{3.24}$$

Then we normalize $\mathbf{F}$ with $(\mathbf{F}^T \mathbf{F})_{ii} = 1, i = 1, \ldots, c$. The clustering results are obtained from the learned $\mathbf{F}$. In addition, the proposed method can be treated as an unsupervised feature selection method. We first map data into the latent subspace by $\mathbf{Q}$ and then select features in the subspace using $\mathbf{P}$.

Classification. Similar to the above analysis, the proposed formulation is also adaptive to semi-supervised and supervised classification. For semi-supervised and supervised classification, we still use the definition of the selection matrix $\mathbf{U}$ in Eq. 3.7, that is, U_{ii} is set to a large enough constant if $\mathbf{x}_i$ is labeled. The changes in the extension to clustering are still applied to classification. That is, we impose orthogonal constraint on $\mathbf{F}$. As a consequence, we obtain the following problem:

$$\min \|\mathbf{Z}\|_{2,1} + \alpha(\text{Tr}[\mathbf{F}^T\mathbf{L}\mathbf{F}] + \text{Tr}[(\mathbf{F} - \mathbf{Y})^T\mathbf{U}(\mathbf{F} - \mathbf{Y})])$$

$$+\beta\text{Tr}[\mathbf{Q}^T\mathbf{X}\mathbf{L}\mathbf{X}^T\mathbf{Q}] + \gamma\|\mathbf{W} - \mathbf{Q}\mathbf{P}\|_F^2 + \lambda\|\mathbf{P}\|_{2,1}$$

$$\text{s.t.} \quad \mathbf{Q}^T\mathbf{Q} = \mathbf{I}_r, \mathbf{F}^T\mathbf{F} = \mathbf{I}_c, \mathbf{F} \geq 0. \tag{3.25}$$

Note that for consistency to $\mathbf{F}$, $\mathbf{Y}$ is made orthogonal by $\mathbf{Y} \leftarrow \mathbf{Y}(\mathbf{Y}^T\mathbf{Y})^{-\frac{1}{2}}$.

The solutions of $\mathbf{P}$, $\mathbf{Q}$, and $\mathbf{W}$ are consistent with those in Sect. 3.3.2. To obtain the solution of $\mathbf{F}$, by relaxing the orthogonal constraint and using the Lagrange function and the KKT condition, we obtain

$$F_{ij} \leftarrow F_{ij} \frac{(\eta\mathbf{F} + \alpha\mathbf{U}\mathbf{Y})_{ij}}{(\mathbf{M}\mathbf{F} + \alpha\mathbf{U}\mathbf{F} + \eta\mathbf{F}\mathbf{F}^T\mathbf{F})_{ij}}. \tag{3.26}$$

Note that in semi-supervised classification, the unlabeled learning data are labeled by the learned $\mathbf{F}$. The testing data are labeled using the learned matrix $\mathbf{W}$ in semi-supervised and supervised classification.

3.4   Performance Evaluation

We present extensive experiments to validate the effectiveness of our method for image understanding tasks, including image tagging, clustering, and classification. The experiments are discussed in detail in terms of image tagging and briefly analyzed for clustering and classification. Statistical significance test is also performed with a significance level of 0.05. The student t test is employed in our experiments.

3.4.1   Image Tagging

3.4.1.1   Data Set

Social photo sharing sites allow users to post, tag, and comment on images. Therefore, social images cover almost all the concepts people are interested in, which makes researchers collect images to build social image data sets for experimental purpose. In this work, we conduct our experiments on two large-scale publicly available social image data sets: MIRFlickr [20] and NUS-WIDE [12]. Table 3.1 summarizes some statistics of these data sets.

MIRFlickr [20]. It contains 25,000 images from Flickr. It contains 1386 tags and provides the ground-truth annotation of 38 concepts. We kept the tags that appear at least 50 times, resulting in a vocabulary of 457 tags, which only contains 18 concepts of those 38 concepts. Thus, we adopt these 18 concepts to validate the performance. We adopt two types of global image descriptors: Gist features and color histograms

Table 3.1 Statistics of the used data sets with image and tag counts in the format mean/maximum

	MIRFlickr data set	NUS-WIDE data set
Tag size	457	2892
Concept size	18	81
Image size	25,000	55,615
Tags per image	2.7/45	9.4/199
Concepts per image	4.7/17	4.2/13
Image per tag	145.4/1483	180.9/9208
Image per concept	3102.8/10,373	2891.5/38,098

with 16 bins in each color channel for LAB and HSV representations and one type of local feature: SIFT feature. The features are available at http://lear.inrialpes.fr/data/.

NUS-WIDE [12]. It contains 55,615 images from Flickr associated with 5018 tags annotated by amateur users. The data set provides the ground-truth annotations of 81 concepts, which are used to evaluate the performance. Note that these 81 concepts are different from the user tags with much irrelevant noise information, while the ground-truth labels are manually labeled. To reduce too noisy tags, we removed tags whose occurrence numbers are below 25 and obtained 2892 unique tags. We download five types of features: 144-D color correlation, 73-D edge direction histogram, 128-D wavelet texture, 64-D color histogram, and 225-D block-wise color moments.

3.4.1.2 Experimental Setting

In our experiments, data are partitioned into two groups: the learning data and the testing data. The learning data are used for model estimation and evaluate the performance of noisy tagged data while the testing data are utilized to test the performance of new data. We randomly select n samples as learning data and the remaining samples are used as testing data. In our experiments, we set $n = 5,000$, $n = 10,000$, respectively, and report all of the results. During the partition process, each label is guaranteed to be associated with at least one image. To alleviate the instability introduced by the randomly selected training data, we independently repeat experiments 10 times to generate different learning and testing data, and report the average results. The results on the noisy tagged learning data and the testing data are both reported.

3.4.1.3 Compared Scheme

To validate the effectiveness of RSSL, we compare it with one baseline and a number of related state-of-the-art approaches, which are enumerated as follows. The parameters of these methods are tuned within the candidate set $[10^{-6}, 10^{-3}, 1, 10^3, 10^6]$.

- **Baseline**: The rigid regression is utilized as the baseline algorithm.
- **ASO** [3]: It learns predictive structures from multiple tasks and unlabeled data.
- **LapRLS** [6]: With the manifold assumption, it uses the least square loss to seek a decision function which is smooth over the whole data distribution according to the graph Laplacian.
- **SDA** [7]: It reduces the dimension of the input visual features and then rigid regression is performed as a classifier.
- **SSLF** [22]: It discovers the correlation information among multiple labels by a low-dimensional subspace learning framework.
- **LSCCA** [42]: The least-squares formulation of canonical correlation analysis is used to predict labels for samples.
- **SFSS** [36]: It predicts labels by considering both label consistence with the training data labels and manifold fitting on the data structure.
- **SFUS** [37]: It annotates images by uncovering the shared subspace of original features based on a sparsity-based model.
- **LMGE** [49]: Images are annotated by integrating shared structure learning and graph-based learning into a joint framework.
- **C2MR** [39]: The underlying latent semantic space is learned by mining both context and content links in social media networks.

3.4.1.4   Evaluation Metric

The area under the receiver operating characteristic (ROC) curve, known as the AUC, is currently considered to be the standard method for model comparison. It is well known that it is a more faithful criterion used in many applications. Following [22, 49], in our experiments we adopt Area Under Cures (AUC) as evaluation metric. As done in [49], both the microaveraging and macroaveraging measures are utilized to evaluate both the global performance across multiple concepts and the average performance of all the concepts. To calculate the microaveraging result, we first concatenate the concept indicator vectors of all concepts as a long vector and then compute the average AUC. For the macroaveraging result, we first compute the mean AUC of each concept and then average the mean AUC values of all the concepts.

Besides, the performance for image tagging is also evaluated using F1 measure, which is defined as follows: $F1 = \frac{2 \times R \times P}{R+P}$, where $R = \frac{|N_c|}{|N_g|}$, and $P = \frac{|N_c|}{|N_t|}$. Here $|N_g|$ be the number of images tagged with one concept w in the ground truth, $|N_t|$ be the number of images tagged with w of our algorithm, and $|N_c|$ be the number of correct tagged images with w by our algorithm. The mean F1 over concepts is presented. Note that in our experiments we annotate each image with five concepts. Furthermore, Mean Average Precision (MAP) is utilized to measure the image retrieval performance.

3.4.1.5 Experimental Results

The mean MicroAUC, mean MacroAUC, and mean F1 of 10 times independent experiments of all the algorithms on the MIRFlickr and NUS-WIDE data sets are presented in Tables 3.2 and 3.3, respectively. Results that are significantly better than others are indicated in boldface. From the results, we have the following observations.

First, from the results in Tables 3.2 and 3.3, we can see that the proposed method gains the best performances among all of the compared algorithms in terms of mean MicroAUC, MacroAUC, and F1 on both the MIRFlicrk and NUS-WIDE data sets. This indicates that the proposed RSSL enables to effectively learn a robust structured subspace from data. Second, compared with the related approaches, i.e., ASO, SSLF, LapRLS, SFSS, SFUS, and LGME, the proposed RSSL achieves significant improvements, which demonstrates the necessity and advantage of the introduced $\ell_{2,1}$-norm and smooth regularization. $\ell_{2,1}$-norm makes RSSL robust to noise and outliers. By mining the local geometric structure, RSSL maps visually similar images close to

Table 3.2 Experimental results (mean microauc, mean macroauc, and mean F1) on the MIRFlickr data set. The best results are highlighted in bold

Method		n = 5000			n = 10,000		
		MicroAUC	MacroAUC	F1	MicroAUC	MacroAUC	F1
Baseline	Learn	0.555	0.544	0.195	0.582	0.588	0.230
ASO	Learn	0.590	0.579	0.229	0.634	0.613	0.2312
LapRLS	Learn	0.578	0.566	0.211	0.598	0.590	0.242
SDA	Learn	0.561	0.553	0.204	0.571	0.550	0.201
SSLF	Learn	0.667	0.638	0.369	0.685	0.649	0.297
LSCCA	Learn	0.574	0.553	0.247	0.586	0.566	0.259
SFSS	Learn	0.676	0.658	0.370	0.708	0.668	0.380
SFUS	Learn	0.677	0.655	0.369	0.701	0.674	0.380
LGME	Learn	0.688	0.658	0.369	0.703	0.673	0.381
C2MR	Learn	0.636	0.616	0.261	0.671	0.647	0.286
RSSL	Learn	**0.703**	**0.675**	**0.498**	**0.724**	**0.685**	**0.512**
Baseline	Test	0.524	0.511	0.162	0.550	0.536	0.185
ASO	Test	0.547	0.5311	0.188	0.566	0.562	0.194
LapRLS	Test	0.561	0.540	0.189	0.570	0.538	0.189
SDA	Test	0.557	0.541	0.192	0.571	0.541	0.189
SSLF	Test	0.634	0.594	0.191	0.646	0.623	0.205
LSCCA	Test	0.561	0.516	0.175	0.563	0.521	0.179
SFSS	Test	0.658	0.603	0.215	0.681	0.622	0.218
SFUS	Test	0.643	0.617	0.214	0.674	0.619	0.218
LGME	Test	0.644	0.627	0.221	0.677	0.613	0.223
C2MR	Test	0.630	0.607	0.193	0.658	0.642	0.197
RSSL	Test	**0.673**	**0.642**	**0.255**	**0.697**	**0.653**	**0.267**

Table 3.3 Experimental results (mean microauc, mean macroauc, and mean F1) on the NUS-WIDE data set. The best results are highlighted in bold

Method		$n = 5000$			$n = 10,000$		
		MicroAUC	MacroAUC	F1	MicroAUC	MacroAUC	F1
Baseline	Learn	0.677	0.594	0.225	0.697	0.612	0.316
ASO	Learn	0.709	0.636	0.327	0.724	0.641	0.343
LapRLS	Learn	0.708	0.663	0.354	0.712	0.664	0.333
SDA	Learn	0.709	0.642	0.310	0.722	0.644	0.347
SSLF	Learn	0.708	0.677	0.326	0.738	0.685	0.341
LSCCA	Learn	0.618	0.724	0.258	0.632	0.732	0.264
SFSS	Learn	0.757	0.722	0.480	0.786	0.736	0.485
SFUS	Learn	0.753	0.727	0.390	0.785	0.725	0.407
LGME	Learn	0.761	0.739	0.453	0.780	0.744	0.471
C2MR	Learn	0.689	0.621	0.301	0.770	0.655	0.351
RSSL	Learn	**0.835**	**0.768**	**0.576**	**0.844**	**0.791**	**0.589**
Baseline	Test	0.658	0.550	0.131	0.674	0.560	0.152
ASO	Test	0.673	0.559	0.157	0.675	0.574	0.159
LapRLS	Test	0.677	0.554	0.140	0.691	0.561	0.151
SDA	Test	0.672	0.613	0.165	0.682	0.633	0.160
SSLF	Test	0.683	0.630	0.173	0.696	0.653	0.189
LSCCA	Test	0.588	0.613	0.158	0.599	0.621	0.192
SFSS	Test	0.706	0.630	0.228	0.731	0.653	0.239
SFUS	Test	0.708	0.633	0.238	0.735	0.662	0.247
LGME	Test	0.711	0.641	0.243	0.729	0.657	0.248
C2MR	Test	0.642	0.620	0.220	0.767	0.641	0.225
RSSL	Test	**0.773**	**0.703**	**0.269**	**0.795**	**0.731**	**0.272**

each other in the hidden subspace. Thus they have consistent feature representations in the hidden subspace, which makes much easier to assign concepts to images in the subspace. Third, RSSL, LGME, and SFSS are superior to other methods in general, such as ASO, SDA, SSLF, and SFUS. It indicates the effectiveness of the local consistent constraint over tags, which gives an intuitive interpretation of better performance of the proposed algorithm since visually similar images can implicitly share common tags. On the other hand, the noise in tags can also be somewhat alleviated by exploiting visual geometric structure. Fourth, by exploring the feature combinations in the prediction process, RSSL, LGME, SFUS, SSLF, and ASO are better than baseline. The proposed model learns a robust latent subspace by exploiting the image tagging information and visual content information simultaneously and can easily assign tags to new images. Sixth, RSSL outperforms LSCCA by jointly uncovering the image tagging information and image content. The proposed framework can reduce the noise-induced uncertainty. In addition, RSSL achieves better results than C2MR, which indicates that it is better to jointly explore the visual geometric structure and the tag local and global consistency.

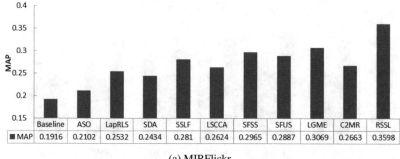

	Baseline	ASO	LapRLS	SDA	SSLF	LSCCA	SFSS	SFUS	LGME	C2MR	RSSL
■ MAP	0.1916	0.2102	0.2532	0.2434	0.281	0.2624	0.2965	0.2887	0.3069	0.2663	0.3598

(a) MIRFlickr

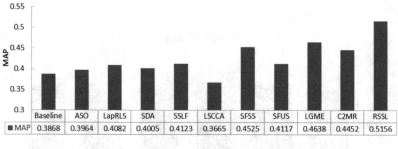

	Baseline	ASO	LapRLS	SDA	SSLF	LSCCA	SFSS	SFUS	LGME	C2MR	RSSL
■ MAP	0.3868	0.3964	0.4082	0.4005	0.4123	0.3665	0.4525	0.4117	0.4638	0.4452	0.5156

(b) NUS-WIDE

Fig. 3.1 Comparison of different algorithms on MIFlickr and NUS-WIDE learning data sets with $n = 5,000$ in terms of MAP

Finally, we present the performance of image retrieval in terms of MAP of all the compared methods on the learning data sets with $n = 5,000$ of the MIRFlcirk and NUS-WIDE data sets in Fig. 3.1. It is observed that RSSL performs significantly better than other methods for image retrieval, which shows that RSSL can rank the relevant tags at the top positions.

3.4.1.6 Parameter Sensitiveness

In the proposed framework, there are several parameters to be tuned. In our experiments, it is observed that the performance is not sensitive to the dimensionality r of the latent subspace and we set $r = 5 \times \lfloor \frac{m-1}{5} \rfloor$, where m is the number of concepts and $\lfloor c \rfloor$ denotes the largest integer not greater than c. When α is larger than 10, the performance of RSSL is good for the two image data sets. Besides, we observe that RSSL is not sensitive to λ when it is in the range of $[10^{-3}, 10^3]$. To validate how the rest parameters affect the performance, we conduct experiments to evaluate their sensitivity. The MIRFlickr and NUS-WIDE data sets with $n = 5,000$ learning data are used. The results show that the tagging performance varies corresponding

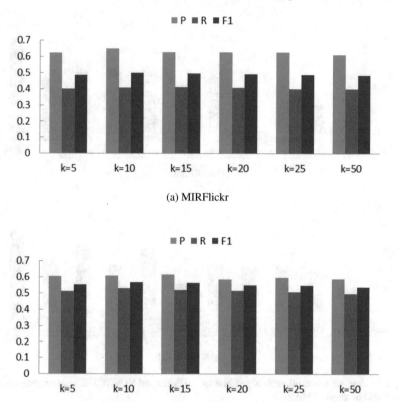

(a) MIRFlickr

(b) NUS-WIDE

Fig. 3.2 The performance in terms of precision, recall, and F1 by varying k to compute **L** on MIFlickr and NUS-WIDE learning data sets with $n = 5,000$

to different values of the parameters β and γ. The performance is good when the parameter β is not too large or small, which demonstrates the necessity of the smooth regularization on the underlying geometric structure between samples in the latent subspace. However, due to images represented by the low-level visual features, large β may introduce inaccurate information, which degrades the performance. For the parameter γ, we can see that it should not be small. Large γ makes the learned **W** satisfy the expected properties, which guarantees that better results are achieved.

The underlying geometric structure preservation in the latent subspace is dependent on the neighbor number k to compute the Laplcian matrix. In this experiment, we tune k within the range of $\{5, 10, 15, 20, 25, 50\}$. The performances in terms of recall, precision, and F1 by varying k on the two databases are presented in Fig. 3.2. We observe that the performance of the proposed RSSL varies slightly with varying k when k is not large. Thus, in our experiments, we fix $k = 15$ for both the MIRFlickr and NUS-WIDE data sets.

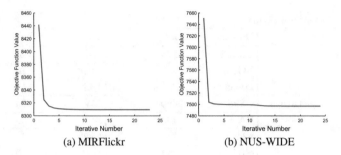

Fig. 3.3 Convergence curves of the objective function value of the proposed algorithm

3.4.1.7   Convergence Study

To solve the proposed formulation, we develop an iterative update algorithm. Now we experimentally validate its convergence and study the speed of convergence. Following the above experiments, the corresponding experiments are conducted on the MIRFlickr and NUS-WIDE data sets with $n = 5,000$ learning data. The convergence rates are shown in Fig. 3.3. From these figures, we can see that the value of our objective function monotonically decreases when the iteration round increases and changes only a little bit after five iterations for these two data sets, demonstrating that the proposed optimization algorithm is effective and converges quickly.

3.4.2   Clustering

In this section, we evaluate the performance of the proposed formulation for unsupervised clustering. The performance in terms of clustering is measured by two widely used evaluation metrics, i.e., Accuracy (ACC) and Normalized Mutual Information (NMI). The experiments are conducted on 7 publicly available data sets, including three face image data sets (i.e., UMIST [1], JAFFE [35], and Pointing4 [15]), two handwritten digit data sets (i.e., a subset of USPS [1] and Binary Alphabet (BA) [1]), and two text data sets (i.e., tr11 [2] and oh15 [2]). Data sets from different areas serve as a good test bed for a comprehensive evaluation. Table 3.4 summarizes the details of these 7 benchmark data sets.

As stated above, the goal of the proposed method is to learn a suitable representation and our method is suitable for clustering. Therefore, we adopt the learned **F** by the proposed method for clustering and denote it as RSSL. Besides, to validate the performance of the proposed method for representation learning, the proposed method is treated as a feature selection algorithm, denoted as RSSL-FS. That is, we first map data into the underlying subspace and then select features in the subspace by **P** to represent data. To demonstrate the performance of our method, we take all the original features for clustering as baseline and compare it with various representative

Table 3.4 Data set description

Domain	Data set	n	d	c
Face image	UMIST	575	644	20
	JAFFE	213	1,024	10
	Poingting4	2,790	1,120	15
Handwritten digits image	USPS	400	256	10
	BA	1,404	320	36
Text data	tr11	414	6,429	9
	oh15	913	3,100	10

algorithms, including Spectral Clustering (SC) [10], PCA [4], LPP [18], and several unsupervised feature selection methods, i.e., MaxVar (Features corresponding to the maximum variance are selected.), Laplacian Score (LS) [16], SPEC [51], MCFS [9], UDFS [48], NDFS [33], and LLCFS [50]. For feature selection methods, the numbers of features used for clustering are set as {5, 10, 20, 50, 100, 150, 200, 250, 300} for all the data sets except USPS. Because the total feature number of USPS is 256, we set the number of selected features as {5, 10, 20, 50, 80, 110, 140, 170, 200}. In our experiments, we adopt Kmeans to cluster samples based on the selected features. The performance of Kmeans depends on initialization. We repeat the clustering 20 times with random initialization for each setup and report the average results. The average results are presented in Tables 3.5 and 3.6.

Table 3.5 Clustering results (ACC%) of different algorithms for clustering on different data sets. The best results are highlighted in bold

Data set	Face			Handwritten digits		Text	
	UMIST	JAFFE	Pointing4	USPS	BA	tr11	oh15
Baseline	41.8	72.5	35.9	62.6	40.3	30.9	30.4
SC	59.6	75.8	64.6	71.5	44.4	31.1	39.4
PCA	43.3	78.2	36.5	65.5	43.4	32.4	34.9
LPP	56.5	69.7	47.1	64.0	44.1	48.2	33.4
MaxVar	45.8	67.3	44.0	63.8	40.7	30.5	32.9
LS	45.9	74.0	37.1	64.9	42.1	31.6	33.8
SPEC	47.9	76.9	38.6	65.5	42.2	35.1	33.8
MCFS	46.3	78.8	46.2	64.4	41.5	36.3	33.8
UDFS	48.6	76.7	45.1	66.2	42.7	35.9	32.9
NDFS	51.3	81.2	48.9	67.3	43.4	37.4	34.8
LLCFS	52.6	81.6	65.7	68.9	41.8	38.0	35.8
RSSL-FS	**65.2**	**91.5**	**69.1**	**76.5**	**47.6**	**57.8**	**48.2**
RSSL	**67.9**	**97.4**	**76.9**	**79.6**	**49.2**	**58.4**	**54.0**

Table 3.6 Clustering results (NMI%) of different algorithms for clustering on different data sets. The best results are highlighted in bold

Data set	Face			Handwritten digits		Text	
	UMIST	JAFFE	Pointing4	USPS	BA	tr11	oh15
Baseline	62.3	80.0	41.7	62.6	40.3	7.0	17.7
SC	77.2	85.6	73.8	69.2	60.3	2.5	30.0
PCA	63.8	83.4	47.4	58.7	58.4	7.7	26.0
LPP	74.2	80.8	56.0	62.4	59.5	40.2	24.0
MaxVar	63.5	70.3	50.8	58.1	56.9	7.6	22.1
LS	63.9	79.4	42.7	58.7	57.3	8.0	23.2
SPEC	65.2	82.8	40.5	59.5	57.9	11.5	23.6
MCFS	66.7	83.4	53.1	59.3	57.5	13.5	23.1
UDFS	67.3	82.3	52.4	60.1	58.1	13.7	21.8
NDFS	69.7	86.3	56.4	61.3	58.8	14.2	24.2
LLCFS	71.2	85.8	73.2	65.8	57.3	31.9	24.9
RSSL-FS	**80.5**	**94.7**	**77.9**	**72.2**	**62.3**	**41.9**	**36.8**
RSSL	**81.4**	**96.2**	**82.4**	**73.4**	**62.7**	**43.2**	**39.3**

It can be observed that our method is significantly superior to other algorithms, which verifies that the proposed RSSL enables to uncover more informative representations. And our method is the only one which has consistently high performance on all seven data sets. Intuitively, this indicates that it is necessary and useful to exploit the latent subspace to find the discriminative representation of data.

3.4.3   Classification

In this section, we apply our method to the problem of classification including semi-supervised classification and supervised classification. To validate the performance, we conduct experiments on four data sets, i.e., UMIST, JAFFE, USPS, and tr11. The performance is measured by the widely used evaluation metric, i.e., Classification Accuracy (AC).

For semi-supervised classification, we randomly choose 50% of samples as training data and the rest as testing data. We further randomly sample $s\%$ of training data as labeled data. In our experiments, we set s as 5, 10, 20, and 50, respectively, and report all of the results. The proposed algorithm is compared with several semi-supervised methods, including LapRLS [6], SDA [7], LSR [46], and SFSS [36]. The experiments are independently repeated 20 times to generate different training and testing data, and the average results are reported. The compared results are presented in Tables 3.7 and 3.8. We can see that the performance of all the algorithms improves as the number of labeled samples increases. Furthermore, it also is observed that our

Table 3.7 Semi-supervised classification results (AC%) of different algorithms on UMIST and JAFFE data sets. The best results are highlighted in bold

Data set		UMIST				JAFFE			
		$s = 5$	$s = 10$	$s = 20$	$s = 50$	$s = 5$	$s = 10$	$s = 20$	$s = 50$
LapRLS	Semi	51.9	56.1	59.3	65.8	81.9	85.3	90.1	91.8
SDA	Semi	34.4	39.0	42.1	46.3	72.3	75.9	82.0	89.2
LSR	Semi	30.9	37.7	46.3	65.2	77.8	85.7	87.9	90.6
SFSS	Semi	41.2	59.3	72.0	89.0	76.7	87.9	96.5	99.9
RSSL	Semi	**60.5**	**71.8**	**82.9**	**93.4**	**92.7**	**97.6**	**99.9**	**100.0**
LapRLS	Test	50.4	56.4	58.5	63.7	82.7	84.1	90.0	90.2
SDA	Test	32.4	37.1	40.8	45.5	70.2	75.6	80.6	85.7
LSR	Test	–	–	–	–	–	–	–	–
SFSS	Test	40.2	58.9	71.6	88.2	76.8	88.1	96.0	99.5
RSSL	Test	**59.7**	**71.2**	**82.2**	**93.9**	**89.5±1.2**	**96.3**	**99.6**	**100.0**

Table 3.8 Semi-supervised classification results (AC%) of different algorithms on USPS and tr11 data sets. The best results are highlighted in bold

Data set		USPS				tr11			
		$s = 5$	$s = 10$	$s = 20$	$s = 50$	$s = 5$	$s = 10$	$s = 20$	$s = 50$
LapRLS	Semi	56.5	63.6	68.9	71.3	40.7	45.9	51.3	56.6
SDA	Semi	44.7	50.4	54.4	61.0	37.2	45.5	52.6	57.2
LSR	Semi	50.2	65.5	70.7	78.4	52.0	62.1	67.6	72.9
SFSS	Semi	50.3	62.1	72.3	80.9	46.6	57.4	69.6	74.9
RSSL	Semi	**68.8**	**76.4**	**83.4**	**91.8**	**64.7**	**75.4**	**81.4**	**86.7**
LapRLS	Test	56.0	63.0	68.5	70.7	40.1	45.4	49.3	56.4
SDA	Test	44.2	47.3	53.0	60.6	37.0	46.7	50.3	57.3
LSR	Test	–	–	–	–	–	–	–	–
SFSS	Test	49.6	60.8	71.1	80.4	44.3	55.5	69.4	73.1
RSSL	Test	**67.4**	**74.7**	**81.5**	**89.5**	**63.5**	**73.3**	**80.3**	**84.5**

framework significantly outperforms all of the compared semi-supervised classification approaches, which indicates that RSSL can effectively learn a representation of data and classifiers from the labeled and unlabeled data.

The performance of the proposed RSSL for supervised classification is also validated on these four data sets. We randomly choose $c\%$ of samples as training data and the rest as testing data. In our experiments, we set c as 5, 10, 20, and 50, respectively. The experiments are independently repeated 20 times to generate different training and testing data, and the average results are reported. To demonstrate the superiority of the proposed RSSL, we compared it with several state-of-the-art methods, i.e., ASO [3], FSNM [38], SSLF [22], LSCCA [42], SFUS [37], and SFSS [36]. The results measured by classification accuracy (AC) are reported in Tables 3.9 and 3.10.

Table 3.9 Classification results (AC%) of different algorithms for supervised classification on UMIST and JAFFE data sets. The best results are highlighted in bold

Data set	UMIST				JAFFE			
	$c = 5$	$c = 10$	$c = 20$	$c = 50$	$c = 5$	$c = 10$	$c = 20$	$c = 50$
ASO	60.4	71.8	85.3	94.8	90.6	95.4	98.8	**100.0**
FSNM	46.3	69.0	85.6	94.6	78.7	92.5	99.0	99.9
SSLF	47.5	72.4	87.4	96.5	87.3	95.6	99.4	**100.0**
LSCCA	47.6	70.1	86.1	94.8	86.3	95.9	99.1	99.9
SFUS	48.4	72.3	87.3	95.6	80.9	96.9	99.5	**100.0**
SFSS	48.3	72.2	87.2	96.9	83.9	95.2	99.2	**100.0**
RSSL	**65.2**	**83.5**	**93.6**	**98.8**	**96.8**	**99.7**	**100.0**	**100.0**

Table 3.10 Classification results (AC%) of different algorithms for supervised classification on USPS and tr11 data sets. The best results are highlighted in bold

Data set	USPS				tr11			
	$c = 5$	$c = 10$	$c = 20$	$c = 50$	$c = 5$	$c = 10$	$c = 20$	$c = 50$
ASO	62.2	69.3	74.2	82.2	54.4	69.7	75.9	82.9
FSNM	60.8	64.48	71.9	81.5	50.8	63.6	76.1	83.3
SSLF	62.9	70.3	74.1	83.4	56.0	73.0	80.15	83.7
LSCCA	61.9	63.3	64.9	66.1	42.4	54.2	67.3	81.0
SFUS	64.5	70.0	77.8	83.3	60.1	73.5	80.4	84.8
SFSS	64.9	72.2	78.6	84.3	58.83	72.5	81.0	85.5
RSSL	**73.9**	**82.9**	**88.5**	**92.6**	**71.7**	**82.3**	**89.9**	**94.8**

From the results, we can see that the proposed RSSL obviously achieves the best performance.

From these experiments, we conclude that our method is well suited to classification problems, including semi-supervised and supervised ones.

3.4.4 Discussion

The proposed formulation (3.10) is a general one and can be used to explain several existing algorithms as special cases.

Connection with Feature Selection Algorithms. By now many feature selection methods have been studied, such as NDFS [33] and SFUS [37].

First, in unsupervised scenarios there is no labeled data. If we set $r = d$ and $\mathbf{Q} = \mathbf{I}_d$, we have $\mathbf{W} = \mathbf{P}$ and the objective function (3.22) is changed to

$$\min_{\mathbf{F},\mathbf{W}} \|\mathbf{F} - \mathbf{X}^T\mathbf{W}\|_{2,1} + \alpha\mathrm{Tr}[\mathbf{F}^T\mathbf{L}\mathbf{F}] + \lambda\|\mathbf{W}\|_{2,1}$$

$$\text{s.t.} \quad \mathbf{F}^T\mathbf{F} = \mathbf{I}_c, \mathbf{F} \geq 0. \tag{3.27}$$

If we use the least-squares loss function, the above formulation is same to the formulation of NDFS [33]. Our formulation is robust to the outliers using the $\ell_{2,1}$-norm-based loss function.

Second, for supervised learning, we set $\zeta \to \infty$ to make $\mathbf{F} = \mathbf{Y}$ since all the data are labeled. If we set $\beta = 0$ and use the regularization term $\|\mathbf{W}\|_{2,1}$ instead of $\|\mathbf{P}\|_{2,1}$ to facilitate feature selection, our formulation leads to

$$\min_{\mathbf{P},\mathbf{Q},\mathbf{W}} \|\mathbf{Y} - \mathbf{X}^T\mathbf{W}\|_{2,1} + \gamma\|\mathbf{W} - \mathbf{Q}\mathbf{P}\|_F^2 + \lambda\|\mathbf{W}\|_{2,1}$$

$$\text{s.t.} \quad \mathbf{Q}^T\mathbf{Q} = \mathbf{I}_r, \tag{3.28}$$

which is the formulation of SFUS [37].

Connection with Semi-Supervised Learning Algorithms. We now discuss the relationship between the proposed formulation and several Semi-supervised Learning (SSL) algorithms.

First, a SSL algorithm is proposed for multitask learning in [3], which is close to the proposed formulation. When $\zeta \to \infty$, we have $\mathbf{F}_{\text{labeled}} = \mathbf{Y}_{\text{labeled}}$. If we set $\beta = 0$ and $\lambda = 0$ and adopt the same loss function, the proposed formulation reduces to the one in [3] in the special case where the input data are the same for all tasks. Besides, if we further set $r = c$ and $\mathbf{P} = \mathbf{I}_c$, we have $\mathbf{W} = \mathbf{Q}$ and the proposed framework leads to LapRLS [6] with linear predictive function.

Second, in [36], a semi-supervised feature analyzing framework for multimedia data understanding is proposed, which is formulated as

$$\min_{\mathbf{F},\mathbf{W}} \alpha(\mathrm{Tr}[\mathbf{F}^T\mathbf{L}\mathbf{F}] + \mathrm{Tr}[(\mathbf{F} - \mathbf{Y})^T\mathbf{U}(\mathbf{F} - \mathbf{Y})])$$

$$+ \|\mathbf{F} - \mathbf{X}^T\mathbf{W}\|_F^2 + \lambda\|\mathbf{W}\|_{2,1}. \tag{3.29}$$

If we set $r = d$ and $\mathbf{Q} = \mathbf{I}_d$, we have $\mathbf{W} = \mathbf{P}$. Then using the least-squares loss function, our formulation leads to the above formulation.

Besides, if we use Frobenius norm rather than $\ell_{2,1}$-norm and impose a regularization term on $\mathbf{W}$ instead of $\mathbf{P}$, by setting $\beta = 0$, our formulation reduces to

$$\min_{\mathbf{F},\mathbf{P},\mathbf{Q},\mathbf{W}} \alpha(\mathrm{Tr}[\mathbf{F}^T\mathbf{L}\mathbf{F}] + \mathrm{Tr}[(\mathbf{F} - \mathbf{Y})^T\mathbf{U}(\mathbf{F} - \mathbf{Y})])$$

$$+ \|\mathbf{F} - \mathbf{X}^T\mathbf{W}\|_F^2 + \gamma\|\mathbf{W} - \mathbf{Q}\mathbf{P}\|_F^2 + \lambda\|\mathbf{W}\|_F^2$$

$$\text{s.t.} \quad \mathbf{Q}^T\mathbf{Q} = \mathbf{I}_r. \tag{3.30}$$

It is same to the objective function in [49]. In [49], the relationships to dimensionality reduction algorithms, transductive classification, and traditional graph regularization have been discussed. Thus, the relationships analyzed in [49] are appropriate to ours.

Connection with Multi-Label Classification. When all data are labeled and $\zeta \to \infty$, we have $\mathbf{F} = \mathbf{Y}$. Then when the regularization parameter $\beta = 0$, the proposed formulation reduces to the one in [22] in the special case where we employ Frobenius norm rather than $\ell_{2,1}$-norm. In [22], it discusses its connections with several algorithms, such as the classical ridge regression. Similarly, we can build the corresponding relationships between those algorithms and ours.

3.5 Discussions

In this chapter, we propose a subspace learning framework which enables to learn understanding-oriented representations for data by incorporating image understanding and feature learning into a unified framework. It exploits the visual geometric structure and the local and global consistencies over labels simultaneously to uncover a underlying subspace robust to the outliers and noise. We apply the proposed framework to several image understanding tasks, i.e., image tagging, clustering, and classification. And the proposed formulation is a general framework that can include several well-known formulations as special cases.

In the social image tagging task, the user-provided tags are utilized to analyze the image-tag associations. The user as one of important entities in the social tagging data is neglected. It is necessary to introduce the user factor for subspace learning and image tagging. The association between images and tags is estimated by taking into account all essential entities, user, image, and tag. And many other real-world tasks can be realized, such as personalized tag recommendation and personalized image search. Personalized tag recommendation is to predict tags for each user on a given web item (image, music, URL, or publication).

In the future, we will investigate the following research directions: (1) extend the proposed model in a nonlinear version, e.g., designing the potential functions with kernels, which can improve the robustness and generalization capability; and (2) consider to incorporate it and deep learning into a unified framework, with potential extensions to more practical applications.

References

1. http://cs.nyu.edu/~roweis/data.html
2. http://tunedit.org/repo/Data/Text-wc
3. Ando, R.K., Zhang, T.: A framework for learning predictive structures from multiple tasks and unlabeld data. J. Mach. Learn. Res. **6**, 1817–1853 (2005)
4. Belhumeur, P.N., Hespanha, J.P., Wu, X., Kriegman, D.J.: Eigenfaces vs. fisherfaces: recognition using class specific linear projection. IEEE Trans. Patt. Anal. Mach. Intell. **19**(7), 711–720 (1997)
5. Belkin, M., Niyogi, P.: Laplacian eigenmaps for dimensionality reduction and data representation. Neural Comput. **15**(6), 1373–1396 (2003)

6. Belkin, M., Niyogi, P., Sindhwani, V.: Manifold regularization: a geometric framework for learning from labeled and unlabeled examples. J. Mach. Learn. Res. **7**, 2399–2434 (2006)
7. Cai, D., He, X., Han, J.: Semi-supervised discriminant analysis. In: Proceedings of of IEEE International Conference on Computer Vision (2007)
8. Cai, D., He, X., Han, J.: Spectral regression: a unified approach for sparse subspace learning. In: Proceedings of International Conference on Data Mining (2007)
9. Cai, D., Zhang, C., He, X.: Unsupervised feature selection for multi-cluster data. In: Proceedings of ACM SIGKDD International Conference on Knowledge Discovery and Data Mining (2010)
10. Chen, W.Y., Song, Y., Bai, H., Lin, C.J., Chang, E.Y.: Parallel spectral clustering in distributed systems. IEEE Trans. Patt. Anal. Mach. Intell. **33**(3), 568–586 (2011)
11. Cheng, Q., Zhou, H., Cheng, J.: The fisher-markov selector: fast selecting maximally separable feature subset for multiclass classification with applications to high-dimensional data. IEEE Trans. Patt. Anal. Mach. Intell. **33**(6), 1217–1233 (2011)
12. Chua, T., Tang, J., Hong, R., Li, H., Luo, Z., Zheng, Y.: Nus-wide: a real-world web image database from national university of Singapore. In: Proceedings of ACM International Conference on Image and Video Retrieval (2009)
13. Chung, F.R.K.: Spectral Graph Theory (CBMS Regional Conference Series in Mathematics, No. 92). American Mathematical Society (1997)
14. Duda, R., Hart, P., Stork, D.: Pattern Recognition, 2nd edn. Wiley, New York, USA (2001)
15. Gourier, N., Hall, D., Crowley, J.: Estimating face orientation from robust detection of salient facial features. In: Proceedings of ICPR Workshop on Visual Observation of Deictic Gestures (2004)
16. He, X., Cai, D., Niyogi, P.: Laplacian score for feature selection. In: Proceedings of Advances in Neural Information Processing Systems (2005)
17. He, X., Cai, D., Yan, S., Zhang, H.J.: Neighborhood preserving embedding. In: Proceedings of International Conference on Computer Vision (2005)
18. He, X., Niyogi, P.: Locality preserving projections. In: Proceedings of Advances in Neural Information Processing Systems (2003)
19. Higham, N.J.: Accuracy and Stability of Numerical Algorithms, 2nd edn. Society for Industrial and Applied Mathematics, Manchester, England (2002)
20. Huiskes, M., Lew, M.: The mir flickr retrieval evaluation. In: Proceedings of ACM International Conference on Multimedia Information Retrieval (2008)
21. Jain, A., Zongker, D.: Feature selection: evaluation, application, and small sample performance. IEEE Trans. Patt. Anal. Mach. Intell. **19**(2), 153–158 (1997)
22. Ji, S., Zhang, L., Yu, S., Ye, J.: A shared-subspace learning framework for multi-label classification. ACM Trans. Knowl. Disc. Data **4**(2), 1817–1853 (2010)
23. Jiang, Y., Liu, J., Li, Z., Li, P., Lu, H.: Co-regularized plsa for multi-view clustering. In: Proceedings of Asian Conference on Computer Vision, pp. 202–213
24. Jiang, Y., Liu, J., Li, Z., Lu, H.: Collaborative plsa for multi-view clustering. In: Proceedings of International Conference on Pattern Recognition, pp. 2997–3000
25. Jiang, Y., Liu, J., Li, Z., Lu, H.: Semi-supervised unified latent factor learning with multi-view data. Mach. Vis. Appl. **25**(7), 1635–1645 (2014)
26. Jin, L., Li, Z., Shu, X., Gao, S., Tang, J.: Partially common-semantic pursuit for rgb-d object recognition. In: Proceedings of ACM International Conference on Multimedia, pp. 959–962
27. Kuhn, H., Tucker, A.: Nonlinear programming. In: Berkeley Symposium on Mathematical Statistics and Probabilistics (1951)
28. Li, Y., Liu, J., Li, Z., Zhang, Y., Lu, H., Ma, S.: Learning low-rank representations with classwise block-diagonal structure for robust face recognition. In: Proceedings of AAAI Conference on Artificial Intelligence, pp. 2810–2816
29. Li, Z., Liu, J., Lu, H.: Structure preserving non-negative matrix factorization for dimensionality reduction. Comp. Vis. Image Underst. **117**(9), 1175–1189 (2013)
30. Li, Z., Liu, J., Tang, J., Lu, H.: Projective matrix factorization with unified embedding for social image tagging. Comp. Vis. Image Underst. **124**, 71–78 (2014)

31. Li, Z., Liu, J., Tang, J., Lu, H.: Robust structured subspace learning for data representation. IEEE Trans. Patt. Anal. Mach. Intell. **37**(10), 2085–2098 (2015)
32. Li, Z., Tang, J.: Weakly-supervised deep nonnegative low-rank model for social image tag refinement and assignment. In: Proceedings of AAAI Conference on Artificial Intelligence (2017)
33. Li, Z., Yang, Y., Liu, J., Zhou, X., Lu, H.: Unsupervised feature selection using nonnegative spectral analysis. In: Proceedings of AAAI Conference on Artificial Intelligence (2012)
34. Liu, J., Jiang, Y., Li, Z., Zhou, Z.H., Lu, H.: Partially shared latent factor learning with multiview data. IEEE Trans. Neural Netw. Learn. Syst. **26**(6), 1233–1246 (2015)
35. Lyons, M.J., Budynek, J., Akamatsu, S.: Automatic classification of single facial images. IEEE Trans. Patt. Anal. Mach. Intell. **21**(12), 1357–1362 (1999)
36. Ma, Z., Nie, F., Yang, Y., Uijlings, J., Sebe, N., Hauptmann, A.: Discriminating joint feature analysis for multimedia data understanding. IEEE Trans. Multimed. **14**(4), 1021–1030 (2012)
37. Ma, Z., Nie, F., Yang, Y., Uijlings, J., Sebe, N., Hauptmann, A.: Web image annotation via subspace-sparsity collaborated feature selection. IEEE Trans. Multimed. **14**(4), 1021–1030 (2012)
38. Nie, F., Huang, H., Cai, X., Ding, C.: Efficient and robust feature selection via joint $\ell_{2,1}$-norms minimization. In: Proceedings of Advances in Neural Information Processing Systems, pp. 1813–1821 (2010)
39. Qi, G.J., Aggarwal, C., Tian, Q., Ji, H., Huang, T.: Exploring context and content links in social media: a latent space method. IEEE Trans. Patt. Anal. Mach. Intell. **34**(5), 850–862 (2012)
40. Roweis, S.T., Saul, L.K.: Nonlinear dimensionality reduction by locally linear embedding. Science **29**(5500), 2323–2326 (2000)
41. Smeulders, A.W.M., Worring, M., Santini, S., Gupta, A., Jain, R.: Content-based image retrieval at the end of the early years. IEEE Trans. Patt. Anal. Mach. Intell. **22**(12), 1349–1380 (2000)
42. Sun, L., Ji, S., Ye, J.: Canonical correlation analysis for multilabel classification: a least-squares formulation, extensions and analysis. IEEE Trans. Patt. Anal. Mach. Intell. **1**(33), 2194–2200 (2011)
43. Tang, J., Jin, L., Li, Z., Gao, S.: Rgb-d object recognition via incorporating latent data structure and prior knowledge. IEEE Trans. Multimed. **17**(11), 1899–1908 (2015)
44. Tenenbaum, J., Silva, V., Langford, J.: A global geometric framework for nonlinear dimensionality reduction. Science **290**(22), 2319–2323 (2000)
45. la Torre, F.D., Black, M.J.: A framework for robust subspace learning. Int. J. Comp. Vis. **54**(1–3), 117–142 (2003)
46. Xiang, S., Nie, F., Zhang, C.: Semi-supervised classification via local spline regression. IEEE Trans. Patt. Anal. Mach. Intell. **32**(11), 2039–2053 (2010)
47. Yan, S., Xu, D., Zhang, B., Zhang, H., Yang, Q., Lin, S.: Graph embedding and extensions: a general framework for dimensionality reduction. IEEE Trans. Patt. Anal. Mach. Intell. **29**(1), 40–51 (2007)
48. Yang, Y., Shen, H.T., Ma, Z., Huang, Z., Zhou, X.: $\ell_{2,1}$-norm regularized discriminative feature selection for unsupervised learning. In: Proceedings of International Joint Conference on Artificial Intelligence (2011)
49. Yang, Y., Wu, F., Nie, F., Shen, H.T., Zhuang, Y., Hauptmann, A.: Web and personal image annotation by mining label correlation with relaxed visual graph embedding. IEEE Trans. Image Process. **21**(3), 1339–1351 (2012)
50. Zeng, H., Cheung, M.Y.: Feature selection and kernel learning for local learning-based clustering. IEEE Trans. Patt. Anal. Mach. Intell. **33**(8), 1532–1547 (2011)
51. Zhao, Z., Liu, H.: Spectral feature selection for supervised and unsupervised learning. In: Proceedings of International Conference on Machine Learning (2007)
52. Zou, H., Hastie, T., Tibshirani, R.: Sparse principal component analysis. J. Comput. Graph. Stat. **15**(2), 262–286 (2006)

Chapter 4
Personalized Tag Recommendation

Abstract Social tagging becomes increasingly important to organize and search large-scale community-contributed photos on social websites. To facilitate generating high-quality social tags, tag recommendation by automatically assigning relevant tags to photos draws particular research interest. In this chapter, we focus on the personalized tag recommendation task and try to identify user-preferred, geo-location-specific as well as semantically relevant tags for a photo by leveraging rich contexts of the freely available community-contributed photos. For users and geo-locations, we assume they have different preferred tags assigned to a photo, and propose a subspace learning method to individually uncover the both types of preferences. Considering the visual feature is a lower level representation on semantics than the textual information, we adopt a progressive learning strategy by additionally introducing an intermediate subspace for the visual domain. Given an untagged photo with its geo-location to a user, the user-preferred and the geo-location-specific tags are found by the nearest neighbor search in the corresponding unified spaces.

4.1 Introduction

Due to the rapid popularization of GPS-enable camera devices and mobile phones, recent years have witnessed an explosive growth of personal photos with rich context like tags, geo-locations[1] and visual attributes (colors and textures) [2]. Furthermore, many photo sharing websites, such as Flickr, Corbis and Picasa, facilitate millions of users to upload and share their personal multimedia data by their smart phones or other Internet access devices. As a consequence, the volume of community-contributed photos increases drastically whether on personal devices or on the social websites.[2] It is challenging and promising to exploit the overwhelming amount of context data for multimedia applications, such as retrieval [16], annotation [18, 39] and recommendation [20].

---

[1]In this chapter, geo-location refers to the city in which each photo was taken. It can be derived according to its longitude and latitude by Flickr API.

[2]http://www.stupros.com.

© Springer Nature Singapore Pte Ltd. 2017
Z. Li, *Understanding-Oriented Multimedia Content Analysis*, Springer Theses,
DOI 10.1007/978-981-10-3689-7_4

Among these applications, assigning proper tags to photos is the crucial task. Obviously, fully manual tag assignment is very time-consuming and impractical due to the massive photos and the limited screen size of the mobile devices. To make it easier, tag recommendation methods [4, 32, 35, 36] are proposed to suggest some relevant tags to a given photo and allow users to select their preferred tags, which cannot only ease the burden for users to upload and share their photos on social websites, but facilitate users to tag and organize their personal images on mobile devices. However, most work attempt to learn the association between tags and photos, while the user preferences are ignored in the recommendation. Users have personal preferences for photos, which can be observed by the following two aspects. First, users favor different types of photos. For instance, some prefer the 'architectures' photos, while others are in favor of the 'natural landscape' ones. Second, different users have different favorite tags. In other words, if very similar photos would be tagged by two users, different tags may be produced, as shown in Fig. 4.1a. Consequently, personalized tag recommendation can provide more appropriate recommendation results by taking user's profile into account.

On the other hand, users are used to spend considerable effort to organize their photo albums geographically by describing photos with tags related to locations where they were taken [1, 31, 33]. Hence, the geographical information of photos should be explored in tag recommendation [9, 21, 22, 25, 34]. Besides, some location-specific tags (e.g., Eiffel Tower and Forbidden City) and location-related tags (e.g., Paris and Beijing) are helpful to disambiguate some visually similar images. As shown in Fig. 4.1b, the two visually similar photos are possibly assigned to the same tags without considering the geographic information even if they are taken by the same user. Therefore, investigating the geo-location preference toward tags from this huge amount of context multimedia data can provide us useful information to recommend the most relevant tags to a given photo.

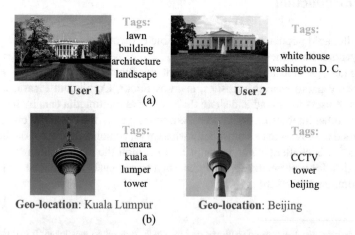

Fig. 4.1 An illustration of preference of users and geo-locations. **a** Users have their specific preferences toward tags for similar photos; **b** two visually similar photos corresponding to different geo-locations are tagged with different tags

To address the above issues, we seek to develop a framework of personalized tag recommendation by jointly exploring the tagging resources and the geo-location information in social web context. We propose a subspace learning method to individually mine user preference from her tagging history and analyze geo-location preference toward tags based on the location-related tagging resources. During the individual subspace learning process, given the tagging photos specific to a user (or a geo-location), we propose to uncover a common structure to link the visual and textual domains, i.e., a unified subspace shared by the both domains, in which visual features and textual representations of photos are comparable. Considering the visual feature is a much lower level representation on semantics than the textual information, we first map the visual features into an intermediate space, which is required to be structure consistent with the textual space. The introduction of the intermediate space for visual domain is to alleviate the semantic gap between the visual and textual domains. Then we attempt to learn a unified space mapping from the intermediate space and the textual space respectively, in which both the visual- and semantic–geometric structures should also be maintained. We integrate the above learning problems about the intermediate space and the unified space together into a united formulation, and propose an effective optimization algorithm followed with its convergence proof. With the learning outputs, we can map an untagged photo given a user (a geo-location) into the unified space corresponding to the user (the location), and use the nearest neighbor search to obtain some user-preferred tags and geo-location-preference tags individually. We further combine the obtained tags and the visual appearance of the photo to discover the semantically and visually related images, and explore the idea of annotation-by-search to rank tags for the untagged photo. Finally, the top ranked tags are recommended to the user. Experiments on a large-scale data set collected from Flickr demonstrate the outperformance of the proposed solution. Most of the work in this chapter has been published in [17].

4.2 Related Work

Generic Tag Recommendation. Generic tag recommendation methods [4, 13–15, 32, 35] are to predict the same list of tags for the same photo, i.e., it is independent of the user factor. Chen et al. [4] proposed an automatic tag recommendation approach that directly predicts the possible tags with models learned from training data. Shen and Fan [32] proposed a multitask structured SVM algorithm to leverage both the inter-object correlations and the loosely tagged images. Images are annotated purely based on image visual content [12]. For an image, it first finds its top-k neighboring images from the community image set and then selects the most frequent tags in the neighbor set as the annotated results. In [35], two approaches, based on Poisson Mixture Models and Gaussian process respectively, are proposed to make effective and efficient tag recommendations. In [36], tag concepts derived based on tag co-occurrence pairs are indexed as textual documents. The candidate tags associated with the matching concepts, which are retrieved with the query of user-given tags of an image, are recommended. There are some work focusing on tagging images by exploiting geo-tags [9, 21, 22, 34]. A typical approach as introduced by Moxley et al. [21] and Kleban et al. [9] is to annotate a given image by constrained k nearest neighbor (k-NN) voting, where the visual neighbors are retrieved from the geo-region of the given image. The fundamental idea in [22] is to learn tag semantics, i.e., categorize tags as places, landmarks, and visual descriptors, in order to post-filter tag the results of tag suggestion. Silva and Martins [34] annotated geo-referenced photos with descriptive tags by exploring the redundancy over the large volume of annotations available at online repositories with other geo-referenced photos. However, the above methods ignore the user preference and suggest same tags to visually similar photos of different users. Different from them, we propose a learning algorithm to effectively uncover user preference from her tagging history.

Personalized Tag Recommendation. Personalized tag recommendation has attracted significant attention recently. In [7], tag recommendation is obtained using both a Naive Bayes classifier on user tagging history and TF-IDF-based global information. In [33], tag co-occurrence for photos is calculated using tags appearing both in the tagging history of a user and in Flickr website, and used to generate recommended tags. Web browsing behavior of a user is exploited to suggest the tags not only to be added to but also to be deleted from the original tags of a photo in Flickr [38]. In [10], image tag recommendation is formulated as a maximum a posteriori problem using a visual folksonomy. With the assumption that favorite images and their associated tags indicate the visual and topical interests of a user, personalized favorite images and their context are used to perform personalized image tag recommendation [6]. A simple personalized image annotation method is designed in [30], which simply annotates an untagged images with the most frequent tags in the user tagging history. Tensor decomposition models have been exploited for tag recommendation [3, 23, 26–28, 37]. Rendle and Thieme [28] propose a special case of the tucker decomposition model, pairwise interaction model, to predict the tag sets. MusicBox [23] tags music based on social tags by capturing the three-way correlations between users–tags–music items using three-order tensors. The low-order tensor decomposition is proposed in [3], which include 0-th, 1-st, 2-nd order polynomials to reconstruct the data. In [26], a tensor factorization and tag clustering model is proposed to recommend items in social tagging systems, which can handle the problems of sparsity, cold start, and learning problem for tag relevance. A personalized method using cross-entropy is proposed to annotate images [11], which personalizes a generic annotation model by learning from a user's tagging history. However, the above methods only focus on photos, users, and tags but ignore the geographical information of photos. Different from the above work, we propose a subspace learning approach to individually uncover user preference by exploiting user's tagging history and geo-location preference by exploiting the geographic information of photos, and then jointly explore the learned subspaces assisted with the search scheme to recommend user-preferred tags to a photo.

4.3 Personalized Geo-Specific Tag Recommendation

4.3.1 Overview of Our Solution

This work focuses on how to ease personalized photo tagging process by exploiting the community-contributed multimedia data with rich contextual information. The proposed framework is illustrated in Fig. 4.2, which contains two primary parts: the offline and online processes.

The offline process is made up of three subdivisions: data collection, user preference learning, and geo-location preference learning. For data collection, we collect a vast amount of photos with their tags, taggers, geo-locations and some relevant text information from Flickr. With the collected resources, we organize the photos according to different taggers (i.e., users) and geo-locations individually. Given a collection corresponding to a user (or a geo-location), we propose a new subspace learning approach to uncover the user's preference (or the geo-location's preference) toward tags. Our goal is to find a unified space for the both visual and textual domains, in which the visual features and the tagging information are comparable, i.e., the correlations between the both heterogeneous representations can be directly constructed. The details about the proposed approach and its optimization will be presented in Sect. 4.3.2.

In the online module (discussed in Sect. 4.3.5), given a new photo with a specific user and a specific geo-location, we first find its top ranked neighboring tags in the user-specific unified space and the geo-specific unified space individually, and combine the both sets of neighboring tags to generate the initial tags, by which semantically relevant photos are chosen from the community-contributed photo set. And then visually similar photos are found by implementing content-based photo retrieval from these semantically relevant photos. Finally, the most frequent tags in the semantically and visually related photos are recommended to the user.

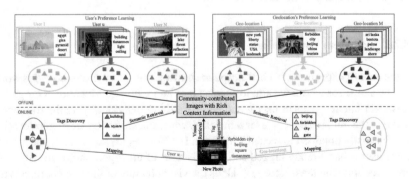

Fig. 4.2 The framework of the proposed personalized tag recommendation algorithm. The *square* and *triangle* denote photo and tag, respectively. The *circle* is corresponding to a new photo. The selected related tags are with *red boundary*

4.3.2   Discovering Intermediate Space and Unified Space

In this section, we first present our motivation for user preference and geo-location preference learning in Sect. 4.3.2.1. The proposed algorithm is formulated in Sect. 4.3.2.2, followed by its optimization and convergence analysis in Sect. 4.3.3. Finally, we introduce how to represent tags in the learned unified space in Sect. 4.3.4.

4.3.2.1   Motivation

We address the personalized tag recommendation task with the help of overwhelming community-contributed information, such as user tag and geo-location. The heart is how to learn the latent correlation between visual features and tags for each user (or geo-location). However, there exists the well-known semantic gap making it challenging. Fortunately, the community-contributed photos are associated with rich text information, which can reduce this gap. The content of the text and the photos are highly correlated. However, the text space and visual space have inherently different structures. To address this problem, it is crucial and necessary to discover a common structure to link them. On the other hand, the visual representation and the text representation of a photo should be consistent, i.e., corresponding representations should be same in the common structure. This naturally motivates an approach to discover a latent unified space, in which the corresponding text features and visual features of the same photo are identical. This can be achieved by two transformations from text features and visual feature respectively to a unified space. However, compared with the tag information, visual feature is a much lower level representation on semantics. To reduce the semantic gap, we adopt a progressive way to first map the visual features into an intermediate space, which is analogous to the tag space, and then perform the transform from the intermediate one to the unified space. By the proposed progressive learning manner, a better latent space is learned, which is validated by our experiments in Sect. 4.4.6.

4.3.2.2   Problem Formulation

For the ease of exposition, we first introduce the notations used throughout this work. Let u be a user for whom we aim to suggest tags and g be a geo-location. Our goal is to discover latent spaces of user u and geo-location g individually. In the following, we derive the unified space of user u in detail, while the unified space of geo-location g can be easily obtained in the same manner. Let $\mathbf{X}_{u,tr} = [\mathbf{x}_1, \mathbf{x}_2, \ldots, \mathbf{x}_n]$ be a set of photos user u has already tagged and $\mathbf{X}_{u,te}$ is a set of untagged photos to which we want to recommend tags. Here $\mathbf{x}_i \in \mathbb{R}^d$ is the visual feature of the i-th photo. d is the dimension of visual feature space. We use w to denote a word in the text space and $\mathbb{V} = \{w_1, w_2, \ldots, w_m\}$ for a large vocabulary. $\mathbf{Y}_u = [\mathbf{y}_1, \mathbf{y}_2, \ldots, \mathbf{y}_n] \in \mathbb{R}^{m \times n}$ is the text representation matrix of photos tagged by user u, where $(Y_u)_{ij}$ is used to represent the relevance between tag w_i and photo $\mathbf{x}_j$ assigned by user u. We use the binary scheme to define $\mathbf{Y}_u$ in our experiments, i.e., $(Y_u)_{ij} = 1$ when photo $\mathbf{x}_j$ is tagged with w_i and $(Y_u)_{ij} = 0$ otherwise. Motivated by the above idea, the unified space of user u is discovered based on three linear transformation matrices $\mathbf{W}_u \in \mathbb{R}^{q \times d}$, $\mathbf{V}_u \in \mathbb{R}^{p \times q}$ and $\mathbf{T}_u \in \mathbb{R}^{p \times m}$. Here q and p are the dimensions of the intermediate space and unified space respectively. For brevity, we use $\mathbf{X}, \mathbf{Y}, \mathbf{W}, \mathbf{V}$ and $\mathbf{T}$ to denote $\mathbf{X}_{u,tr}, \mathbf{Y}_u, \mathbf{W}_u, \mathbf{V}_u$ and $\mathbf{T}_u$ respectively from here on.

With transformation matrices $\mathbf{W}$ and $\mathbf{V}$, we can easily obtain the latent representations $\mathbf{G} = [\mathbf{g}_1, \mathbf{g}_2, \ldots, \mathbf{g}_n] \in \mathbb{R}^{q \times n}$ and $\mathbf{U} = [\mathbf{u}_1, \mathbf{u}_2, \ldots, \mathbf{u}_n] \in \mathbb{R}^{p \times n}$ of the original visual features in the intermediate space and the unified space, respectively.

$$\mathbf{G} = \mathbf{WX} \tag{4.1}$$

$$\mathbf{U} = \mathbf{VG} = \mathbf{VWX} \tag{4.2}$$

Similarly, the latent representations $\mathbf{Z} = [\mathbf{z}_1, \mathbf{z}_2, \ldots, \mathbf{z}_n] \in \mathbb{R}^{p \times n}$ of the original text features are obtained by

$$\mathbf{Z} = \mathbf{TY}. \tag{4.3}$$

In the following, we first introduce our optimization problem without setting any canonical form for the loss functions. The specific forms will be explained with the proposed optimization algorithm in Sect. 4.3.3. To derive the effective transformation matrices, the unified space is expected to connect the visual structure and text structure. For this purpose, we require that

$$\mathbf{U} = \mathbf{Z} \Rightarrow \mathbf{VWX} = \mathbf{TY}. \tag{4.4}$$

The above equation is overdetermined and usually there is no exact solutions. Therefore, we employ a cost function f as a measure of disagreement between them

$$\min_{\mathbf{U},\mathbf{Z}} f(\mathbf{U}, \mathbf{Z}). \tag{4.5}$$

We also expect that the intermediate space is analogous to the text space with semantic structure. To this end, we design another cost function h to measure the semantic difference between the structures of the intermediate space $\mathbf{G}$ and the text space $\mathbf{Y}$ as follows.

$$\min_{\mathbf{W}} h(\mathbf{G}, \mathbf{Y}) \tag{4.6}$$

Considering the above two aspects simultaneously, we have the following optimization problem to learn the transformation matrices.

$$\min_{\mathbf{W},\mathbf{V},\mathbf{T}} f(\mathbf{U}, \mathbf{Z}) + \alpha h(\mathbf{G}, \mathbf{Y}) + \lambda \Omega(\mathbf{W}, \mathbf{V}, \mathbf{T}) \tag{4.7}$$

where the third term $\Omega(\mathbf{W}, \mathbf{V}, \mathbf{T})$ is the regularization term about these three transformations, which can avoid overfitting problem. α and λ are the trade-off parameters, which balance the three terms in the objective function.

Besides, the above objective function overlooks the preservation of the geometric structures in the original visual and text spaces. Theoretically, geometric information can benefit the effective discovery of the latent space. Thereupon, it is necessary to add corresponding regularization terms in the objective function in Eq. 4.7. There are many strategies to preserve the local structure, such as LPP [8], LLE [29], and NFS embedding [5]. For simplicity, in this work we adopt LPP to preserve the local structures without loss of generality. Let $\mathbf{S} \in \mathbb{R}^{n \times n}$ and $\mathbf{C} \in \mathbb{R}^{n \times n}$ denote the similarity matrices in the original visual and text spaces, respectively. We take $\mathbf{S}$ to sketch the details.

To preserve the geometric structure, we hope that visually similar photos should be located closely in the unified space. A reasonable criterion is to minimize the following objective function:

$$\frac{1}{2} \sum_{i=1}^{n} \sum_{j=1}^{n} S_{ij} \left\| \frac{\mathbf{u}_i}{\sqrt{D_{ii}}} - \frac{\mathbf{u}_j}{\sqrt{D_{jj}}} \right\|^2 = \mathrm{Tr}[\mathbf{U} \mathbf{L}^S \mathbf{U}^T], \qquad (4.8)$$

where $D_{ii} = \sum_{j=1}^{n} S_{ij}$ is engaged for normalization purpose. $\mathbf{D} = \mathrm{diag}(D_{11}, D_{22}, ..., D_{nn})$ is a diagonal matrix and $\mathbf{L}^S = \mathbf{D}^{-1/2} (\mathbf{D} - \mathbf{S}) \mathbf{D}^{-1/2}$ is the normalized graph Laplacian matrix. $\mathrm{Tr}[.]$ denotes the trace operation. In the same manner, the corresponding regularization for local semantic geometry preservation is $\mathrm{Tr}[\mathbf{Z} \mathbf{L}^C \mathbf{Z}^T]$. We adopt Gaussian kernel similarity and cosine similarity to calculate $\mathbf{S}$ and $\mathbf{C}$ respectively.

Combining the objective function in Eq. 4.7 and the above two regularization terms for preserving local structures, we obtain the following optimization problem.

$$\min_{\mathbf{W},\mathbf{V},\mathbf{T}} f(\mathbf{U}, \mathbf{Z}) + \alpha h(\mathbf{G}, \mathbf{Y}) + \beta \mathrm{Tr}[\mathbf{U} \mathbf{L}^S \mathbf{U}^T] + \gamma \mathrm{Tr}[\mathbf{Z} \mathbf{L}^C \mathbf{Z}^T] + \lambda \Omega(\mathbf{W}, \mathbf{V}, \mathbf{T})$$

$$(4.9)$$

Here β and γ are non-negative trade-off parameters. Our goal is to discover the underlying unified space by predicting the three transformation matrices. It can be achieved by optimizing the above objective function, which will be discussed in the next subsection.

4.3.3 Optimization

We first introduce the optimization algorithm for the above objective function and then analyze its convergence. First of all, we make use of the least square loss function $f(a, b) = (a - b)^2$ to measure the disagreement between $\mathbf{U}$ and $\mathbf{Z}$. For the function h, in this work we only expect that the intermediate space has the same local geometric structure as the text space for simplicity. That is, the difference between $\mathbf{G}$ and $\mathbf{Y}$ is constrained by the Laplacian regularization: $h(\mathbf{G}, \mathbf{Y}) = \mathrm{Tr}[\mathbf{G}\mathbf{L}^C\mathbf{G}^T]$, which is computed in the same manner as in Eq. 4.8. For $\Omega(\mathbf{W}, \mathbf{V}, \mathbf{T})$, we use the conventional squared norm to regularize $\mathbf{V}$ and $\mathbf{T}$ and the $\ell_{2,1}$ norm to regularize $\mathbf{W}$. That is,

$$\Omega(\mathbf{W}, \mathbf{V}, \mathbf{T}) = \|\mathbf{W}\|_{2,1} + \|\mathbf{V}\|_F^2 + \|\mathbf{T}\|_F^2, \tag{4.10}$$

in which $\| \cdot \|_F$ denotes the Frobenius norm and the $\ell_{2,1}$ norm is defined as $\|\mathbf{W}\|_{2,1} = \sum_{i=1}^q \sqrt{\sum_{j=1}^d W_{ij}^2}$. The $\ell_{2,1}$ norm regularization is utilized to use features across all data points with joint sparsity, i.e., each feature either has small scores or large scores over all data points. It is necessary for our task because some visual features are noisy and unhelpful.

Substituting the above expressions, the objective function of Eq. 4.9 can be rewritten as

$$\min_{\mathbf{W},\mathbf{V},\mathbf{T}} \mathscr{L} = \|\mathbf{U} - \mathbf{Z}\|_F^2 + \alpha\mathrm{Tr}[\mathbf{G}\mathbf{L}^C\mathbf{G}^T] + \beta\mathrm{Tr}[\mathbf{U}\mathbf{L}^S\mathbf{U}^T]$$
$$+ \gamma\mathrm{Tr}[\mathbf{Z}\mathbf{L}^C\mathbf{Z}^T] + \lambda(\|\mathbf{W}\|_{2,1} + \|\mathbf{V}\|_F^2 + \|\mathbf{T}\|_F^2) \tag{4.11}$$

The $\ell_{2,1}$-norm regularization term is non-smooth and the objective function is not convex over $\mathbf{W}$, $\mathbf{V}$ and $\mathbf{T}$ simultaneously.

To optimize the proposed objective function, we employ the gradient method to update these transformation matrices iteratively. The derivatives of $\mathscr{L}$ with respect to $\mathbf{W}$, $\mathbf{V}$ and $\mathbf{T}$ can be calculated as follows:

$$\frac{\partial \mathscr{L}}{\partial \mathbf{W}} = 2(\mathbf{V}^T(\mathbf{U} - \mathbf{Z})\mathbf{X}^T + \alpha\mathbf{G}\mathbf{L}^C\mathbf{X}^T + \beta\mathbf{V}^T\mathbf{U}\mathbf{L}^S\mathbf{X}^T + \lambda\mathbf{A}\mathbf{W}) \tag{4.12}$$

$$\frac{\partial \mathscr{L}}{\partial \mathbf{V}} = 2((\mathbf{U} - \mathbf{Z})\mathbf{G}^T + \beta\mathbf{U}\mathbf{L}^S\mathbf{G}^T + \lambda\mathbf{V}) \tag{4.13}$$

$$\frac{\partial \mathscr{L}}{\partial \mathbf{T}} = 2(-(\mathbf{U} - \mathbf{Z})\mathbf{Y}^T + \gamma\mathbf{Z}\mathbf{L}^C\mathbf{Y}^T + \lambda\mathbf{T}) \tag{4.14}$$

Here $\mathbf{A} \in \mathscr{R}^{q \times q}$ is a diagonal matrix with $A_{ii} = \frac{1}{2\|\mathbf{w}_i\|_2}$,[3] where $\mathbf{w}_i$ is the ith row of $\mathbf{W}$. Based on the above analysis, we summarize the detailed optimization algorithm in Algorithm 4. Next, the convergence of the proposed iterative procedure will be proved.

---

[3]In practice, $\|\mathbf{w}_i\|_2$ could be close to zero but not zero. Theoretically, it could be zeros. For this case, we can regularize $A_{ii} = \frac{1}{2\sqrt{(\mathbf{w}_i^T\mathbf{w}_i + \varepsilon)}}$, where ε is very small constant.

Algorithm 4 Transformations Discovery Algorithm

Input:
 Visual Representation $\mathbf{X}$ and Text Representation $\mathbf{Y}$; Parameters α, β, γ, λ, p and q; The step
 length η.
1: Calculate $\mathbf{L}^S$ and $\mathbf{L}^C$;
2: Randomly initialize $\mathbf{W}^t$, $\mathbf{V}^t$ and $\mathbf{T}^t$; Set $\mathbf{A}^t$ as an identity matrix, and the iteration step $t = 1$;
3: **repeat**
4: Update W: $\mathbf{W}^{t+1} = \mathbf{W}^t - \eta \frac{\partial \mathscr{L}(\mathbf{W}^t, \mathbf{V}^t, \mathbf{T}^t)}{\partial \mathbf{W}^t}$;
5: Update V: $\mathbf{V}^{t+1} = \mathbf{V}^t - \eta \frac{\partial \mathscr{L}(\mathbf{W}^{t+1}, \mathbf{V}^t, \mathbf{T}^t)}{\partial \mathbf{V}^t}$;
6: Update T: $\mathbf{T}^{t+1} = \mathbf{T}^t - \eta \frac{\partial \mathscr{L}(\mathbf{W}^{t+1}, \mathbf{V}^{t+1}, \mathbf{T}^t)}{\partial \mathbf{T}^t}$;
7: Update the diagonal matrix $\mathbf{A}$ as

$$\mathbf{A}^{t+1} = \begin{bmatrix} \frac{1}{2\|\mathbf{w}_1^t\|_2} & & \\ & \cdots & \\ & & \frac{1}{2\|\mathbf{w}_q^t\|_2} \end{bmatrix};$$

8: t=t+1;
9: **until** Convergence criterion satisfied
Output:
 Transformation matrices $\mathbf{W} = \mathbf{W}^{t-1}$, $\mathbf{V} = \mathbf{V}^{t-1}$ and $\mathbf{T} = \mathbf{T}^{t-1}$.

Theorem 4.1 *The alternate updating rules in Algorithm 4 monotonically decrease
the objective function value of (4.11) in each iteration.*

Proof In the iterative procedure, for $\mathbf{W}$, $\mathbf{V}$ and $\mathbf{T}$ we update one while keeping the
other two fixed. In the tth step, with $\mathbf{V}$ and $\mathbf{T}$ fixed, for the ease of representation let
us denote

$$F(\mathbf{W}) = \|\mathbf{V}^t \mathbf{G} - \mathbf{T}^t \mathbf{Y}\|_F^2 + \alpha \text{Tr}[\mathbf{G}\mathbf{L}^C \mathbf{G}^T] + \beta \text{Tr}[\mathbf{V}^t \mathbf{G}\mathbf{L}^S(\mathbf{V}^t \mathbf{G})^T] \qquad (4.15)$$

It can easily verified that we have

$$\mathbf{W}^{t+1} = \min_{\mathbf{W}} F(\mathbf{W}) + \lambda \text{Tr}[\mathbf{W}^T \mathbf{A}^t \mathbf{W}]$$

$$\Rightarrow F(\mathbf{W}^{t+1}) + \lambda \text{Tr}[(\mathbf{W}^{t+1})^T \mathbf{A}^t \mathbf{W}^{t+1}] \leq F(\mathbf{W}^t) + \lambda \text{Tr}[(\mathbf{W}^t)^T \mathbf{A}^t \mathbf{W}^t]$$

$$(4.16)$$

That is to say,

$$F(\mathbf{W}^{t+1}) + \lambda \sum_i \frac{\|\mathbf{w}_i^{t+1}\|_2^2}{2\|\mathbf{w}_i^t\|_2} \leq F(\mathbf{W}^t) + \lambda \sum_i \frac{\|\mathbf{w}_i^t\|_2^2}{2\|\mathbf{w}_i^t\|_2}$$

$$\Rightarrow F(\mathbf{W}^{t+1}) + \lambda \|\mathbf{W}^{t+1}\|_{2,1} - \lambda(\|\mathbf{W}^{t+1}\|_{2,1} - \sum_i \frac{\|\mathbf{w}_i^{t+1}\|_2^2}{2\|\mathbf{w}_i^t\|_2})$$

$$\leq F(\mathbf{W}^t) + \lambda \|\mathbf{W}^t\|_{2,1} - \lambda(\|\mathbf{W}^t\|_{2,1} - \sum_i \frac{\|\mathbf{w}_i^t\|_2^2}{2\|\mathbf{w}_i^t\|_2}). \qquad (4.17)$$

According to the Lemmas in [24], $\|\mathbf{W}^{t+1}\|_{2,1} - \sum_i \frac{\|\mathbf{w}_i^{t+1}\|_2^2}{2\|\mathbf{w}_i^t\|_2} \leq \|\mathbf{W}^t\|_{2,1} - \sum_i \frac{\|\mathbf{w}_i^t\|_2^2}{2\|\mathbf{w}_i^t\|_2}$. Thus, we obtain

$$F(\mathbf{W}^{t+1}) + \lambda\|\mathbf{W}^{t+1}\|_{2,1} \leq F(\mathbf{W}^t) + \lambda\|\mathbf{W}^t\|_{2,1}. \tag{4.18}$$

That is, we arrive at

$$\mathcal{L}(\mathbf{W}^{t+1}, \mathbf{V}^t, \mathbf{T}^t) \leq \mathcal{L}(\mathbf{W}^t, \mathbf{V}^t, \mathbf{T}^t). \tag{4.19}$$

With $\mathbf{W}^{t+1}$ and $\mathbf{T}^t$ fixed, the gradient descent method guarantees that

$$\mathcal{L}(\mathbf{W}^{t+1}, \mathbf{V}^{t+1}, \mathbf{T}^t) \leq \mathcal{L}(\mathbf{W}^{t+1}, \mathbf{V}^t, \mathbf{T}^t). \tag{4.20}$$

In this manner, we have

$$\mathcal{L}(\mathbf{W}^{t+1}, \mathbf{V}^{t+1}, \mathbf{T}^{t+1}) \leq \mathcal{L}(\mathbf{W}^{t+1}, \mathbf{V}^{t+1}, \mathbf{T}^t). \tag{4.21}$$

Based on the above three inequalities, we obtain

$$\begin{aligned}\mathcal{L}(\mathbf{W}^{t+1}, \mathbf{V}^{t+1}, \mathbf{T}^{t+1}) &\leq \mathcal{L}(\mathbf{W}^{t+1}, \mathbf{V}^{t+1}, \mathbf{T}^t)\\ &\leq \mathcal{L}(\mathbf{W}^{t+1}, \mathbf{V}^t, \mathbf{T}^t) \leq \mathcal{L}(\mathbf{W}^t, \mathbf{V}^t, \mathbf{T}^t).\end{aligned} \tag{4.22}$$

Thus, $\mathcal{L}(\mathbf{W}, \mathbf{V}, \mathbf{T})$ monotonically decreases using the updating rules in Algorithm 4 and Theorem 4.1 is proved.

According to Theorem 4.1, we can see that the iterative optimization in Algorithm 4 can converge to local optimal values of $\mathbf{W}$, $\mathbf{V}$ and $\mathbf{T}$. Actually, in the proposed learning algorithm, each matrix can be updated column by column. Therefore, the algorithm can be parallelized. In the experiments, we observed that the proposed optimization converges to the minimum after about 20 iterations. Figure 4.3 shows the changing values of the objective function in the convergence process. We perform our experiments on the MATLAB in a PC with 2.13 GHz CPU and 16 GB memory.

4.3.4 Tag Representation in Unified Space

Thus far, we have discovered the unified space and are able to embed untagged photos with visual features into this space. However, our target is to estimate the correlations between photos and tags. Hence, we also need to obtain the representation of each tag in the unified space, so as to adopt a similarity measure to calculate the correlations directly. For a tag, we propose to represent it with the feature reconstruction of the photos tagged with the tag. In the reconstruction, the textual representations of the photos are considered, because they have more semantic relevance to tags than visual features. Thus, the reconstructed representation $\mathbf{t}_i$ of a tag w_i is defined as

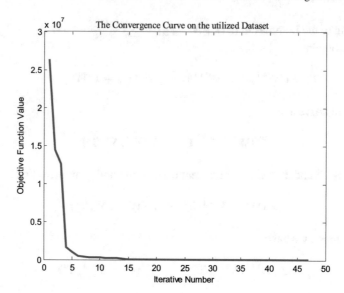

Fig. 4.3 The convergence curve of the proposed optimization algorithm in Algorithm 4

$$\mathbf{t}_i = \frac{1}{\sum_{j=1}^{n} Y_{ij}} \sum_{j=1}^{n} Y_{ij} \mathbf{z}_j \qquad (4.23)$$

Here, Y_{ij} is the indicator whether the jth photo is tagged with the tag w_i, and $\mathbf{z}_j$ is the embedded textual representation of the jth photo in the unified space.

4.3.5 Tag Recommendation

In this section, we will introduce how to recommend tags for a new photo with the user and geo-location information. Using the above proposed learning algorithm, we can learn the corresponding underlying space for each user (or geo-location) and obtain the tag representations in the space. For each new uploaded photo $\mathbf{x}_{te}$ taken in geo-location g by user u, we first map it into the unified spaces of its corresponding user and geo-location individually, and obtain a set of initial tags relevant to the photo. Then we perform semantic photo retrieval and select the semantically relevant photos from a large-scale community-contributed dataset. Finally, visual image retrieval is implemented to identify the semantically and visually relevant photos, and top ranked tags are suggested based on the voting strategy.

First, we elaborate the selection of initial tags. We adopt the same strategy in the user-specific unified space and the geo-specific unified space, and detail the process performed in the user-specific one. With the learned transformation matrices $\mathbf{W}$ and $\mathbf{V}$, we first embed the visual feature $\mathbf{x}_{te}$ of an untagged photo into the unified space $\mathbf{U}$ and obtain the latent feature vector $\mathbf{u}_{te}$.

$$\mathbf{u}_{te} = \mathbf{VW}\mathbf{x}_{te} \tag{4.24}$$

Then we use the embedded visual representation to calculate its relevance to each tag, which has been embedded into the unified space as discussed in Sect. 4.3.4. Specially, we adopt the cosine similarity as the relevance measure. The relevance vector of the photo to each tag is denoted as $\mathbf{s}_u$. In the same way, we can obtain the relevance scores of the photo to tags in terms of the given geo-location, denoted as $\mathbf{s}_g$. The relevant scores of this photo to tags are obtained by

$$\mathbf{s} = \rho \frac{\mathbf{s}_u}{\sum_i s_u(i)} + (1 - \rho) \frac{\mathbf{s}_g}{\sum_i s_g(i)}, \tag{4.25}$$

where ρ is a non-negative parameter to weight the importance of these two terms. We set it to 0.6 in our experiments for simplicity. Top ranked tags larger than a specified threshold are utilized to perform tag-based photo retrieval in our large-scale community-contributed photo set collected from Flickr. By this procedure, the top r_s semantically similar photos are selected as the database for the next content-based photo retrieval. To perform content-based photo retrieval, we extract visual features of all photos in advance and employ ℓ_2 distance metric to measure the visual similarities among images. Then the top r_v visually similar images are selected among the top r_s semantically similar photos ($r_v = 100$, $r_s = 1000$ in our implementation).

4.4 Performance Evaluation

4.4.1 Dataset

We collect a vast amount of photos with rich context information from Flickr using Flickr API. For each photo, we downloaded this photo together with its tag, geo-location (i.e., longitude and latitude), title, description, and comments. For each tag, we also kept its tagger. We obtained 3,309,698 photos with 231,662 users and 20,806 geo-locations.[4] We summarize the detailed statistical information in Fig. 4.4.

We want photos to be tagged by at least one tag because photos without any tag are not helpful for our task. We preserve the tags assigned to no less than 100 photos and the photos with at least one tag. Consequently, we obtain a dataset $\mathbf{X}_{all}$ with the remaining about 2.7 M photos and a vocabulary $\mathcal{V}$ with 15,554 unique tags. To learn and evaluate our approach, we select the users tagging no less than 300 photos and the geo-locations with more than 100 photos. As a result, 559 users and 1351

---

[4]We first derived the longitude and latitude of each photo and then identified the corresponding place name from Flickr using Flickr API. In this work, the city-level place names are extracted. That is, we obtained 20,806 cities finally.

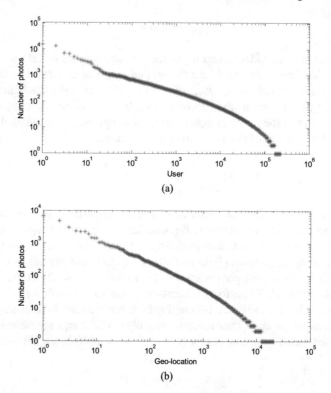

Fig. 4.4 The statistic of users and geo-locations. **a** The number of photos per user; **b** the number of photos per geo-location

geo-locations are chosen. To illustrate our motivation, we analyze characteristics of tags used by each user (or geo-location), as shown in Fig. 4.5a, b. It is observed that tag-preferences of users (geo-locations) are different, which verifies the motivation of this work.

For each user u, we divide her photos into two distinct subsets denoted as $\mathbf{X}_{u,tr}$ and $\mathbf{X}_{u,te}$, which are used for training and evaluation, respectively. In our experiments, 100 photos are chosen to compose $\mathbf{X}_{u,te}$, and the rest photos are included in $\mathbf{X}_{u,tr}$. Note that each test photo is treated as untagged and its original tags are merely used as the ground truths for evaluation. For each geo-location g, the photos relevant the geo-location, except the ones within $\bigcup_u \mathbf{X}_{u,te}$, constitute the training dataset $\mathbf{X}_g$. Besides, the dataset $\mathbf{X}_c = \mathbf{X}_{all} \setminus \bigcup_u \mathbf{X}_{u,te}$ is used as our community-contributed photo set for photo retrieval. To represent the visual content of photos, we construct 1000-dimensional bag-of-visual-words representation by extracting local features from photos using SIFT descriptor [19]. In the text space, photos are represented by binary vectors over tags.

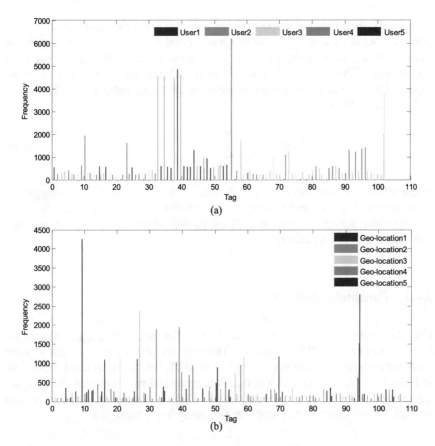

Fig. 4.5 Illustration of tag preference of users and geo-locations. We randomly select 5 users (geo-locations) and show the frequencies of top 25 frequently used tags for each user and geo-location

4.4.2   Evaluation Measures

For each photo, we remain the top k tags (k is from 1 to 10) as the recommendation result and evaluate its performance with Recall (R), Precision (P) and $F1$, which are defined as

$$R@k = \frac{|R_C@k|}{|R_G|} \tag{4.26}$$

$$P@k = \frac{|R_C@k|}{k} \tag{4.27}$$

$$F1@k = \frac{2(R@k \times P@k)}{R@k + P@k} \tag{4.28}$$

Here, $|R_G|$ is the number of tags assigned by its tagger in the groundtruth, and $|R_C@k|$ is the number of correct tags in the k tags suggested by recommendation algorithm. Besides, we use Average Precision (AP) to evaluate the tag ranking performance. It corresponds to the average of the precision at each position where an accurate tag appears. Let $P(k)$ measure the percentage of accurate tags within the top k positions of the ranking. We have

$$\text{AP} = \frac{1}{|R_G|} \sum_{k=1}^{m} P(k) \times rel(k), \tag{4.29}$$

where $rel(k)$ is an indicator function equaling 1 if the tag at rank k is tagged by the corresponding user, and zero otherwise. For the above measures, we report the corresponding values averaged over all test photos for each user and then averaged over all users in our experiments.

4.4.3   Parameter Setting

There are some parameters to be set in advance. For our learning algorithm, we set $\lambda = 0.005$ and $\eta = 0.05$ for simplicity. The trade-off parameters α, β, and γ in our proposed method are tuned in the range $\{0.01, 0.01, 0.1, 1, 10\}$ by cross-validation, and we set $\alpha = 1, \beta = 0.1$, and $\gamma = 0.1$. For the dimensions of the intermediate space and the unified space, we set $q = 500$ and $p = 300$ to leverage the performance and the cost. We will discuss the parameter sensitivity in the following.

4.4.4   Compared Methods

To prove the effectiveness of our work, we compared it with state-of-the-art models, including generic tag recommendation and personalized tag recommendation. The details of the compared schemes are listed as follows.

- **CommunityPreference (CP)**: It is to suggest the most frequent tags within the community set.
- **Visual** [12]: It chooses relevant tags purely based on visual content of photos. Top k visual similar photos from the community image set are first obtained and then the most frequent tags in the similar set are used as the recommendation result.
- **GeoVisual** [9]: It first identifies a correct geo-tag using the visual content of a new photo and user feedback. Then, it collects images with the same geo-tag and selects tags from the collected images using kNN density estimation based on visual features.

- **PersonalPreference (PP)** [30]: Given a new image uploaded by a user u, it simply recommends the most frequent tags used by the user u in the past, i.e., suggests the most frequent tags in $\mathbf{X}_{u,tr}$.
- **GTV** [25]: It recommends tags to users by accumulating votes from the candidate images including visually similar images, images captured in the same geographical coordinates or in the same period of time, which are selected from their history images.
- **Tensor** [3]: It adopts a low-order tensor decomposition approach to model the user-image-tag correlation data, and predicts relevant tags of an image for a specific user.
- **CEPIA** [11]: It predicts personalized tags by learning from user tagging history based on a cross-entropy based learning algorithm.
- **UIU**: Our proposed method only using user tagging information, corresponding to the case of $\rho = 1$ in Eq. 4.25.
- **GIU**: Our proposed method only using geographic information, corresponding to the case of $\rho = 0$ in Eq. 4.25.
- **UGU**: Our proposed method without importing the intermediate space, i.e., directly mapping visual features into the unified space using one transformation matrix.
- **IU-G**: Our proposed method only to learn the geo-specific intermediate space and unified space, but the corresponding uniform ones for all users.
- **IU-U**: Our proposed method only to learn the user-specific intermediate space and unified space, but the corresponding uniform ones for all geo-locations.
- **UGIU**: Our proposed algorithm considering user tagging history and geographic information with the intermediate space and the unified space mining.

4.4.5 Parameter Sensitivity Analysis

There are some parameters involved in the proposed learning model, i.e., three trade-off parameters α, β and γ, and the dimensions of the intermediate space and the unified space. Now we discuss their influence on the performance.

First, we discuss the sensitivity analysis of the trade-off parameters α, β and γ. We tune these three parameters in the range of $\{0, 0.0001, 0.001, 0.01, 0.1, 1.0, 10, 100\}$. The corresponding results in terms of $F1@5$ are illustrated in Fig. 4.6. By examining these results, we have the following observations: (1) The parameter α has the most remarkable impact on the performance. When α is very small (less than 0.01) or very large (more than 10), the performance in term of $F1@5$ decreases dramatically. It demonstrates that the introduced intermediate space is not only necessary but also supposed to reflect the semantic information, which is coincident with our intuition. (2) It is necessary to preserve the local semantic structure and the local visual structure for the unified subspace learning. When $\beta = 0$ or $\gamma = 0$, i.e., we do not consider the local structure preservation, the results of tag recommendation become worse. (3) The

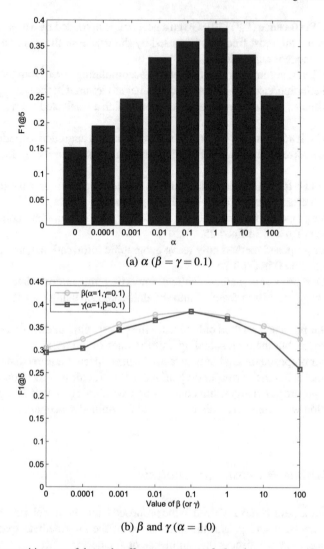

Fig. 4.6 The sensitiveness of the trade-off parameters: **a** α; **b** β and γ

semantic structure preservation is important than the visual structure preservation in the unified subspace learning procedure since the performance has less change with varying the value of β than that of γ.

The dimensions of the intermediate space and the unified space are two important parameters, which affect the user preference and geo-location preference learning. We conduct experiments to test their effects on the performance of tag recommendation and present results in terms of $F1@5$ in Fig. 4.7a, b, respectively. We can see that the performance varies with different values of the dimension p of the unified space and the dimension q of the intermediate space. The performance is improved

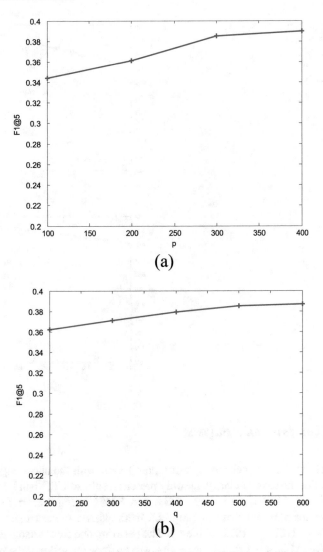

Fig. 4.7 Impact of parameters: **a** the dimension p of the unified space and **b** the dimension q of the intermediate space

by increasing p and q to some extent and arrive relatively stable $F1$ values when $q \geq 500$ and $p \geq 300$, respectively. Considering high dimension corresponds to an expensive computing cost, we set $q = 500$ and $p = 300$ to leverage the performance and the cost.

Fig. 4.8 Performance
comparisons in terms
of **a** $P@k$, **b** $R@k$
and **c** $F1@k$ with
$k = 1, 2, \ldots, 10$

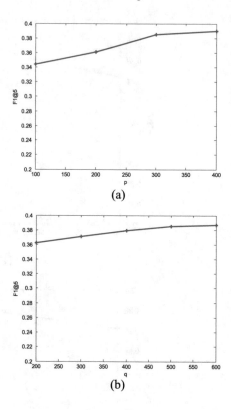

(a)

(b)

4.4.6   Experimental Analysis

We conduct extensive experiments to compare UGUI with the above algorithms in
Sect. 4.4.4. For the sake of clarity, we only present results of CP, Visual, PP, CEPIA,
Tensor and UGIU in terms of $P@k$, $R@k$, and $F1@k$ in Fig. 4.8a–c, respectively.
To compare the variations of our proposed methods, we present results in terms
of $F1@k$ ($k = 1, 2, \ldots, 10$) in Table 4.1. The performance comparison on averaged
APs is shown in Fig. 4.9. From these results, we can draw the following observations.

First, compared to generic models (i.e., CP, Visual and GeoVisual), personalized
models prevalently achieve better results, which is consistent with the observations
made by [11, 30]. The simple PP model gains a relative improvement over CP, which
reveals that the user tagging history is helpful to personalized tag recommendation. It
can be also demonstrated by the comparison of GTV versus GeoVisual, UGIU versus
IU-G, and UGIU versus GIU. Besides, visual content cannot be ignored, which
is observed from the better performance of Visual by considering visual content
compared with CP.

Second, to demonstrate the necessity of exploiting geographic information and
learning geo-location penchant toward tags, we conduct the comparisons of Geo-
Visual versus Visual, UIU versus IU-U, and IU-U versus UGIU. First, GeoVisual

Table 4.1 Performance comparison in terms of $F1@k$ ($k = 1, 2, \ldots, 10$). The best results are highlighted in bold

$F1@k$	$k = 1$	$k = 2$	$k = 3$	$k = 4$	$k = 5$	$k = 6$	$k = 7$	$k = 8$	$k = 9$	$k = 10$
CP	0.0245	0.0271	0.0280	0.0366	0.0366	0.0369	0.0456	0.0460	0.0480	0.0498
Visual [12]	0.0362	0.0740	0.1116	0.1489	0.1848	0.211	0.2304	0.2424	0.2518	0.2583
GeoVisual [9]	0.1029	0.1695	0.2328	0.2921	0.3513	0.4027	**0.4359**	0.4652	0.4859	0.5005
PP [30]	0.0864	0.1664	0.2310	0.2990	0.3342	0.3672	0.4069	0.4404	0.4725	0.4964
GTV [25]	0.1067	0.1813	0.2310	0.3142	0.3374	0.3883	0.4303	0.4543	0.4894	0.5250
CEPIA [11]	0.1210	0.1842	0.2505	0.3145	0.3605	0.3785	0.4260	0.4543	0.4856	0.5092
Tensor [3]	0.094	0.1157	0.2253	0.2842	0.3439	0.3610	0.4338	0.4518	0.4730	0.5124
UIU	0.0638	0.1164	0.1967	0.2829	0.3468	0.3741	0.4120	0.4498	0.4670	0.5082
GIU	0.0128	0.0280	0.0405	0.0506	0.0599	0.0674	0.0768	0.0861	0.0952	0.104
UGU	0.0994	0.1843	0.2510	0.3273	0.3694	0.4041	0.4176	0.4829	0.5009	0.5299
IU-G	0.0905	0.1662	0.2392	0.2998	0.3356	0.3714	0.4126	0.4441	0.4742	0.5010
IU-U	0.0972	0.1851	0.2590	0.3173	0.3613	0.3876	0.4122	0.4794	0.4893	0.5099
UGIU	**0.1366**	**0.1990**	**0.2630**	**0.3373**	**0.3851**	**0.4115**	0.4327	**0.4885**	**0.5124**	**0.5491**

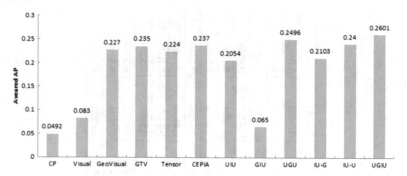

Fig. 4.9 Performance comparison about averaged AP

gains the better performance than the Visual model by additionally considering geo-context. Similarly, IU-U has the better result in terms of $F1$ than UIU. This reveals that the geographic information can provide helpful cues for tag recommendation. Second, from the comparison between IU-U and UGIU, the better results are obtained by UGIU. Thus, we can claim that the geo-location preference is useful to filter tags for recommendation.

Third, by introducing an intermediate space, UGIU considerably surpasses UGU. This is consistent with our earlier presentations that a better latent space can be learned by the proposed progressive manner. The visual features is a much lower level representation on semantics and the gap between the visual features and the semantic concepts is too large. It is not suitable to directly map the visual features into the underlying unified space. By introducing an intermediate space which is analogous to the tag space, the semantic gap is bridged progressively and a better latent space is learned.

Finally, our proposed UGIU achieves the best performance among all the compared method, specially the personalized models. Compared to the three personalized algorithms GTV, Tensor and CEPIA, UGIU obtains 14, 12 and 7% gains in terms of $F1@5$ respectively. It is noted that GTV and the proposed method UGIU both consider the user history and geographical information. However, UGIU is significantly better than GTV, which demonstrates the superiority of the proposed learning algorithm.

From the above experimental results, we can see that the improvement of the proposed method over the compared methods becomes narrow when $k \geq 4$. Thus, to demonstrate the significance of the improvement, we perform the statistical analysis of the variance of GeoVisual, GTV, CEPIA, Tensor, and UGIU in terms of $F1@k$ ($k \geq 4$), and present the results in Table 4.2. It is clearly observed that the proposed method UGIU statistically outperforms the compared methods.

Table 4.2 The variance analysis in terms of $F1@k$ ($k \geq 4$). The best results are highlighted in bold

$F1@k$	4	5	6	7	8	9	10
GeoVisual [9]	0.2921	0.3513	0.4027	**0.4359**	0.4652	0.4859	0.5005
GTV [25]	0.3142	0.3374	0.3883	0.4303	0.4543	0.4894	0.5250
CEPIA [11]	0.3145	0.3605	0.3785	0.4260	0.4543	0.4856	0.5092
Tensor [3]	0.2842	0.3439	0.3610	0.4338	0.4518	0.4730	0.5124
UGIU	**0.3373**	**0.3851**	**0.4115**	0.4327	**0.4885**	**0.5124**	**0.5491**

4.5 Discussions

In this chapter, we propose to mine the personalized tags for new updated photos using users' tagging histories and geographic information. We propose a new subspace learning algorithm to individually discover the user preference and the geo-location preference toward tags. In the proposed method, the visual features and text features of photos are mapped into a unified space by three transformation matrices: two for visual features and one for text features. To bridge the semantic gap, we propose to first map visual features into an intermediate space having the consistent semantic structure with the text space. For an untagged photo, we first map it into the unified spaces in terms of the user and geographic information to find relevant tags, and then perform semantic and visual photo retrieval to find relevant photos. Finally, the most frequent tags in the relevant photos are suggested to users.

With the learned user preference and geo-specific preference to tags or semantic concepts, we can develop some verticalized social applications, such as personalized product recommendation, geo-location-based traveling suggestion, personalized geo-specific news report, and so on. Besides, how to investigate the joint or partially joint connections among user, geo-location, social tags, and photos to enhance the latent subspace learning performance, is also a potential research topic.

References

1. Ames, M., Naaman, M.: Why we tag: motivations for annotation in mobile and online media. In: Proceedings of the SIGCHI Conference on Human Factors in Computing Systems, pp. 971–980 (2007)
2. Berg, T.L., Berg, A.C., Shih, J.: Automatic attribute discovery and characterization from noisy web images. In: Proceedings of European Conference on Computer Vision, pp. 663–676 (2010)
3. Cai, Y., Zhang, M., Luo, D., Ding, C., Chakravarthy, S.: Low-order tensor decompositions for social tagging recommendation. In: Proceedings of ACM International Conference on Web Search and Data Mining, pp. 695–704 (2011)
4. Chen, H.M., Chang, M.H., Chang, P.C., Tien, M.C., Hsu, W.H., Wu, J.L.: Sheepdog: group and tag recommendation for flikr photos by automatic search-based learning. In: Proceedings of ACM Conference on Multimedia, pp. 737–740 (2008)

5. Chen, Y.N., Han, C.C., Wang, C.T., Fan, K.C.: Face recognition using nearest feature space embedding. IEEE Trans. Pattern Anal. Mach. Intell. **33**(6), 1073–1086 (2011)
6. Eom, W., Lee, S., Neve, W.D., Ro, Y.M.: Improving image tag recommendation using favorite image context. In: Proceedings of IEEE International Conference on Image Processing, pp. 2445–2448 (2011)
7. Garg, N., Weber, I.: Personalized, interactive tag recommendation for flickr. In: Proceedings of ACM Recommender Systems, pp. 67–74 (2008)
8. He, X., Yan, S., Ho, Y., Niyogi, P., Zhang, H.J.: Face recognition using laplacianfaces. IEEE Trans. Pattern Anal. Mach. Intell. **27**(3), 328–340 (2005)
9. Kleban, J., Moxley, E., Xu, J., Manjunath, B.: Global annotation on georeferenced photographs. In: Proceedings of ACM International Conference on Image and Video Retrieval, pp. 14:1–14:8 (2009)
10. Lee, S., Neve, W.D., Plataniotis, K.N., Ro, Y.M.: Map-based image tag recommendation using a visual folksonomy. Pattern Recognit. Lett. **31**(9), 976–982 (2010)
11. Li, X., Gavves, E., Snoek, C.G.: Personalizing automated image annotation using cross-entropy. In: Proceedings of ACM International Conference on Multimedia, pp. 233–242 (2011)
12. Li, X., Snoek, C., Worring, M.: Unsupervised multi-feature tag relevance learning for social image retrieval. In: Proceedings of ACM International Conference on Image and Video Retrieval, pp. 10–17 (2010)
13. Li, Z., Liu, J., Lu, H.: Nonlinear matrix factorization with unified embedding for social tag relevance learning. Neurocomputing **105**, 38–44 (2013)
14. Li, Z., Liu, J., Xu, C., Lu, H.: Mlrank: multi-correlation learning to rank for image annotation. Pattern Recognit. **46**(10), 2700–2710 (2013)
15. Li, Z., Liu, J., Zhu, X., Liu, T., Lu, H.: Image annotation using multi-correlation probabilistic matrix factorization. In: Proceedings of ACM Conference on Multimedia, pp. 1187–1190 (2010)
16. Liu, J., Li, Z., Lu, H.: Sparse semantic metric learning for image retrieval. Multimed. Syst. **20**(6), 635–643 (2014)
17. Liu, J., Li, Z., Tang, J., Jiang, Y., Lu, H.: Personalized geo-specific tag recommendation for photos on social websites. IEEE Trans. Multimed. **16**(3), 588–600 (2014)
18. Liu, J., Zhang, Y., Li, Z., Lu, H.: Correlation consistency constrained probabilistic matrix factorization for social tag refinement. Neurocomputing **119**, 3–9 (2013)
19. Lowe, D.G.: Distinctive image features from scale-invariant keypoints. Int. J. Comput. Vis. **60**(2), 91–110 (2004)
20. Mei, T., Hsu, W.H., Luo, J.: Knowledge discovery from community-contributed multimedia. IEEE Multimed. **17**(4), 16–17 (2010)
21. Moxley, E., Kleban, J., Manjunath, B.S.: SpiritTagger: a geo-aware tag suggestion tool mined from Flickr. In: Proceedings of ACM International Conference on Multimedia Information Retrieval, pp. 24–30 (2008)
22. Moxley, E., Kleban, J., Manjunath, B.S.: Not all tags are created equal: learning Flickr tag semantics for global annotation. In: Proceedings of IEEE International Conference on Multimedia and Expo, pp. 1452–1455 (2009)
23. Nanopoulos, A., Rafailidis, D., Manolopoulos, Y.: Musicbox: personalized music recommendation based on cubic analysis of social tags. IEEE Trans. Audio Speech Lang. Process. **18**(2), 407–412 (2010)
24. Nie, F., Huang, H., Cai, X., Ding, C.: Efficient and robust feature selection via joint $\ell_{2,1}$-norms minimization. In: Proceedings of Advances in Neural Information Processing Systems, pp. 1813–1821 (2010)
25. Qian, X., Liu, X., Zheng, C., Du, Y., Hou, X.: Tagging photos using users' vocabularies. Neurocomputing **111**, 144–153 (2013)
26. Rafailidis, D., Daras, P.: The TFC model: tensor factorization and tag clustering for item recommendation in social tagging systems. IEEE Trans. Syst. Man Cybern.: Syst. **43**(3), 673–688 (2013)

27. Rendle, S., Marinho, L.B., Nanopoulos, A., Schmidt-Thieme, L.: Learning optimal ranking with tensor factorization for tag recommendation. In: Proceedings of ACM SIGKDD International Conference on Knowledge Discovery and Data Mining, pp. 727–736 (2009)
28. Rendle, S., Thieme, L.S.: Pairwise interaction tensor factorization for personalized tag recommendation. In: Proceedings of ACM International Conference on Web Search and Data Mining, pp. 81–90 (2010)
29. Roweis, S., Saul, L.: Nonlinear dimensionality reduction by locally linear embedding. Science 290(22), 2323–2326 (2000)
30. Sawant, N., Datta, R., Li, J., Wang, J.: Quest for relevant tags using local interaction networks and visual content. In: Proceedings of ACM International Conference on Multimedia Information Retrieval, pp. 231–240 (2010)
31. Serdyukov, P., Murdock, V., van Zwol, R.: Placing flickr photos on a map. In: Proceedings of ACM SIGIR Conference on Research and Development in Information Retrieval, pp. 484–491 (2009)
32. Shen, Y., Fan, J.: Leveraging loosely-tagged images and inter-object correlations for tag recommendation. In: Proceedings of ACM Conference on Multimedia, pp. 5–14 (2010)
33. Sigurbjörnsson, B., van Zwol, R.: Flickr tag recommendation based on collective knowledge. In: Proceedings of International conference on World Wide Web, pp. 327–336 (2008)
34. Silva, A., Martins, B.: Tag recommendation for georeferenced photos. In: Proceedings of ACM SIGSPATIAL International Workshop on Location-Based Social Networks, pp. 57–64 (2011)
35. Song, Y., Zhang, L., Giles, C.L.: Automatic tag recommendation algorithms for social recommender systems. ACM Trans. Web 5(1), 4 (2011)
36. Sun, A., Bhowmick, S.S., Chong, J.A.: Social image tag recommendation by concept matching. In: Proceedings of ACM Conference on Multimedia, pp. 1181–1184 (2011)
37. Symeonidis, P., Nanopoulos, A., Manolopoulos, Y.: Tag recommendations based on tensor dimensionality reduction. In: Proceedings of ACM International Conference on Web Search and Data Mining, pp. 43–50 (2008)
38. Takashita, T., Itokawa, T., Kitasuka, T., Aritsugi, M.: Tag recommendation for flickr using web browsing behavior. In: Proceedings of International Conference on Computational Science and Its Applications, pp. 412–421 (2010)
39. Tang, J., Li, M., Li, Z., Zhao, C.: Tag ranking based on salient region graph propagation. Multimed. Syst. 21(3), 267–275 (2015)

Chapter 5
Understanding-Oriented Multimedia News Retrieval

Abstract Online news reading becomes an important channel for information acquisition in our daily lives. Users have to consume much time in finding the news they are interested in from such huge volumes of information. To facilitate users to access news quickly and comprehensively, we design understanding-oriented multimedia news search and browsing systems, in which the news elements of "Where", "Who", "What" and "When" are enhanced. The result ranking and visualization are conducted to present search results relevant to a target news query.

5.1 Introduction

Online news reading services, such as Google News and Yahoo! News, have become increasingly prevalent as the Internet provides fast access to news information from various sources around every corner of the world. Consequently, online news reading becomes an important channel for information acquisition in our daily lives. According to the report by the Pew Research Center's Project for Excellence in Journalism,[1] 58.2% of Americans receive news online, overtaking newspaper readership (about 35%) by the end of 2011. However, with the explosive growth of the World Wide Web, vast amounts of news resources are generated every day. Users have to consume much time in finding the news they are interested in from such huge volumes of information. Therefore, how to help users access their desired news quickly and comprehensively is a key issue of online news services.

A news article is defined as a specific event arose by specific people or an organization which happens at a certain time and place. That is, a news article corresponding to a specific news event can be identified according to the following "4W" elements:

©Li, Z., Liu, J., Zhu, X., Lu, H. "Multi-modal Multi-correlation Person-centwric News Retrieval", ACM Conference on Information and Knowledge Management, ©2010 ACM, Inc. Reprinted by permission. https://doi.org/10.1145/1871437.1871464.

[1] http://www.journalism.org/.

© Springer Nature Singapore Pte Ltd. 2017
Z. Li, *Understanding-Oriented Multimedia Content Analysis*, Springer Theses,
DOI 10.1007/978-981-10-3689-7_5

Fig. 5.1 An illustrate
example of connections
among news entities and
news events

Who (person or organization), When (time), Where (locations), and What (event). In particular, "Who" as a news entity should be paid special attention because the social network among different persons can be viewed as a kind of indirect connection among news events as well as their textual relevance. Accordingly, news event and news person should be considered as the two basic items in news retrieval, special for person-centric news retrieval in this section. The both items are correlated to each other. Specifically, different news articles may be relevant when the news events happen on the same or related persons, and the persons appearing in the same news event should also be related by certain social interaction. As shown in Fig. 5.1, the five news articles are related to some extent due to a shared person (*Yao Ming*), and different persons appearing in these articles are connected with specific social relationships, such as *Yao Ming* is the teammate of *McGrady* and *Battier*, the husband of *Ye Li*, and the rival of *Howard*. It is an important and challenging problem to effectively explore the both items and their within- and inter-correlations to organize and search possible relevant news events on Internet, so as to enable an informative overview about a target news topic. On the other hand, existing studies demonstrate that users usually have high priority in getting news about some specific places, such as their countries, working cities, and hometowns [35]. However, the existing online news services, such as Yahoo! News and Ask News, lack the ability of organizing news documents according to locations. Although some projects and Yahoo News Map have attempted to geo-organize news, the granularity for news localization and the interactivity for news browsing with respect to these projects are often unsatisfied. Besides, the toponyms contained in news documents are usually noisy and incomplete, and this degrades the performance. Thus, we should focus on the problems of how to precisely construct the correlations between news documents and locations, and further to facilitate users to search and browse news about their interested places.

Besides, it has been revealed that the recognition process of the human brain needs multimedia information to form a comprehensive understanding [27]. Furthermore, as the saying goes, a picture is worth a thousand words. However, pictures contained in news documents are usually very few. It can be observed from the statistical analysis shown in Fig. 5.2b on a news data set that more than half of news documents

 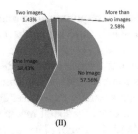

(I)   (II)

Fig. 5.2 **a** Examples for showing how images complement the text information of news documents. By providing illustrative images, users can get more information. **b** The distribution of the number of pictures contained in a news document. It can be observed that the pictures in news documents are usually limited

do not contain any picture and only less than 5% of news documents contain more than one picture. Thus, enriching news documents with illustrative images is necessary for users to access news more quickly and vividly.

In this chapter, we present news retrieval and browsing systems to explore the "4W" elements and multimedia information. First, we investigate the element "Who", and propose a framework of multi-modal multi-correlation Person-centric news retrieval (MMPNR) by integrating news event correlations, news entity correlations, and event-entity correlations simultaneously and seamlessly and employing both text information and image information. Different from a typical news browser, which only presents a ranking list of relevant news items, we additionally provide user a query-oriented multi-correlation map as an intuitive and concise resulting presentation. Second, we propose to organize news based on geographic information and visualize news documents with a set of web images. It is well known that the key part of a news document is "4W" elements: "Who", "When", "Where", and "What". The enhancement of "Where" is obvious as we can estimate the location relevance for the news document. The elements of "Who" and "What" are enhanced by image enrichment as shown in Fig. 5.2a. With enriched images, users can quickly understand who and what the news documents are about. Besides, the time information, namely the element of "When", is considered in the result ranking procedure. Most of the work in this chapter has been published in [19, 20].

5.2 Related Work

In this section, we review some related methods with the analysis of news retrieval. To enhance the "4W" elements, the element should be extracted first. The task of relation extraction has been traditionally studied as to extract predefined semantic relations between pairs of entities in text. The supervised methods [12, 39] require a set of labeled training examples of the predefined relations to learn an extractor. However, the labeled examples are scarce and expensive. The bootstrapping approaches

[10] relax the requirement on training data through iteratively discovering extraction patterns and identifying entity relations with a small number of seeds. Probabilistic relation model [11, 24] has been proposed to estimate the relations among entities. Relational techniques such as PRMs [11] extended generative methods to deal with various combinations of probabilistic dependency among entities. Such methods can be computationally expensive, and may not scale to the large amount of data typically collected by social media websites. Some work focus on relational learning methods [24] through pairwise relationships among entities, which involve loss of information when data has high-order interactions. Sekine et al. [33] proposed 150 types of named entity, which were useful in information extraction and Question and Answering (Q&A) in the newspaper domain. KnowItAll [9] is a system for automating the tedious process to extract large collections of facts from the web, which is based on generic extraction rules to generate candidates, co-occurrence statistic, and a naive Bayes classifier. It learned an effective pattern to extract relevant entities from relevant and irrelevant terms for expected entities. It found entity names in the same class as a given example by using several syntactic patterns. However, it required large numbers of search queries and downloaded web pages.

The relevance of location to news document is exploited for news retrieval with location queries. Currently, there are several systems that support news browsing with geographic information, such as World News Map and Yahoo News Map. However, the geo-location in these system is only performed at the country level based on simple heuristics. Geographical Information Retrieval (GIR) [1, 2, 26] is the augmentation of Information Retrieval (IR) with geographic metadata and has received major attention from IR researchers in the last few years. For document geo-localization, there are a variety of applications that arise from connecting linguistic content (a word, phrase, document or entire corpus) to geography. Leidner [18] provided a systematic overview of geography-based language applications over the previous decade, with a special focus on the problem of toponym resolution–identifying and disambiguating the references to locations in texts.

Moreover, we try to find appropriate images to illustrate the text contents [14]. It is related to text visualization, whose goal is to visually represent large collections of text information. WordsEye [7] employs semantic representation to synthesize 3D scenes from text. Joshi et al. [16] proposed a Story Picturing Engine that is able to find pictures to describe a fragment of a text. In their approach, key phrases are extracted from the text to retrieve images, which are then ranked using lexical annotations and visual content. Document Cards [34] try to find a suitable and representative small-scale overview of a document by extracting important key terms and images from the document. Video collage [5] is to represent multiple video documents with text and images extracted from these videos. News video is labeled by Wikipedia entries to extend information of Wikipedia entries by news stories in [28]. To visualize news TV, a combination with two or three keywords from a few keywords to create links between news videos and related articles on the web, and TF-IDF model and cosine distance are used to select relevant links. The most related work is [8], which adds images for each sentence to assist users in reading news. There are some work focusing on illustrative image selection [4]. They queried images with location names recognized in the texts and tested different methods for the selection of photos. Representative photo is selected from photo set based on mutual relation between near-duplicate photo pairs or context cues.

Factor analysis has been widely utilized in many fields [23, 25, 32, 42]. Zhu et al. [42] proposed a joint matrix factorization combining both linkage and document-term matrices to improve the hypertext classification. The content information and link strictures were seamlessly combined through a single set of latent factors. The discovered latent factors (bases) explained both content information and link structures, and were used to classify the web pages. Probabilistic Matrix Factorization (PMF) [32] was proposed to find only point estimates of model parameters and hypermeters, instead of inferring the full posterior distribution over them. It models the user-item matrix as a product of two low-rank user and item matrices. The computation cost of PDF is linear with the number of observations. A social recommendation has been proposed based on the probabilistic matrix factorization model, named as SoRec [25]. It fused the user-item matrix with the users' social trust networks by sharing a common latent low-dimensional user feature matrix.

5.3 Person-Centered Multimedia News Retrieval

In this section, we propose a framework of multi-modal multi-correlation Person-centric news retrieval (MMPNR) by integrating news event correlations, news entity correlations, and event-entity correlations simultaneously and seamlessly and employing both text information and image information.

5.3.1 Overview of the Proposed MMPNR System

In this section, we will briefly overview the framework of the proposed MMPNR (shown in Fig. 5.3), which includes four components, namely data preprocessing, correlation initialization, correlation reconstruction, and result ranking and visualization.

First, we collect and preprocess news data. A large scale of news articles are crawled from some distinguished news sites including ABCNews.com,[2] BBC.co.uk[3] and CNN.com.[4] We first parse these news articles into news titles, summaries, texts, URLs and images of news pages. Necessary text preprocessing including word separation and stop-words filtering are conducted. Then we extract news entities (Time,

---

[2]http://abcnews.go.com/.

[3]http://www.bbc.co.uk/.

[4]http://edition.cnn.com/.

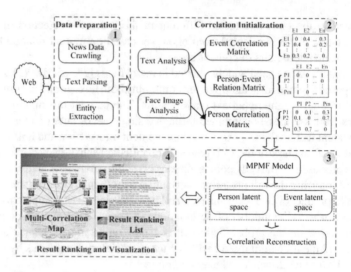

Fig. 5.3 The framework of the proposed MMPNR

Person or Organization, and Location) according to [33]. In this section, we view Person (or Organization) as entities, while the time and location are used to identify news events.

The second component introduced in Sect. 5.3.2 aims to initialize three kinds of correlations: the event correlation, the person correlation, and the person-event correlation. In particular, the event correlation is estimated via the TF-IDF model on text information (news title, summary, and details) from news web pages. For the person correlation, a linear combination of the two co-occurrences of person name entities within text information and faces on person images respectively. We utilize the occurrence of a specific person in an event to obtain a binary relationship between the person and the event.

The third component is the basic component in MMPNR, which is demonstrated in Sect. 5.3.3. We apply the multi-correlation probabilistic matrix factorization model to mine the hidden relations. We connect these three different correlations simultaneously and seamlessly through the shared person latent feature space and event latent feature space, that is, the person latent feature space in the news person relational matrix is the same in the person-event correlation matrix and the event latent feature space in the news event similarity matrix is the same in the person-event correlation matrix. By performing factor analysis via MPMF, the low-dimension person latent features and event latent features are learned, which can be used to reconstruct the news person-event correlations.

The fourth component described in Sect. 5.3.4 is the result ranking and visualization in MMPNR, which obtains and displays query-related search results to the end users. To give users vivid and informative organization of news results, we divide the user interface into two parts. The left part gives users a query-oriented relation graph, in which the relations between the query and events (or persons) are illustrated. In the right part, we present a ranking list of related news events with their titles, and the most relevant persons and events respectively.

5.3.2 Correlation Initialization

In this section, we will explain how to estimate the three correlations from multi-modal information on news web pages. The estimated correlations is viewed as the initialized inputs of the MPMF model, which will be introduced in Sect. 5.3.3. The details about the estimation are presented as follows.

Person-Event Correlation Matrix. As mentioned above, we employ the binary relationship to measure the person–event correlation $\mathbf{R}$, that is, if a news person i appears in a news event j, $R_{ij} = 1$ and $R_{ij} = 0$ otherwise. Because the amount of online news articles is too large, the person–event relation matrix R is very sparse, which is one of the reasons we employ the probabilistic matrix factorization model.

Event Correlation Matrix. From the aspect of utilizing the contents, TF-IDF [31] is still the dominant technique to represent document, and cosine similarity is the generally used similarity metric. Therefore, we adopt the TF-IDF model and cosine similarity to measure the news event similarity matrix $\mathbf{S}$. Considering the difference of the importance of news article's title, summary and text to a news event, we process them separately and linearly combine them. Besides, the information of title is the most important to the news event and the information of summary is more important than the information of text to the news event. In our experiments, we combine these three kinds of similarities as

$$\mathbf{S} = \alpha \mathbf{S}^{title} + \beta \mathbf{S}^{summary} + (1 - \alpha - \beta)\mathbf{S}^{text}, \tag{5.1}$$

where $\mathbf{S}$, $\mathbf{S}^{title}$, $\mathbf{S}^{summary}$ and $\mathbf{S}^{text}$ represent the similarity of event, title, summary and text, respectively.

Person Correlation Matrix. In view of current news web pages containing images and persons always appearing in images of news articles, we are supposed to utilize not only the text information, but also the information of images to calculate the co-occurrence of people in news events. Thus, we combine the text information and the image information to calculate the relationship among news persons. First, we use the formula $C_{iq}^{Text} = 2f(i, q)/(f(i) + f(q))$ to calculate the co-occurrence based on the textual information, where $f(i, q)$, $f(i)$ and $f(q)$ denote the number of news articles including person i and person q simultaneously, the count of news articles containing person i, and the count of news articles containing person q, respectively. We apply the face detection and matching methods to process the information of image, which will be explained in detail as follows. We employ the same formula to calculate the co-occurrence based on the image information C_{iq}^{Img}.

Fig. 5.4 An illustrative example of face detection and matching. *a* The names of news persons; *b* the faces detected in images crawled from Wikipedia by submitting names in *a*; *c* the face matching results; *d* the co-occurrence matrix based on *c*. The *red, green, blue* and *yellow boxes* represent "Barack Obama", "Michelle Obama", "Joy Biden", and "Jill Biden", respectively

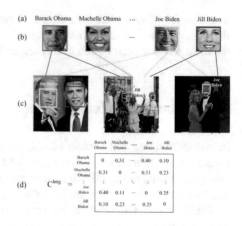

We first submit names of persons to Wikipedia,[5] crawl and parse the corresponding returned web pages, and download images in the resume tables. And then we adopt the face detection approaches to detect the face parts in images. To determine whether a specific person appears in the news images or not, we adopt SIFT flow [22] to match the face part of the specific person's image from Wikipedia with any face part detected in the image from news web page. An illustrate example is given in Fig. 5.4. The face parts (b), which are the face parts of images derived by submitting persons' names in (a), are used to be matched with the face parts in image (c) from news web pages. The matched results by SIFT flow algorithm are presented in (c). According to the matching results, we can derive the image co-occurrence matrix as shown in (d).

The SIFT flow approach assumes SIFT descriptors extracted at each pixel location are constant with respect to the pixel displacement field and allows a pixel in one image to match any other pixel in the other image. We still want to encourage smoothness of the pixel displacement field by encouraging close-by pixels to have similar displacements. It formulates the correspondence search as a discrete optimization problem on the image lattice with the following cost function

$$l(\mathbf{w}) = \sum_{\mathbf{p}} \|s_1(\mathbf{p}) - s_2(\mathbf{p} + \mathbf{w})\|_1 + \frac{1}{\sigma^2} \sum_{\mathbf{p}} (u_{\mathbf{p}}^2 + v_{\mathbf{p}}^2)$$

$$+ \alpha \sum_{(\mathbf{p},\mathbf{q}) \in \varepsilon} \min(|u(\mathbf{p}) - u(\mathbf{q})|, \frac{d}{\alpha}) + \min(|v(\mathbf{p}) - v(\mathbf{q})|, \frac{d}{\alpha}), \qquad (5.2)$$

where $\mathbf{w}(\mathbf{p}) = (u(\mathbf{p}), v(\mathbf{p}))$ is the displacement vector at pixel location $\mathbf{p} = (x, y)$, $s_i(\mathbf{p})$ is the SIFT descriptor extracted at location $\mathbf{p}$ in image i and q is the spatial neighborhood of a pixel. Parameters $\sigma = 300$, $\alpha = 0.5$ and $d = 2$ are fixed in our experiments. Based on the results of matching, we decide whether a person emerges in the news images. Finally, we obtain an indicator matrix with each column

---

[5]http://en.wikipedia.org/wiki/Main_Page.

representing whether a news person appears in news images or not. We statistic term frequency and calculate the co-occurrence similar to text processing. We linearly integrate these two co-occurrences as follows:

$$C_{iq} = (1 - \gamma) \times C_{iq}^{Text} + \gamma \times C_{iq}^{Img}. \tag{5.3}$$

5.3.3 Correlation Reconstruction

Through the initializing component, we have accomplished the preparation for the following correlation reconstruction i.e., the complement and refinement of the initialized correlations. For clarity, we first introduce the standard Probabilistic Matrix Factorization (PMF) model [32]. Then, we present our proposed Multi-correlation PMF model (MPMF) with additional consideration of the within correlations about events and entities respectively.

PMF [32] was proposed to handle very large, sparse, and imbalanced data set in collaborative filtering, based on the assumption that users who have rated similar sets of movies are likely to have similar preferences. Following, let us take collaborative filtering for example to illustrate the probabilistic matrix factorization model. In order to learn the characteristic of the users, matrix factorization is employed to factorize the user-item matrix. Suppose we have m users, n movies, and the rating values within the interval $[0, 1]$. If the rating values are integer from 1 to Q (a bigger integer value more than 1, such as 3 and 5), we can map the ratings $1, \ldots, Q$ to the internal $[0, 1]$ using the function $h(x) = (x - 1)/(Q - 1)$. Let R_{ij} denote the rating of user i for movie j, $\mathbf{R} \in \mathbb{R}^{m \times n}$ denote the rating matrix. The basic idea of probabilistic matrix factorization is to derive two high-quality d-dimensional (d is lower than $\min(m, n)$.) latent feature spaces $\mathbf{P} \in \mathbb{R}^{d \times m}$ and $\mathbf{E} \in \mathbb{R}^{d \times n}$, which denote the latent user and movie feature spaces respectively. The column vectors $\mathbf{p}_i$ and $\mathbf{e}_j$ represent user-specific and movie-specific latent feature vectors, which are not unique. A probabilistic model with Gaussian observation noise is employed as shown in Fig. 5.5, and the conditional distribution over the observed rating is defined as

$$p(\mathbf{R}|\mathbf{P}, \mathbf{E}, \sigma_R^2) = \prod_{i=1}^{m} \prod_{j=1}^{n} [\mathcal{N}(R_{ij}|g(\mathbf{p}_i^T \mathbf{e}_j), \sigma_R^2)]^{I_{ij}}, \tag{5.4}$$

where $\mathcal{N}(x|\mu, \sigma^2)$ denotes the probabilistic density function, in which the conditional distribution is defined as the Gaussian distribution with mean μ and variance σ^2, and I_{ij} is the indicator function that is equal to 1 if user i rated movie j and equal to 0 otherwise. The function $g(x)$ is a logistic function defined as $g(x) = 1/(1 + exp(-x))$, which makes it possible to bound the range of $\mathbf{p}_i^T \mathbf{e}_j$ within the interval $[0, 1]$. Zero-mean spherical Gaussian priors are placed on user and movie feature vectors

Fig. 5.5 Graphical model
for Probabilistic Matrix
Factorization (PMF)

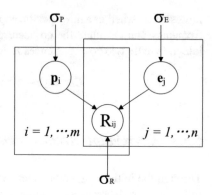

$$p(\mathbf{P}|\sigma_P^2) = \prod_{i=1}^{m} \mathcal{N}(\mathbf{p}_i|0, \sigma_P^2 \mathbf{I}), \qquad (5.5)$$

$$p(\mathbf{E}|\sigma_E^2) = \prod_{j=1}^{n} \mathcal{N}(\mathbf{e}_j|0, \sigma_E^2 \mathbf{I}), \qquad (5.6)$$

where $\mathbf{I}$ is an identity matrix.

Through a Bayesian inference, the posterior distribution over the user and movie features is given by

$$p(\mathbf{P}, \mathbf{E}|\mathbf{R}, \sigma_R^2, \sigma_P^2, \sigma_E^2) \propto p(\mathbf{R}|\mathbf{P}, \mathbf{E}, \sigma_R^2) p(\mathbf{P}|\sigma_P^2) p(\mathbf{E}|\sigma_E^2)$$
$$= \prod_{i=1}^{m} \prod_{j=1}^{n} [\mathcal{N}(R_{ij}|g(\mathbf{p}_i^T \mathbf{e}_j), \sigma_R^2)]^{I_{ij}} \prod_{i=1}^{m} \mathcal{N}(\mathbf{p}_i|0, \sigma_P^2 \mathbf{I}) \prod_{j=1}^{n} \mathcal{N}(\mathbf{e}_j|0, \sigma_E^2 \mathbf{I}).$$
$$(5.7)$$

Thus, we can derive the log of the posterior distribution given by Eq. 5.7, described as

$$\ln p(\mathbf{P}, \mathbf{E}|\mathbf{R}, \sigma_R^2, \sigma_P^2, \sigma_E^2) = -\frac{1}{2\sigma_R^2} \sum_{i=1}^{m} \sum_{j=1}^{n} I_{ij}^R (R_{ij} - g(\mathbf{p}_i^T \mathbf{e}_j))^2 - \frac{1}{2\sigma_P^2} \sum_{i=1}^{m} \mathbf{p}_i^T \mathbf{p}_i$$
$$- \frac{1}{2\sigma_E^2} \sum_{j=1}^{n} \mathbf{e}_j^T \mathbf{e}_j - \frac{1}{2} (\sum_{i=1}^{m} \sum_{j=1}^{n} I_{ij}^R \ln \sigma_R^2 + md \ln \sigma_P^2 + nd \ln \sigma_E^2) + \mathscr{C}, \qquad (5.8)$$

where $\mathscr{C}$ is a constant that does not depend on the parameters. Maximizing the log-posterior distribution over user and movie features given by Eq. 5.8 with hyperparameters (i.e., the observation noise variance and prior variances) kept fixed is equivalent to minimizing the following sum-of-squared-errors objective functions with quadratic regularization terms:

$$L(\mathbf{P}, \mathbf{E}) = \frac{1}{2} \sum_{i=1}^{m} \sum_{j=1}^{n} I_{ij}^{R} (R_{ij} - g(\mathbf{p}_i^T \mathbf{e}_j))^2 + \frac{\lambda_P}{2} \|\mathbf{P}\|_F^2 + \frac{\lambda_E}{2} \|\mathbf{E}\|_F^2, \quad (5.9)$$

in which $\lambda_p = \sigma_R^2/\sigma_P^2$, $\lambda_E = \sigma_R^2/\sigma_E^2$, and $\|\cdot\|_F^2$ denotes the Frobenius norm. Equation 5.9 can be solved using gradient methods, such as the conjugate gradient, quasi-Newton methods and steepest descent method. Through performing gradient descent in $\mathbf{P}$ and $\mathbf{E}$ as described in Eqs. 5.10 and 5.11, we can find a local minimum of the objective function given by Eq. 5.9.

$$\frac{\partial L}{\partial \mathbf{p}_i} = \sum_{j=1}^{n} I_{ij}^{R} g'(\mathbf{p}_i^T \mathbf{e}_j)(g(\mathbf{p}_i^T \mathbf{e}_j) - R_{ij})\mathbf{e}_j + \lambda_P \mathbf{p}_i \quad (5.10)$$

$$\frac{\partial L}{\partial E_j} = \sum_{i=1}^{m} I_{ij}^{R} g'(\mathbf{p}_i^T \mathbf{e}_j)(g(\mathbf{p}_i^T \mathbf{e}_j) - R_{ij})\mathbf{p}_i + \lambda_E \mathbf{e}_j \quad (5.11)$$

$g'(x)$ is the derivative of logistic function $g'(x) = exp(x)/(1 + exp(x))^2$.

In the problem of person-centric news retrieval, we consider two issues: news person and event. We can have three kinds of relations: person-event correlation, person correlation, and event correlation. The person-event relation in the problem of person-centric news retrieval can be analogous to user-item relation in recommender system. Furthermore, due to the fast explosion of online news articles, the correlations among news persons and news events are usually very sparse. The probabilistic matrix factorization algorithm as a natural and feasible option is employed to conduct our work. However, the standard probabilistic matrix factorization model can only employ one relation. Then we extend the model to integrate the news person correlation and news event correlation, named as Multi-correlation Probabilistic Matrix Factorization (MPMF). We employ the probabilistic factor analysis to factorize person-event correlation matrix, person correlation matrix and event correlation matrix, and connect these three different data resources through the shared person latent feature space, that is, the person latent feature space in the person-event correlation matrix is the same in the person correlation space, and the shard event latent feature space, that is, the event latent feature space in the person-event correlation matrix is the same in the event correlation matrix.

To learn the person and event latent feature spaces, we model our problem using the graphical model described in Fig. 5.6. Suppose we have m persons and n events. Let $\mathbf{R} \in \mathbb{R}^{m \times n}$, $\mathbf{C} \in \mathbb{R}^{m \times m}$ and $\mathbf{S} \in \mathbb{R}^{n \times n}$ denote the person–event relation matrix, person correlation matrix and event similarity matrix respectively. Let R_{ij} represent the relation of person i and event j within the range $[0, 1]$, $C_{iq} \in [0, 1]$ denote the relation between person i and person q, and $S_{jk} \in [0, 1]$ denote the similarity between event j and event k. Let $\mathbf{P} \in \mathbb{R}^{d \times m}$, $\mathbf{E} \in \mathbb{R}^{d \times n}$, $\mathbf{X} \in \mathbb{R}^{d \times m}$ and $\mathbf{Z} \in \mathbb{R}^{d \times n}$ be person, event, person factor and event factor latent feature matrices, with column vectors $\mathbf{p}_i, \mathbf{e}_j, \mathbf{x}_q$ and $s\mathbf{z}_k$ representing person-specific, event-specific, person factor-specific and event factor-specific latent feature vectors, respectively.

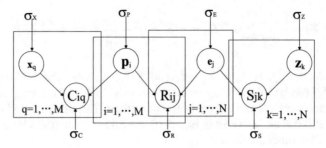

Fig. 5.6 Graphical model for MPMF

The probabilistic model with Gaussian observation noise is adopted and the conditional distributions are defined as

$$p(\mathbf{R}|\mathbf{P}, \mathbf{E}, \sigma_R^2) = \prod_{i=1}^{m} \prod_{j=1}^{n} [\mathcal{N}(R_{ij}|g(\mathbf{p}_i^T \mathbf{e}_j), \sigma_R^2)]^{I_{ij}^R}, \tag{5.12}$$

$$p(\mathbf{C}|\mathbf{P}, \mathbf{X}, \sigma_C^2) = \prod_{i=1}^{m} \prod_{q=1}^{m} [\mathcal{N}(C_{iq}|g(\mathbf{p}_i^T \mathbf{x}_q), \sigma_C^2)]^{I_{iq}^C}, \tag{5.13}$$

$$p(\mathbf{S}|\mathbf{E}, \mathbf{Z}, \sigma_S^2) = \prod_{j=1}^{n} \prod_{k=1}^{n} [\mathcal{N}(S_{jk}|g(\mathbf{e}_j^T \mathbf{z}_k), \sigma_S^2)]^{I_{jk}^S}, \tag{5.14}$$

where I_{ij}^R is the indicator function that is equal to 1 if the relation between news person i and news event j is more than 0 and equal to 0 otherwise. I_{iq}^C and I_{jk}^S are defined similarly.

We also place zero-mean spherical Gaussian priors on person, event, person factor and event factor feature vectors.

$$p(\mathbf{P}|\sigma_P^2) = \prod_{i=1}^{m} \mathcal{N}(\mathbf{p}_i|0, \sigma_P^2 \mathbf{I}) \tag{5.15}$$

$$p(\mathbf{E}|\sigma_E^2) = \prod_{j=1}^{n} \mathcal{N}(\mathbf{e}_j|0, \sigma_E^2 \mathbf{I}) \tag{5.16}$$

$$p(\mathbf{X}|\sigma_X^2) = \prod_{q=1}^{m} \mathcal{N}(\mathbf{x}_q|0, \sigma_X^2 \mathbf{I}) \tag{5.17}$$

$$p(\mathbf{Z}|\sigma_Z^2) = \prod_{k=1}^{n} \mathcal{N}(\mathbf{z}_k|0, \sigma_Z^2 \mathbf{I}) \tag{5.18}$$

Hence, similar to Eq. 5.8, through a simple Bayesian inference, we can obtain the log of the posterior distribution

$$\ln p(\mathbf{P}, \mathbf{E}, \mathbf{X}, \mathbf{Z} | \mathbf{R}, \mathbf{C}, \mathbf{S}, \sigma_R^2, \sigma_C^2, \sigma_S^2, \sigma_P^2, \sigma_E^2, \sigma_X^2, \sigma_Z^2) =$$

$$-\frac{1}{2\sigma_R^2} \sum_{i=1}^m \sum_{j=1}^n I_{ij}^R (R_{ij} - g(\mathbf{p}_i^T \mathbf{e}_j))^2 - \frac{1}{2\sigma_C^2} \sum_{i=1}^m \sum_{q=1}^m I_{iq}^C (C_{iq} - g(\mathbf{p}_i^T \mathbf{x}_q))^2$$

$$-\frac{1}{2\sigma_S^2} \sum_{j=1}^n \sum_{k=1}^n I_{jk}^S (S_{jk} - g(\mathbf{e}_j^T \mathbf{z}_k))^2 - \frac{1}{2\sigma_P^2} \sum_{i=1}^m \mathbf{p}_i^T \mathbf{p}_i - \frac{1}{2\sigma_E^2} \sum_{j=1}^n \mathbf{e}_j^T \mathbf{e}_j$$

$$-\frac{1}{2\sigma_X^2} \sum_{q=1}^m \mathbf{x}_q^T \mathbf{x}_q - \frac{1}{2\sigma_Z^2} \sum_{k=1}^n \mathbf{z}_k^T \mathbf{z}_k - \frac{1}{2}((\sum_{i=1}^m \sum_{j=1}^n I_{ij}^R) \ln \sigma_R^2 + (\sum_{i=1}^m \sum_{q=1}^m I_{iq}^C) \ln \sigma_C^2)$$

$$-\frac{1}{2} \sum_{j=1}^n \sum_{k=1}^n \mathbf{I}_{jk}^S \ln \sigma_S^2 - \frac{1}{2}md \ln \sigma_P^2 - \frac{1}{2}(nd \ln \sigma_E^2 + md \ln \sigma_X^2 + nd \ln \sigma_Z^2) + \mathscr{C}.$$

$$(5.19)$$

As described above, the equivalent optimization problem is to minimize the following objective function

$$L(\mathbf{P}, \mathbf{E}, \mathbf{X}, \mathbf{Z}) = \frac{1}{2} \sum_{i=1}^m \sum_{j=1}^n I_{ij}^R (R_{ij} - g(\mathbf{p}_i^T \mathbf{e}_j))^2 + \frac{\lambda_C}{2} \sum_{i=1}^m \sum_{q=1}^m I_{iq}^C (C_{iq} - g(\mathbf{p}_i^T \mathbf{x}_q))^2$$

$$+ \frac{\lambda_S}{2} \sum_{j=1}^n \sum_{k=1}^n I_{jk}^S (S_{jk} - g(\mathbf{e}_j^T \mathbf{z}_k))^2 + \frac{\lambda_P}{2} \|\mathbf{P}\|_F^2 + \frac{\lambda_E}{2} \|\mathbf{E}\|_F^2 + \frac{\lambda_X}{2} \|\mathbf{X}\|_F^2 + \frac{\lambda_Z}{2} \|\mathbf{Z}\|_F^2,$$

$$(5.20)$$

where $\lambda_C = \sigma_R^2/\sigma_C^2$, $\lambda_S = \sigma_R^2/\sigma_S^2$, $\lambda_P = \sigma_R^2/\sigma_P^2$, $\lambda_X = \sigma_R^2/\sigma_X^2$, $\lambda_E = \sigma_R^2/\sigma_E^2$, and $\lambda_Z = \sigma_R^2/\sigma_Z^2$. A local minimum of the objective function given by Eq. 5.20 can be found by performing gradient descent in $\mathbf{p}_i$, $\mathbf{e}_j$, $\mathbf{x}_q$ and $\mathbf{z}_k$, respectively.

$$\frac{\partial L}{\partial \mathbf{p}_i} = \sum_{j=1}^n I_{ij}^R g'(\mathbf{p}_i^T \mathbf{e}_j)(g(\mathbf{p}_i^T \mathbf{e}_j) - R_{ij})\mathbf{e}_j + \lambda_C \sum_{q=1}^m I_{iq}^C g'(\mathbf{p}_i^T \mathbf{x}_q)(g(\mathbf{p}_i^T \mathbf{x}_q) - C_{iq})\mathbf{x}_q + \lambda_P \mathbf{p}_i$$

$$(5.21)$$

$$\frac{\partial L}{\partial \mathbf{e}_j} = \sum_{i=1}^m I_{ij}^R g'(\mathbf{p}_i^T \mathbf{e}_j)(g(\mathbf{p}_i^T \mathbf{e}_j) - R_{ij})\mathbf{p}_i + \lambda_S \sum_{k=1}^n I_{ik}^S g'(\mathbf{e}_j^T \mathbf{z}_k)(g(\mathbf{e}_j^T \mathbf{z}_k) - S_{jk})\mathbf{z}_k + \lambda_E \mathbf{z}_j$$

$$(5.22)$$

$$\frac{\partial L}{\partial \mathbf{x}_q} = \lambda_C \sum_{i=1}^m I_{iq}^C g'(\mathbf{p}_i^T \mathbf{x}_q)(g(\mathbf{p}_i^T \mathbf{x}_q) - C_{iq})\mathbf{p}_i + \lambda_X \mathbf{x}_q \qquad (5.23)$$

$$\frac{\partial L}{\partial \mathbf{z}_k} = \lambda_S \sum_{j=1}^n I_{jk}^S g'(\mathbf{e}_j^T \mathbf{z}_k)(g(\mathbf{e}_j^T \mathbf{z}_k) - S_{jk})\mathbf{e}_j + \lambda_Z \mathbf{z}_k \qquad (5.24)$$

To reduce the model complexity, in all of our experiments, we set $\lambda_P = \lambda_E = \lambda_X = \lambda_Z$.

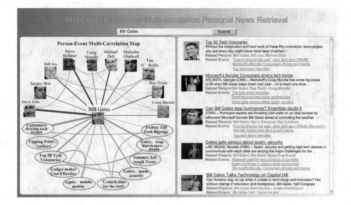

Fig. 5.7 Interface of MMPNR

5.3.4   Ranking and Visualization

Provided with the latent feature spaces by MPMF, we can give users more information than the traditional news engines, which can only present the list of related
news articles. Figure 5.7 gives the interface of our MMPNR system. It presents the
discovered relations and the relative news events to the end users in a visualized view.
Basically, it comprises two types of views: relation view and relative event view.

In the relation view, we give users three relations to answer their queries: person
relation, event relation, and query person-event relation. In the person relation part,
we present a social network about the most relevant persons, which enables users to
explore highly relevant information during searching to discover interesting relationships about persons associated with their queries. We also show users a news event
relation map about the most related events in the event relation part. Through MPMF,
we have got the latent spaces $\mathbf{P}$, $\mathbf{E}$, $\mathbf{X}$ and $\mathbf{Z}$, which can be utilized to reconstruct the
three correlation matrices by the following formulas:

$$\hat{\mathbf{R}} = g(\mathbf{P}^T\mathbf{E}) \quad \hat{\mathbf{C}} = g(\mathbf{P}^T\mathbf{X}) \quad \hat{\mathbf{S}} = g(\mathbf{E}^T\mathbf{Z}). \tag{5.25}$$

If user submits a query corresponding to the person i in our data set, we can rank
persons and events by sorting the ith column of $\hat{\mathbf{C}}$ and $\hat{\mathbf{R}}$ by descending order. We
can also derive the relevant events to the query from the matrix $\hat{S}$. We only present
the top 10 relevant persons in the social network and the top 10 relevant events in the
news event relation map. As shown in the left part of Fig. 5.7, we give names and
face images of persons and keywords of events. The weighted edges between persons
or events denote the relations between them. The thicker the line between persons
or events, the stronger the relation they have. The query person-event view shows
the relations between the relative news events and the query person using weighted
edges. Users can also see the detailed information about a specific event or person
through putting the mouse pointer on the suitable position.

In the relative events view, as done in a traditional news searcher, we also present a ranking list of relative news events with general introduction. We present news event not only with the title and a shot part of summary similar to the traditional news searcher, but also with the top three relevant persons and the top three relevant news events, which can be obtained by sorting the reconstructed event correlation matrix $\hat{S}$. Users can browse more information through clicking the title of events.

5.4 Multimedia News Contextualization

In addition to "Who", we design another news search and browsing system named GeoVisNews, in which the news elements of "Where", "What", and "When" are enhanced via news geo-localization, image enrichment and joint ranking, respectively. For news geo-localization, an Ordinal Correlation Consistent Matrix Factorization (OCCMF) model is proposed to maintain the relevance rankings of locations to a specific news document and simultaneously capture intra-relations among locations and documents. To visualize news, we develop a novel method to enrich news documents with appropriate web images.

5.4.1 Overview of GeoVisNews

In this section, we will briefly overview the framework of GeoVisNews, which is shown in Fig. 5.8. The whole system mainly contains four components: data preprocessing, location relevance analysis, image enrichment, and result ranking and visualization.

First, we collect and process large-scale multimedia news data. Each news document is first parsed into title, main body, URL and image. Then necessary text preprocessing steps, including word separation and stop-words filtering, are performed. We extract named entities including location and time using the OpenNLP software package.

The second component is the location relevance analysis detailed in Sect. 5.4.2. To refine news location relevance, a new matrix factorization approach is proposed, called as Ordinal Consistent Constraint Matrix Factorization (OCCMF), to exploit the hidden relevance of news locations to news documents while exploiting the document similarity and location co-occurrence simultaneously.

The third component is image enrichment introduced in Sect. 5.4.3. To find suitable images to represent news documents, we collect images from the Internet. Since the current image search engines cannot handle long queries, we propose a strategy to first generate multiple queries of different lengths from news documents, and then adopt a rank aggregation method to rank the retrieved images by these queries.

The last component is result ranking and visualization. We consider three aspects: relevance, timeliness, and popularity, to rank news documents. A preliminary User

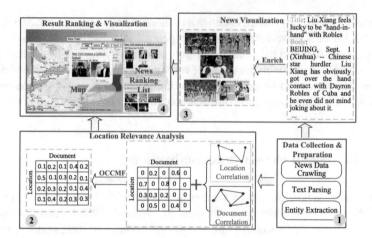

Fig. 5.8 The schematic illustration of GeoVisNews

Interface (UI) is developed based on Google Map API. News can be retrieved by submitting a location query or clicking a place on the map. The details will be presented in Sect. 5.4.4.

5.4.2   News Document Geo-Localization

In this section, we first introduce our toponym filtration and expansion strategy to disambiguate toponyms. Then, we elaborate the proposed OCCMF to refine the location-document relevance.

5.4.2.1   Toponym Filtration and Expansion

Under the toponym filtration and expansion approach, the most promising toponyms are extracted from documents with the help of external knowledge resources. We focus on handling two difficulties, i.e., common nouns misdetected as place names and the ambiguity of toponyms.

First, a list of candidate toponyms is extracted from news documents. We employ the OpenNLP toolbox to extract named entities from news documents. There are some common nouns treated as toponyms. Therefore, in the second step, we filter out common nouns with assistance of Wikipedia.[6] We query Wikipedia with each toponym candidate and remove candidates whose corresponding articles do not contain "infobox" with geo-coordinates. The next step is to expand the toponym list and eliminate geographical ambiguity. For example, there are two places named

---

[6]http://www.wikipedia.org/.

"Paris", one in France and the other in US. We submit each toponym candidate to GeoNames,[7] which will return a list of related places. We collect the corresponding "Name", "Country", "Latitude" and "Longitude" information for each returned item. We parse the returned items and de-duplicate toponyms based on the information of "Country" and geo-coordinates. Meanwhile, we employ the information of "Country" and geo-coordinates to eliminate ambiguity among the toponym candidates.

5.4.2.2 Relevance Analysis by OCCMF

Now we have obtained a toponym list including a set of locations. However, locations found in such way are usually noisy and incomplete. It comes from two facts. First, several locations contained in a news document are not very relevant. For example, considering a document that describes the wedding of a celebrity, the document may contain some locations about the bride, such as where she was born and the home-town name of the bride, but these locations are not relevant enough in comparison with the location where the wedding is hold. The second fact is that several rele-vant locations may not appear in the documents. Clearly, to accurately analyze the most relevant location requires some understanding of the news documents, which is a challenging NLP problem. Existing studies demonstrate that the semantic space spanned by text keywords can be approximated by a smaller subset of salient words of the original space [37, 41]. News content has low-rank property as well. Therefore, considering a relevance score matrix $\mathbf{R}$ of which the (i, j)th element indicates the relevance of the ith toponym to the jth document, it could be approximated by the product of two low-rank matrices $\mathbf{P}$ and $\mathbf{E}$. These two factor matrices are the latent feature representations of locations and news contents. Thus, the relevance analysis problem becomes the task of estimating the location-document relevance matrix with information loss minimization, and we employ matrix factorization to estimate the location-document relevance matrix. Different from traditional matrix factorization models, we propose a novel ranking based optimization scheme to design the objec-tive function. We further explore correlations of locations and news documents, i.e., the relevance scores of highly correlated locations or similar documents should be close. Therefore, we propose an Ordinal Correlation Consistent Matrix Factorization (OCCMF) algorithm to simultaneously integrate the multiple assumptions.

Assume there are M toponyms and N news documents. We use H to denote the rank of $\mathbf{R}$, which usually has the property that $H < \min(M, N)$. Let $\mathbf{R} \in \mathbb{R}^{M \times N}$, $\mathbf{P} \in \mathbb{R}^{H \times M}$, $\mathbf{E} \in \mathbb{R}^{H \times N}$, $\mathbf{C} \in \mathbb{R}^{M \times M}$ and $\mathbf{S} \in \mathbb{R}^{N \times N}$ denote the location-document relevance matrix, location latent feature matrix, document latent feature matrix, location correlation matrix, and document correlation matrix, respectively. $\mathbf{P}$ and $\mathbf{E}$ indicate latent feature matrices that we need to estimate in the matrix factorization approach.

Ordinal Matrix Factorization. An efficient and effective approach to explore the relations is to factorize the observed relational matrix into two low-rank latent

---

[7]http://www.geonames.org/.

matrices, and the factor matrices are utilized to make further relation reconstruction. The premise behind a low-dimensional factor model is that there is only a small number of topics in the news documents and that a document's vector is determined by how each topic applies to that document.

A matrix factorization approach with the least-squares loss function seeks to approximate $\mathbf{R}^0$ by a multiplication of H-rank factors as follows.

$$\min_{\mathbf{P},\mathbf{E}} \sum_{i=1}^{M} \sum_{j=1}^{N} \delta_{ij}(R_{ij}^0 - \mathbf{p}_i^T \mathbf{e}_j)^2 \tag{5.26}$$

Here $\delta_{ij} = 1$ if $R_{ij}^0 > 0$, and 0 otherwise. $\mathbf{R}^0$ is usually initialized by the binary strategy [21]. However, the above model is unreasonable for our task. First, the unobserved values in $\mathbf{R}^0$ are not exploited, which ignores a large amount of information since $\mathbf{R}^0$ is extremely sparse. For each document, the observed locations tend to be more relevant than the unobserved ones, which should be considered in the process of estimating the location-document relevance. Second, in the ranking task, trying to fit to the numerical values is an unnecessary constraint. Instead only the relative ranking relationship is important.

To this end, we propose a new ordinal matrix factorization model to preserve as many ranking constraints as possible. The pairwise ranking constraint can be described as

$$R_{ik} > R_{jk} \Leftrightarrow R_{ik}^0 > R_{jk}^0, \tag{5.27}$$

where $\mathbf{R} = \mathbf{P}^T \mathbf{E}$ is the estimated location-document relevance matrix. Our optimization criterion is to satisfy as many ranking constraints as possible, which leads to the following objective function.

$$\min_{\mathbf{P},\mathbf{E}} \sum_{k=1}^{N} \sum_{i=1}^{M} \sum_{j=1}^{M} \delta_{ijk} f(R_{jk} - R_{ik}) \tag{5.28}$$

Here δ_{ijk} is the indicator function that satisfies $\delta_{ijk} = 1$ if $R_{ik}^0 - R_{jk}^0 > 0$, and otherwise $\delta_{ijk} = 0$. $f : \mathbf{R} \mapsto [0, 1]$ is a monotonic increasing function. In our experiments, we adopt the logistic sigmoid function. To avoid overfitting, two regularization terms are added into Eq. 5.28. Hence, our objective is to minimize the following equation over $\mathbf{P}$ and $\mathbf{E}$.

$$\mathscr{L}_{OMF}(\mathbf{P}, \mathbf{E}) = \sum_{k=1}^{N} \sum_{i=1}^{M} \sum_{j=1}^{M} \delta_{ijk} f(R_{jk} - R_{ik}) + \frac{\lambda_P}{2} \|\mathbf{P}\|_F^2 + \frac{\lambda_E}{2} \|\mathbf{E}\|_F^2, \tag{5.29}$$

Moreover, the title is more important than the main body part for a news document. To distinguish the importance of locations with different frequencies appearing in the title and the main body part, we define $\mathbf{R}^0$ by considering location frequency and distinguishing the title and the main body part

$$R_{ij}^0 = \gamma Y_{ij}^t + (1 - \gamma) Y_{ij}^b. \tag{5.30}$$

Here γ is a parameter to balance the importance of the title and the main body part, which is set to 0.6 empirically. Y_{ij}^t and Y_{ij}^b are the importance scores of the ith location in the title and the main body of the jth news document, respectively. The corresponding Y_{ij} is defined

$$Y_{ij} = \frac{n_{ij}}{\sum_k n_{kj}}, \tag{5.31}$$

where n_{ij} is the frequency of the ith location in the corresponding part of the jth document.

5.4.2.3 Correlation Consistent Regularization

As aforementioned, highly correlated locations are always relevant to news documents closely and very similar documents always contain the nearly same locations. However, the above ordinal matrix factorization method does not consider these two observations. Based on this intuition, we propose our correlation consistent regularization for OMF to further consider the correlations of locations and documents.

To guarantee the above intuition, we utilize the similarity graph **S** of news documents and **C** of toponyms. We take **S** to elaborate the details. For any two news documents i and j, S_{ij} is the textual similarity between them (How to define S_{ij} will be introduced in the rest of this section.). To make sure that all similar documents have similar relevance scores to locations, we minimize the following term:

$$F_S(\mathbf{R}) = \frac{1}{2} \sum_{k=1}^{M} \sum_{i,j=1}^{N} \left(\frac{R_{ki}}{D_{ii}^S} - \frac{R_{kj}}{D_{jj}^S} \right)^2 S_{ij} = \text{Tr}[\mathbf{R}\mathbf{L}^S\mathbf{R}^T], \tag{5.32}$$

in which $\text{Tr}[\cdot]$ denotes the trace operation on a matrix and $\mathbf{L}^S$ is the normalized graph Laplacian defined as $\mathbf{L}^S = (\mathbf{D}^S)^{-\frac{1}{2}}(\mathbf{D}^S - \mathbf{S})(\mathbf{D}^S)^{-\frac{1}{2}}$, where $\mathbf{D}^S = diag(D_{ii}^S)$ is a diagonal matrix with $D_{ii}^S = \sum_{j=1}^{N} S_{ij}$. Similarly, we compute $\mathbf{L}^C$ and minimize the following term.

$$F_C(\mathbf{R}) = \text{Tr}[\mathbf{R}^T\mathbf{L}^C\mathbf{R}] \tag{5.33}$$

Combining the above two formulations, OMF embeds the correlations of locations and documents as two consistency constraints in the low-rank matrix factorization framework. Therefore, our proposed OCCMF is formulated to minimize the following equation:

$$\mathcal{L} = \sum_{k=1}^{N} \sum_{i,j=1}^{M} \delta_{ijk} f(R_{jk} - R_{ik}) + \frac{\lambda_P}{2} \|\mathbf{P}\|_F^2 + \frac{\lambda_E}{2} \|\mathbf{E}\|_F^2 + \frac{\lambda_C}{2} \mathrm{Tr}[\mathbf{R}^T \mathbf{L}^C \mathbf{R}] + \frac{\lambda_S}{2} \mathrm{Tr}[\mathbf{R}\mathbf{L}^S \mathbf{R}^T]$$

(5.34)

Here λ_C and λ_S are two positive trade-off parameters. To optimize the above objective function, we utilize an iterative gradient descent strategy over $\mathbf{p}_l$ and $\mathbf{e}_k$. Let $\mathbf{l}_k$ denote the kth column of $\mathbf{L}$.

$$\frac{\partial \mathcal{L}}{\partial \mathbf{p}_l} = \sum_{k=1}^{N} \sum_{i=1}^{M} (\delta_{ilk} f'(R_{lk} - R_{ik}) - \delta_{lik} f'(R_{ik} - R_{lk}))\mathbf{e}_k + \lambda_P \mathbf{p}_l + \lambda_C \mathbf{E}\mathbf{E}^T \mathbf{P}\mathbf{l}_l^C + \lambda_S \mathbf{E}\mathbf{L}^S \mathbf{E}^T \mathbf{p}_l$$

(5.35)

$$\frac{\partial \mathcal{L}}{\partial \mathbf{e}_k} = \sum_{i,j=1}^{M} \delta_{ijk} f'(R_{jk} - R_{ik})(\mathbf{p}_j - \mathbf{p}_i) + \lambda_E \mathbf{e}_k + \lambda_C \mathbf{P}\mathbf{L}^C \mathbf{P}^T \mathbf{e}_k + \lambda_S \mathbf{P}\mathbf{P}^T \mathbf{E}\mathbf{l}_k^S$$

(5.36)

To implement OCCMF, we need to define $\mathbf{C}$ and $\mathbf{S}$, i.e., the correlation matrices for locations and documents. For location correlation, we adopt Google distance [6]. Let d_{ij} denote the Google distance between the ith and jth locations and then C_{ij} is defined as

$$C_{ij} = \exp(-d_{ij}^2/\sigma_C^2), \qquad d_{ij} = \frac{\max(\log g(i), \log g(j)) - \log g(i, j)}{\log(T) - \min(\log g(i), \log g(j))}, \qquad (5.37)$$

where σ_C is set to the median value of the pairwise distances between all locations. $g(i)$, $g(j)$ and $g(i, j)$ denote the number of pages containing the ith, jth, both ith and jth location, respectively. T is the total number of web pages indexed by Google. For $\mathbf{S}$, we first calculate the textual similarity matrices on the titles ($\mathbf{S}^t$) and the main bodies ($\mathbf{S}^b$) respectively, and then combine them in a linear form as:

$$\mathbf{S} = \alpha \mathbf{S}^t + (1 - \alpha)\mathbf{S}^b.$$

(5.38)

where α is set to 2/3 simply. We use the TF-IDF histograms to represent the corresponding text information, and calculate their cosine similarities for $\mathbf{S}^t$ and $\mathbf{S}^b$.

It is worth mentioning that different from the initial relevance matrix which is usually highly sparse, $\mathbf{R}$ may not be sparse. However, we can easily sparsify $\mathbf{R}$ by setting the elements below a threshold to 0. This can facilitate the inverted indexing structure in large-scale search.

5.4.3 Image Enrichment

To enrich news documents with images, we utilize the external image sources to identify proper pictures. However, existing image search engines usually cannot

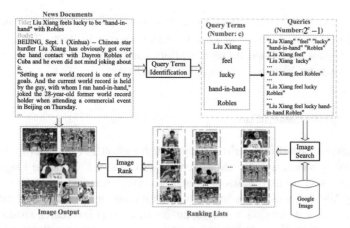

Fig. 5.9 The schematic illustration of the proposed image enrichment approach

handle long queries well. For example, if we directly use documents (or their titles) as queries to search images, usually there are very limited or no results [13, 17]. Therefore, we design an intelligent method to collect images. Figure 5.9 shows a schematic flow diagram of our approach. We first identify a set of query terms from the titles and the main bodies and then generate all possible queries by combining them. We perform image search with these queries and then adopt a rank aggregation method to generate a final ranking list, from which a set of images is selected for image enrichment.

5.4.3.1 Query Term Identification

We first perform stemming and removal of punctuation and stop-words for the whole news documents, and then identify several query terms from each news document. However, a news document is usually too long, making the query term selection difficult. Given the fact that the title of a news document is usually a good summarization of the whole document that is manually constructed by a specialist, it is reasonable to select the query terms from the title. Considering there are several documents with fairly long titles, we rank the title terms according to their correlation with the content of the main body and only select top ones. Denote by $\mathscr{T} = \{\text{term}_1, \dots, \text{term}_u\}$ and $\mathscr{B} = \{\text{term}'_1, \dots, \text{term}'_v\}$ the set of terms in the title and main body, respectively. The importance score of term_i can thus be estimated as

$$\text{score}(\text{term}_i) = \frac{1}{v} \sum_{j=1}^{v} \exp(-\frac{d^2(\text{term}_i, \text{term}'_j)}{\sigma^2}). \tag{5.39}$$

Here $d(\text{term}_i, \text{term}'_j)$ is the Google distance defined by Eq. 5.37 and σ is the median value of all $d(\text{term}_i, \text{term}'_j)$. For each document, we select c terms. The terms in $\mathscr{T}$ with the highest scores have the highest priority. In case that $u < c$, we simply select $c - u$ terms from $\mathscr{B}$ with the highest TF-IDF values.

5.4.3.2   Query Generation

The intuitive approach is to perform image search with all the c query terms. However, as previously mentioned, current search engines cannot well-handle long queries, and usually very limited results or even no result are returned for complex queries [13, 17]. We face a dilemma here: using more query terms for search can obtain more accurate and descriptive images, but it will also get less search results or even no result returned. For example, we consider a query term set {"Barack Obama", "GreatWall", "bids", "China", "farewell"}. If we use each term to search, such as "Barack Obama" or "GreatWall", the resulted images are not descriptive for the news document. If we use the combination of multiple terms such as "Barack Obama China GreatWall" to search, better results can be collected. But if we use all the terms, i.e., "Obama GreatWall bids China farewell tour", the returned results are limited and are also irrelevant to the whole story. Figure 5.10 shows the comparison of the top results of different queries. To address this problem, we propose an approach that first generates all the combinations of the c terms as queries for search and then fuse the search results by assigning appropriate weights to the queries. Clearly, from the c terms, we generate $L = \sum_{k=1}^{c} \binom{c}{k} = 2^c - 1$ queries with their lengths varying from 1 to c. In our experiments, we set $c = 5$.

5.4.3.3   Rank Aggregation

We issue each query on the Google image search engine and collect the top h ranked results. Thus our next task is to fuse the L ranking lists, which is a rank aggregation problem. Generally there are two approaches for rank aggregation, namely, score-based fusion and rank-based fusion [29, 38, 40]. Here we adopt the score-based

(a) Barack Obama

(b) GreatWall

(c) Barack Obama GreatWall

(d) Obama GreatWall bids China farewell tour

Fig. 5.10 Top image search results of a "Barack Obama", b "GreatWall", c "Barack Obama Great-Wall", and d "Obama Great Wall tour bids China farewell". From the results we can see the dilemma: the descriptiveness of the results from too few query terms is not good due to the lack of context information, and long queries cannot return reasonable results due to the limitation of search engines in handling complex queries

fusion approach. All the L lists are merged and we also remove the duplicates based on their URL information. For each image in a ranking list, we can define its relevance score based on its position. But note that there are several news documents that originally contain pictures and we also take their information into the relevance score estimation. That is, search results that are closer to the original pictures will be assigned higher scores. Considering the ith image $z_{k,i}$ of the kth document, it may occur in more than one list. If it is at the lth ($l \geq 1$) position of the jth ranking list, its relevance score is defined as

$$s_j(z_{k,i}) = \mu(1 - \frac{l-1}{h}) + (1 - \mu)\max_{z \in \mathscr{O}_k} \text{sim}(z, z_{k,i}), \qquad (5.40)$$

where $\mathscr{O}_k$ is the set of original pictures contained in the kth news document and $\text{sim}(z, z_{k,i})$ is the visual similarity between web image $z_{k,i}$ and the original news picture $z \in O_k$. To calculate the image similarity, we extract 1000-dimensional bag-of-visual-words features from each image and adopt cosine similarity. Here we simply set the parameter μ to 0.5.

In rank aggregation, all lists are merged to obtain the fused scores. The fused score of $z_{k,i}$ is

$$f(z_{k,i}) = \sum_{j=1}^{L} \eta_j s_j(z_{k,i}), \qquad (5.41)$$

where η_j is the to-be-learned weight, which actually indicates the search quality of the jth list. In our task, the queries extracted from different documents vary widely and adopting fixed weights η_j is not reasonable. Different from [21], in which only the query length is considered to learn the weights, we extract the following three features that enable to reflect search quality and learn the weights based on the features.

1. Query length. As aforementioned, search quality is correlated with the complexity of queries. Therefore, we adopt the query length as a feature to learn the weights.
2. Image number. The number of images returned also reflects the search quality [43]. Therefore, we regard the number of search results as a feature to learn the weights.
3. Part of Speech. We analyze each query with a Part of Speech (POS) tagger and a 3D histogram is generated by counting the nouns, adjectives and verbs. The histogram is utilized as a type of features as it reflects the structure of the query.

We concatenate the above three types of features and form a 5D feature vector for each query. Denote by $\mathbf{f}_{k,j}$ the feature vector of the jth query of the kth news document. The weight of the query is then generated based on the feature vector, which can be denoted as

$$\eta_{k,j} = \mathbf{w}^T \mathbf{f}_{k,j}. \qquad (5.42)$$

Therefore, the task becomes learning the 5D vector $\mathbf{w}$. We adopt an approach that is analogous to ranking SVM [15].

For the ith image of the kth news document, its ranking score is

$$f(z_{k,i}) = \sum_{j=1}^{L} \eta_{k,j} s_j(z_{k,i}) = \sum_{j=1}^{L} \mathbf{w}^T \mathbf{f}_{k,j} s_j(z_{k,i}) = \mathbf{w}^T \sum_{j=1}^{L} \mathbf{f}_{k,j} s_j(z_{k,i}). \qquad (5.43)$$

For simplicity, let $\mathbf{x}_{k,i}$ denote $\sum_{j=1}^{L} \mathbf{f}_j s_j(z_{k,i})$. Thus, $f(z_{k,i}) = f(\mathbf{x}_{k,i}) = \mathbf{w}^T \mathbf{x}_{k,i} = \langle \mathbf{w}, \mathbf{x}_{k,i} \rangle$. To learn $\mathbf{w}$, we manually labeled the ground truth for each image collected of a document in a given set of news documents. For the kth document, if image $z_{k,i}$ is more relevant than $z_{k,j}$, $f(\mathbf{x}_{k,i}) > f(\mathbf{x}_{k,j})$. That is,

$$\delta(\mathbf{x}_{k,i} \succ \mathbf{x}_{k,j}) \langle \mathbf{w}, \mathbf{x}_{k,i} - \mathbf{x}_{k,j} \rangle > 0. \qquad (5.44)$$

Here $\succ$ denotes the relevancy to the corresponding documents and $\delta(\cdot) = 1$ if the condition is true and -1 otherwise.

Constructing the SVM model with the Hinge Loss is equivalent to solving the following quadratic optimization problem

$$\min_{\mathbf{w}} \frac{1}{2} \|\mathbf{w}\|^2 + C \sum_{k,i,j} \xi_{k,i,j} \qquad (5.45)$$

$$\text{s.t.} \quad \delta(\mathbf{x}_{k,i} \succ \mathbf{x}_{k,j}) \langle \mathbf{w}, \mathbf{x}_{k,i} - \mathbf{x}_{k,j} \rangle > 1 - \xi_{k,i,j} \qquad (5.46)$$

$$\xi_{k,i,j} > 0, \forall k \forall i \forall j \qquad (5.47)$$

C is a parameter that allows trading-off margin size against training error. It can be solved using decomposition algorithms similar to those used for SVM classification.

Suppose that $\mathbf{w}^*$ is the weights in the SVM solution. We utilize $\mathbf{w}^*$ to form a ranking function for ranking instances: $f(\mathbf{x}) = \langle \mathbf{w}^*, \mathbf{x} \rangle$. We rank the collected images based on the ranking function f, and then adopt the approach in [36] to perform duplicate detection for all these images and for each duplicate pair we remove the one with lower rank. After that, for the kth news document, we select the top $v - |\mathcal{O}_k|$ images to complement the original pictures in $\mathcal{O}_k$, where $|\mathcal{O}_k|$ is the size of $\mathcal{O}_k$. Therefore, for each document we have v images. v is set to 5 in our experiments.

5.4.4 Result Ranking and Visualization

Based on the proposed news location analysis and image enrichment approaches, we design a news browsing system, GeoVisNews, as shown in Sect. 5.4.1. We now introduce how to rank and present the relevant results to users' queries.

5.4.4.1 Result Ranking

According to users' queries, the news search and browsing system returns the relevant results to users. The retrieval system should place the users' desired results in the rank front. To this end, we consider three properties for news presentation and search: relevance, timeliness, and popularity. The relevance is measured by the relevance score calculated by OCCMF between the query location and each document. We utilize the time information of news documents to consider the timeliness. For popularity, it is reasonable to assume that the popular news event is intensively reported by many documents. That is, the popularity of a news document can be estimated by its similarity to other news documents. Here we adopt a PageRank [30] approach with considering these three aspects.

The time information is an important aspect for news. We quantize the time stamp of each document as a number of "YYYYMMDD". For example, the time "Sep. 12 2010" is quantized to be 20100912. Denote by date_k the quantized date of the kth document and we then normalize date_k with two steps

$$\text{date}_k = \frac{\text{date}_k - \min_j(\text{date}_j)}{\max_j(\text{date}_j) - \min_j(\text{date}_j)}; \tag{5.48}$$

$$\text{date}_k = \frac{\text{date}_k}{\sum_j \text{date}_j}. \tag{5.49}$$

Through OCCMF, we have obtained relevance scores between locations and documents, denoted as $\text{rs}_k (k = 1, \ldots, N)$. We normalize them: $\text{rs}_k = \text{rs}_k / \sum_j \text{rs}_j$.

In the PageRank method [30], we set the static ranking score of the kth document to

$$r_k^0 = \frac{\text{date}_k + \text{rs}_k}{2}. \tag{5.50}$$

An iterative process is then implemented by performing

$$r_k^{\text{iter}} = (1 - y)r_k^0 + y \sum_j \frac{S_{kj}}{\sum_m S_{mj}} r_j^{\text{iter}-1}, \tag{5.51}$$

until $\text{iter} \geq 1$ achieves the pre-determined number. Here, S_{ij} is the similarity between the ith and jth document, and y is the damping factor (we simply set it to 0.85 [3]).

5.4.4.2 User Interface

A preliminary User Interface (UI) of GeoVisNews is presented in Fig. 5.11, which is developed based on Google Map API. By submitting a location query (in the top textbox) or clicking a place on the map, the highest ranked news document with its title and the top 2 illustrative images is presented as a pop-up window positioning

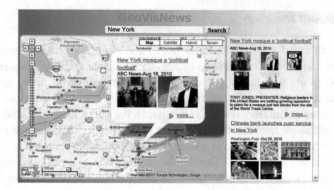

Fig. 5.11   The user interface of GeoVisNews

on the queried location of the map. The detailed ranking results about this location are shown in the right part with title, summary and illustrative images (including the original pictures and the images enriched by our approach), through which users can quickly master the main points of each document. In this way, users can quickly get information about the news without reading its main body. If they are interested in it, they can browse the full content by clicking the title or the "More" button. Although UI is a very important part for such a system, a more detailed investigation is beyond our current scope and we leave it to our future work.

5.5   Discussions

In this chapter, we propose understanding-oriented multimedia news retrieval and browsing systems to enhance the news elements of "Where", "Who", "What", and "When". A news retrieval system named MMPNR (Multi-modal Multi-correlation Person-centric News Retrieval) is designed based on multimodal analysis and multi-correlation exploration. Besides, GeoVisNews supports users in browsing and retrieving news with a map. This system is based on news geo-localization and image enrichment.

The proposed models open a broad way for future improvement and extension. For example, personalized news search is to return news for each user on a given query. Users' preference and browsing histories should be covered to mine the underlying relationships for multimedia news search. Another application is multimedia news question and answer. The current system is to return a list of multimedia documents to users according to their queries. Users have to find their desired information from the returned list, which may take much time and energy. A better way is to provide multimedia answers for users' questions.

It is well known that a story has several topics. Another element, i.e., "How", can be highlighted by analyzing the latent topics. Thus, we will study how to organize the news with a topic discovery component by developing a multimedia news summarization system. It will uncover the underlying topics among the query-related news information and thread the news events within each topic to generate a query-related brief overview.

References

1. Amitay, E., Sivan, R., Soffer, A.: Web-a-Where: geotagging web content. In: Proceedings of ACM SIGIR Conference on Research and Development in Information Retrieval, pp. 273–280 (2004)
2. Andogah, G.: Geographically constrained information retrieval. Ph.D. thesis, University of Groningen (2010)
3. Brin, S., Page, L.: The anatomy of a large-scale hypertextual web search engine. In: Proceedings of International Conference on World Wide Web, pp. 107–117 (1998)
4. Candeias, R., Martins, B.: Associating relevant photos to georeferenced textual documents through rank aggregation. In: Proceedings of the Terra Cognita 2011 Workshop (2011)
5. Christel, M.G., Hauptmann, A.G., Wactlar, H.D., Ng, T.D.: Collages as dynamic summaries for news video. In: Proceedings of ACM International Conference on Multimedia, pp. 561–569 (2002)
6. Cilibrasi, R.L., Vitanyi, P.M.B.: The Google similarity distance. IEEE Trans. Knowl. Data Eng. **19**(3), 370–383 (2007)
7. Coyne, B., Sproat, R.: WordsEye: an automatic text-to-scene conversion system. In: Proceedings of Computer Graphics and Interactive Techniques, pp. 487–496 (2001)
8. Delgado, D., Magalhaes, J., Correia, N.: Assisted news reading with automated illustrations. In: Proceedings of ACM International Conference on Multimedia, pp. 1647–1650 (2010)
9. Etzioni, O., Cafarella, M.J., Downey, D., Kok, S., Popescu, A.M., Shaked, T., Soderland, S., Weld, D.S., Yates, A.: Web-scale information extraction in knowitall: (preliminary results). In: Proceedings of International Conference on World Wide Web, pp. 100–110 (2004)
10. Etzioni, O., Cafarella, M.J., Downey, D., Popescu, A.M., Shaked, T., Soderland, S., Weld, D.S., Yates, A.: Unsupervised named-entity extraction from the web: an experimental study. Artif. Intell. **165**(1), 91–134 (2005)
11. Friedman, N., Getoor, L., Koller, D., Pfeffer, A.: Learning probabilistic relational models. In: Proceedings of International Joint Conference on Artificial Intelligence, pp. 1300–1309 (1999)
12. Harabagiu, A., Bejan, C.A., Morarescu, P.: Shallow semantics for relation extraction. In: Proceedings of International Joint Conference on Artificial Intelligence, pp. 1061–1066 (2005)
13. Huston, S., Croft, W.B.: Evaluating verbose query processing techniques. In: Proceedings of ACM SIGIR Conference on Research and Development in Information Retrieval, pp. 291–298 (2010)
14. Jiang, Y., Liu, J., Li, Z., Xu, C., Lu, H.: Chat with illustration: a chat system with visual aids. In: Proceedings of International Conference on Internet Multimedia Computing and Service, pp. 96–99 (2012)
15. Joachims, T.: Optimizing search engines using clickthrough data. In: Proceedings of ACM SIGKDD International Conference on Knowledge Discovery and Data Mining, pp. 133–142 (2002)
16. Joshi, D., Wang, J.Z., Li, J.: The story picturing engine: finding elite images to illustrate a story using mutual reinforcement. In: Proceedings of ACM Workshop on Multimedia Information Retrieval, pp. 119–126 (2004)
17. Kumaran, G., Carvalho, V.R.: Reducing long queries using query quality predictors. In: Proceedings of ACM SIGIR Conference on Research and Development in Information Retrieval, pp. 564–571 (2009)

18. Leidner, J.L.: Toponym resolution in text: annotation, evaluation and applications of spatial grounding of place names. Dissertation.Com (2008)
19. Li, Z., Liu, J., Wang, M., Xu, C., Lu, H.: Enhancing news organization for convenient retrieval and browsing. ACM Trans. Multimed. Comput. Commun. Appl. **10**(1), 1:1–1:20 (2013)
20. Li, Z., Liu, J., Zhu, X., Lu, H.: Multi-modal multi-correlation person-centric news retrieval. In: Proceedings of ACM Conference on Information and Knowledge Management, pp. 179–188 (2010)
21. Li, Z., Wang, M., Liu, J., Xu, C., Lu, H.: News contextualization with geographic and visual information. In: Proceedings of ACM International Conference on Multimedia, pp. 133–142 (2011)
22. Liu, C., Yuen, J., Torralba, A., Sivic, J., Freeman, W.T.: Sift flow: dense correspondence across different scenes. In: Proceedings of European Conference on Computer Vision, pp. 28–42 (2008)
23. Liu, Q., Li, Z.: Projective nonnegative matrix factorization for social image retrieval. Neurocomputing **172**, 19–26 (2016)
24. Long, B., Zhang, Z., Yu, P.: A probabilistic framework for relational clustering. In: Proceedings of ACM SIGKDD International Conference on Knowledge Discovery and Data Mining, pp. 470–479 (2007)
25. Ma, H., Yang, H., Lyu, M.R., King, I.: Sorec: social recommendation using probabilistic matrix factorization. In: Proceedings of ACM Conference on Information and Knowledge Management, pp. 931–940 (2008)
26. Martins, B.: Geographically aware web text mining. Ph.D. thesis, University of Lisbon (2009)
27. Mcgurk, H., Macdonald, J.: Hearing lips and seeing voices. Nature **264**(5588), 746–748 (1976)
28. Okuoka, T., Takahashi, T., Deguchi, D., Ide, I., Murase, H.: Labeling news topic threads with Wikipedia entries. In: Proceedings of IEEE International Symposium on Multimedia, pp. 501–504 (2009)
29. Olivares, X., Ciaramita, M., van Zwol, R.: Boosting image retrieval through aggregating search results based on visual annotations. In: Proceedings of ACM International Conference on Multimedia, pp. 189–198 (2008)
30. Page, L., Brin, S., Motwani, R., Winograd, T.: The PageRank citation ranking: bringing order to the web. Technical report, Stanford Digital Library Technologies Project (1999)
31. Rajaraman, A., Ullman, J.D.: Mining of Massive Datasets. Cambridge University Press, Cambridge (2011)
32. Salakhutdinov, R., Mnih, A.: Probabilistic matrix factorization. In: Proceedings of Advances in Neural Information Processing Systems, pp. 1257–1264 (2007)
33. Sekine, S., Sudo, K., Nobata, C.: Extended named entity hierarchy. In: Proceedings of Third International Conference on Language Resources and Evaluation, pp. 1818–1824 (2002)
34. Strobelt, H., Oelke, D., Rohrdantz, C., Stoffel, A., Keim, D.A., Deussen, O.: Document cards: a top trumps visualization for documents. IEEE Trans. Vis. Comput. Graph. **15**(6), 1145–1152 (2009)
35. Sturm, J.F.: Site matters: the value of local newspaper web sites. Technical report, NAA. http://www.naa.org/TrendsandNumbers/Research.aspx (2009)
36. Wang, B., Li, Z., Li, M., Ma, W.Y.: Large-scale duplicate detection for web image search. In: Proceedings of IEEE International Conference on Multimedia and Expo, pp. 353–356 (2006)
37. Wang, Z.X., Li, Z., Ding, X.F., Tang, J.: Overlapping community detection based on node location analysis. Knowl. Based Syst. **105**, 225–235 (2016)
38. Yan, R., Hauptmann, A.G.: The combination limit in multimedia retrieval. In: Proceedings of ACM International Conference on Multimedia, pp. 339–342 (2003)
39. Zelenko, D., Aone, C., Richardella, A.: Kernel methods for relation extraction. J. Mach. Learn. Res. **3**, 1083–1106 (2003)
40. Zhang, L., Chen, L., Jing, F., Deng, K., Ma, W.Y.: Enjoyphoto: a vertical image search engine for enjoying high-quality photos. In: Proceedings of ACM International Conference on Multimedia, pp. 367–376 (2006)

41. Zhao, R., Grosky, W.I.: Narrowing the semantic gap—improved text-based web document retrieval using visual features. IEEE Trans. Multimed. **4**(2), 189–200 (2002)
42. Zhu, S., Yu, K., Chi, Y., Gong, Y.: Combining content and link for classification using matrix factorization. In: Proceedings of ACM SIGIR Conference on Research and Development in Information Retrieval, pp. 487–494 (2007)
43. Zong, W., Wu, D., Sun, A., Lim, E.P., Goh, D.H.L.: On assigning place names to geography related web pages. In: Proceedings of ACM/IEEE-CS Joint Conference on Digital Libraries, pp. 354–362 (2005)

Chapter 6
Understanding-Oriented Multimedia News Summarization

Abstract People now live in a sea of massive multimedia data. Given results from multimedia news search, there are several underlying topics to cover the stories of the returned results. The element "How" can be enhanced by uncovering the underlying topics. In this chapter, we develop a novel understanding-oriented approach of multimedia news summarization for searching results on Internet. It uncovers the underlying topics among the query-related news information and threads the news events within each topic to generate a query-related brief overview. And we design a friendly interface to present users the understanding-oriented hierarchical summarization of their required news information.

6.1 Introduction

With the proliferation of news articles on Internet, an increasing number of people access news information online rather than from newspapers.[1] According to the report of the Pew Research Center's Project for Excellence in Journalism,[2] 58.2% of Americans browse news online, overtaking newspaper readership (about 35%) by the end of 2011. Unfortunately, it takes much time for users to find the news they are interested in from such huge volumes of information. As a consequence, it urges the necessity to uncover compact presentations of possibly noisy and redundant news, and provide the understanding-oriented summarization of the news information.

In the last chapter, we provide news search systems by focusing on the elements of "Who", "Where", "When", and "What". They attempt to provide updated news to users. However, these systems only return a list of related news articles for each query and do not present users a summary view, which prevents users from accessing the

---

©Li, Z., Liu, J., Wang, M., Xu, C., Lu, H. "Enhancing News Organization for Convenient Retrieval and Browsing", ACM Trans. on Multimedia Computing, Communications and Applications, Vol. 10(1): 1 (1–20), ©2013 ACM, Inc. Reprinted by permission. doi:10.1145/2488732

[1]http://mashable.com/2011/03/15/online-versus-newspaper-news/.
[2]http://www.journalism.org/.

© Springer Nature Singapore Pte Ltd. 2017   131
Z. Li, *Understanding-Oriented Multimedia Content Analysis*, Springer Theses,
DOI 10.1007/978-981-10-3689-7_6

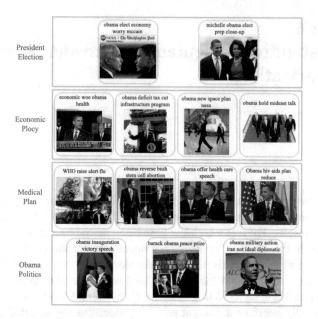

Fig. 6.1 The illustration of the topic structure discovered in the news data related to the query "Barack Obama"

desired information quickly and comprehensively. Considering different concerns in various news articles and varying stages during news development, an idea system for news search can present an informative and complete news story including news origin, developing process, and its result about certain news subject. That is to say, the element of "How" should be investigated. Here we present an illustrative example in Fig. 6.1, which is the topic structure of the related news documents to the query "Barack Obama". It is observed that there exist four topics: "President Election", "Economic Policy", "Medical Plan", and "Obama Politics". Therefore, how to search and summarize such news information is necessary and important for news search, which is the focus of this chapter. On the other hand, most news web pages contain multimodal information, such as image, video, and text. There is a saying that "a picture is worth a thousand words." Thus, visual content should be exploited to complement the textual content of news to provide users vivid and comprehensive information. Which images are selected and how to organize them in a compact form deserve our attention in this chapter.

As mentioned above, it is desirable to generate a vivid and informative news story relevant to a specific query, which can make users quickly get a brief and comprehensive overview about their desired information. Towards this end, this work develops a multimedia news summarization framework focusing on the query-related news articles and their associated multimedia information. The proposed framework is illustrated in Fig. 6.2. For each query, the related news articles can be found by many approaches for news retrieval. This work utilizes the proposed correlation

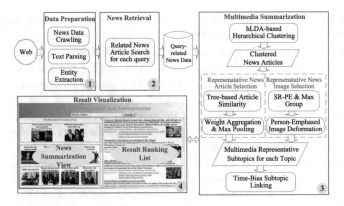

Fig. 6.2 The framework of our system

mining MPMF method in the last chapter [11]. In the following, the returned corpus of related news data is summarized into a hierarchical presentation. First, we adopt hierarchical latent Dirichlet allocation (hLDA) [1] to uncover the hierarchical topic structure among those query-related news documents, and propose an approach based on weighted aggregation and max pooling to identify one typical news event for each topic. Besides, one representative image is also selected for each topic to complement the textual contents, and the chosen images are deformed to emphasize news persons in the news images. Next, a time-bias maximum spanning tree (MST) approach is proposed to link subtopics of one topic. Finally, a vivid and informative user interface is designed to display the multimodel news summary view as well as a ranking list of related news documents for each query. Most of the work in this chapter has been published in [12].

6.2   Previous Work

Extensive research efforts have been devoted to news categorization, automatic topic detection, summarization, and retrieval. We will briefly review the related work on topic detection, summarization, and retrieval, respectively.

Hierarchical topic detection (HTD) task was proposed and evaluated in 2004, in which stories are classified in a hierarchy of topic clusters. The traditional topic detection task was replaced by a hierarchical structure [30], and a hierarchical agglomerative clustering (HAC) algorithm achieved the highest performance in the evaluation [31]. A notable technique under the bag-of-words assumption for document classification is latent Dirichlet allocation (LDA) [2]. Probabilistic latent semantic analysis [7] is the predecessors of LDA. A hierarchical topic algorithm was proposed to address the issue of variable topics, named hierarchical LDA (hLDA) [1].

Given any text document, automatic summarization attempts to abstract important information in text and present it in a condensed form sensitive to the user's or applications' needs [16]. Methods for text summarization can be generally classified into two categories: single-document summarization [21] and multiple-document summarization [15]. Many approaches have been proposed for clustering and summarizing multiple documents [23, 27], which exploit meaningful relations among documents. It is a nature application of multi-document summarization algorithms to provide summarization for web pages. Several systems [19, 26] have been developed to perform web page clustering and generic summarization based on relevant results from a search engine. Techniques particularly on news articles have also been proposed in [18, 24, 25]. NewsBlaster [18] provides summaries that give a representative of a cluster. NewsInEssence [24] generates online document clusters and summaries for user-specified requirement. Some other work generate structured representation for news event as timeline summarization [29, 32, 33] to provide better information for users than the traditional one. Hierarchical summarization [3, 6] has been studied to generate a summary of multiple documents based on sentences. Different from them, the proposed summarization scheme uncovers the hierarchical topics and represents topics based on documents and images.

Some popular news services, such as Google News, present clusters of related articles, allowing readers to easily find all stories on a given topic. Google news provides the summarization, such as topic cluster, representative images, news articles, and news videos. However, the topics in Google news are predefined according to the location or the categories such as sports, economy, politics and so on. Besides, the latest articles, images, and videos are simply selected. Google News Timeline[3] provides a preset time period overview of news using a timeline interface. Another Google system, named Fast Flip,[4] provides an interface for browsing news resembling hard-copy newspaper reading. The Yahoo! Correlator[5] associates a search item with all its related "events". EMM NewsBrief[6] is a news summarization service.

Current web pages always contain multimodal information. In [8], web pages are visually summarized by selecting images from the internal and external images. The work in [11] jointly exploits textual news content and news image information to estimate inter- and intra-correlations among news persons and news events. Multi-correlation probabilistic matrix factorization (MPMF) was proposed to reconstruct person-event, person and event correlation matrices simultaneously by the shared latent person and event matrices. Based on the reconstructed correlations, the work can provide person-centric news search results. Li et al. [13] focused on the relations between news documents and news geo-locations, and news enrichment with web images. The latent relations between news documents and news geo-location are uncovered by the proposed matrix factorization methods. Furthermore, they designed approaches to extract queries from news documents for image search

---

[3]http://newstimeline.googlelabs.com.

[4]http://fastflip.googlelabs.com.

[5]http://correlator.sandbox.yahoo.net.

[6]http://emm.newsbrief.eu.

and then selected suitable images to visualize news contents. However, the above methods do not summarize the information and cannot provide readers a condensed view. In addition, they ignore the topics hidden in the events.

6.3 Multimedia News Summarization

In this section, we elaborate the understanding-oriented multimedia news summarization by uncovering the underlying topic structure and multimedia information.

6.3.1 Hierarchical Topic Structure

Given the corpus of related news articles to one query, the latent topic structure is first discovered since the related news articles always cover several aspects. The number of topics hidden in the news data is usually uncertain. To address the issue of variable topics, the hierarchical latent Dirichlet allocation (hLDA) model [1] is adopted to discover multiple topics along a hierarchical structure. The hierarchical structure presents a top-down organization of news data, in which the lower node has the more specific (or abstract) interpretation. Therefore, it is appealing to show a compact news summary with such a hierarchically coarse-to-fine manner, which is unable for a "flat" model.

The hLDA model represents topic distribution with a tree of fixed depth L. Each node is associated with a topic distribution over words, and a topic is a distribution across words. An article is generated by selecting a path from the root to a leaf, repeatedly sampling topics along the path and selecting words from the sampled topics. The tree structure is learned along with the topics using a nested Chinese restaurant process (nCRP) [1] method, which assigns probability distributions to infinitely branching and infinitely deep tree. The basic process is specified as follows. A sequence of n news articles arrive. Similar to the case that the first customer sits at the first table, the first article takes the initial path, starting with a single-branch tree. The n_tth subsequent article is assigned to a path drawn from the following distribution

$$p(\text{an existing path} c | n_c, n_t) = \frac{n_c}{\gamma + n_t - 1}, \tag{6.1}$$

$$p(\text{a new path} c | n_c, n_t) = \frac{\gamma}{\gamma + n_t - 1}, \tag{6.2}$$

where n_c is the number of previous articles assigned to path c and n_t is the total number of articles observed in the tree. γ is a parameter to control how often an article chooses a path versus creates a new path.

In hLDA, articles in a corpus are drawn from the following generative process:

- For each topic $t \in \mathbb{T}$ in the tree
  - Draw a distribution $\beta_t \sim \text{Dirichlet}(\eta)$.
- For each article $d \in \mathbb{D} = \{d_1, d_2, \ldots, d_n\}$
  - Draw a path $c_d \sim \text{nCRP}(\gamma)$.
  - Draw a distribution over levels in the tree, $\theta_d \sim \text{Dirichlet}(\alpha)$.
  - For each word a,
    Choose level $t_{d,a} | \theta_d \sim \text{Discrete}(\theta_d)$.
    Choose word $w_{d,a} | \{t_{d,a}, c_d, \beta\} \sim \text{Discrete}(\beta_{c_d}[t_{d,a}])$, which is parameterized by the topic in position $t_{d,a}$ on the path c_d.

Intuitively, the parameters γ and η control the size of the tree. A model with larger γ and smaller η will tend to find a tree with more topics. In the hierarchical topic model, the internal nodes are not the summaries of their children, but reflect the shared terminology of the articles assigned to the paths that contain them. We also present an example of the topic structure discovered by hLDA in Fig. 6.3. The corpus of news articles consists of the top 1,000 related news articles to the query "Barack Obama".

6.3.2 Multimedia Topic Representation

In this section, we will elaborate how to obtain a multimedia representation for each latent topic based on the hierarchical topic structure.

6.3.2.1 Representative News Article Selection

In the hierarchical tree, each article is represented as a path and each path is shared by many articles. The articles sharing the same path belong to the same topics, and

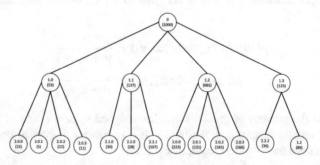

Fig. 6.3 The hLDA-based topic structure to the query "Barack Obama". The *numbers in the brackets* present the numbers of news articles which have the nodes in their paths

thus they are more similar to each other. Motivated by [3, 5], if the degree of an article is larger than the degree of any other article belonging to the same topic, it can better describe the topic. We adopt the degree as the score of the news article, which is calculated based on the news article similarity. In this chapter, the news article similarity is calculated by combining the text information and the hierarchical structure, which is defined as

$$S_{comb} = \varepsilon S^{text} + (1 - \varepsilon) S^{tree}. \tag{6.3}$$

Here S^{text} is the similarity matrix based on text information or mined by other methods, such as MPMF [11], and S^{tree} is the similarity calculated based on the hierarchical tree. ε is a parameter to balance their importance. We propose a new algorithm to calculate the similarly S^{tree} based on the hierarchical tree and choose a representative news article for each topic using weighted aggregation and max pooling.

Tree-Based Article Similarity Gibbs sampling is a particular Markov Chain Monte Carlo algorithm to approximate the posterior for hLDA. Let $\mathbf{t}$ denote the level assignment for all words and $\mathbf{c}$ denote the path assignment for all articles conditioned on the observed words $\mathbf{w}$. Given the assignment of words $\mathbf{w}$ to levels $\mathbf{t}$ and assignments of articles to paths $\mathbf{c}$, the expected posterior probability of a word w at a given topic $\mathbf{t} = t$ of a path $\mathbf{c} = c$ is proportional to the number of times that w was generated by topic t

$$p(w|\mathbf{t}, \mathbf{c}, \mathbf{w}, \eta) \propto \#[\mathbf{t} = t, \mathbf{c} = c, \mathbf{w} = w] + \eta, \tag{6.4}$$

Similarly, the posterior probability of a particular topic t in a given article d is

$$p(t|\mathbf{t}, \mathbf{c}, \alpha) \propto \#[\mathbf{t} = t, \mathbf{c} = c_d] + \alpha. \tag{6.5}$$

$\#[\cdot]$ is the count of elements of an array satisfying the given condition. The posterior should be normalized with total counts and their parameters.

$S^{tree}(d, g)$ between news articles d and g is measured based on the distribution of words at each topic t on path c and distribution of topic t on path c. Based on Eq. 6.4, we can obtain the distribution $p_{t,d} = p(\mathbf{w}_{t,d}|\mathbf{z}_d = t, c, \mathbf{w} = v_t)$, where $\mathbf{w}_{t,d}$ and $\mathbf{w} = v_t$ are the set of words in d that are generated from topic t and a vocabulary with words generated by the topic t, respectively. Similarly, $p_{t,g} = p(\mathbf{w}_{t,g}|\mathbf{z}_g = t, c, \mathbf{w} = v_t)$ is the probability of words $\mathbf{w}_g$ in g of the same topic t. We adopt the Jensen–Shannon divergence [14] to measure the distance between $p_{t,d}$ and $p_{t,g}$

$$div_{d,g,t} = \frac{1}{2}(KL(p_{t,d}||\frac{p_{t,d} + p_{t,g}}{2}) + KL(p_{t,g}||\frac{p_{t,d} + p_{t,g}}{2})), \tag{6.6}$$

where $KL(d||g) = \sum_i d_i \log(d_i/g_i)$ is the Kullback–Leibler (KL) divergence. Then the divergence is transformed into a similarity measure [17]

$$S_1^{tree}(d, g, t) = 10^{-div_{d,g,t}}. \tag{6.7}$$

We introduce the topic-based similarities based on article-topic mixing proportions. We calculate the topic proportion between d and g, represented by $p_{t_d} = p(z_d|t, c, \alpha)$ and $p_{t_g} = p(\mathbf{z}_g|t, c, \alpha)$ via Eq. 6.5. $S_2^{\text{tree}}(d, g)$ between these two distributions is measured based on Eqs. 6.6 and 6.7. Two articles on the same path would have different words, and hence have different posterior topic probabilities.

Algorithm 5 Tree-Based Article Similarity

Input:
    Tree $\mathbb{T}$ from hLDA, Articles: $\mathbb{D} = \{d_1, \ldots, d_n\}$;
Output:
    The article similarity matrix based on the hierarchical tree: $\mathbf{S}^{\text{tree}}$.
1: **for** each article $d \in \mathbb{D}$
2:   **for** each article $g \in \mathbb{D}$
3:     Find their sharing topic set $\mathbb{T}_{d,g}$
4:     **for** each topic $t \in \mathbb{T}_{d,g}$
5:       Find the level l_t
6:       Calculate $S_1^{\text{tree}}(d, g, t)$ and $S_2^{\text{tree}}(d, g, t)$
7:     **end**
8:     Calculate $S^{\text{tree}}(d, g)$ using Eq. 6.8
9:   **end**
10: **end**

S_1^{tree} provides information about the similarity between two articles based on topic-word distribution. Similarly, S_2^{tree} provides information on the similarity between the weights of the topics in each article. They jointly effect the article similarity and then are combined in one measure in all levels and all possible paths

$$S^{\text{tree}}(d, g) = \frac{1}{|\mathbb{T}_{d,g}|} \sum_{t \in \mathbb{T}_{d,g}} S_1^{\text{tree}}(d, g, t) * S_2^{\text{tree}}(d, g, t) * l_t, \qquad (6.8)$$

where $\mathbb{T}_{d,g}$ denotes the set of topics shared by articles d and g. $|\mathbb{T}|$ is the size of set $\mathbb{T}$ and l_t is the level of topic t. If $\mathbb{T}_{d,g} = \emptyset$, $S^{\text{tree}}(d, g) = 0$. We summarize the algorithm in Algorithm 5.

Weighted Aggregation We have obtained the similarity graph based on the combined similarity $\mathbf{S}_{\text{comb}}$. Representative news articles for topics are selected from the bottom to up of the hierarchical tree. Let $\mathbb{D}_l$ and $\mathbb{D}_{c,l}$ denote the article set at the lth level and the article set of the topic $t_{c,l}$ at the lth level on path c, respectively, where $\mathbb{D}_l = \bigcup_c \mathbb{D}_{c,l}$.

For article $d \in \mathbb{D}_{c,l}$, we assign a score to d to represent its importance in the set $\mathbb{D}_{c,l}$

$$\text{score}(d) = \sum_{g \in \mathbb{D}_{c,l}} S_l(d, g), \qquad (6.9)$$

where $\mathbf{S}_l$ denotes the similarity matrix at level l, specially, $\mathbf{S}_L = \mathbf{S}_{\text{comb}}$. A representative article denoted as $td_{c,l}$ is chosen to stand for the topic $t_{c,l}$ using max pooling

$$\text{td}_{c,l} = \arg \max_{d \in \mathbb{D}_{c,l}} \text{score}(d). \tag{6.10}$$

We employ a sparse interpolation matrix $\mathbf{W}_l$ to build the relations between $\mathbb{D}_l$ and $\mathbb{D}_{l-1}$. $\mathbf{W}_l$ is defined as

$$W_l(d, g) = \begin{cases} 0 & \text{if } d, g \in \mathbb{D}_{l-1} \text{ and } d \neq g \\ 1 & \text{if } d, g \in \mathbb{D}_{l-1} \text{ and } d = g \\ \frac{S_l(d,g)}{\sum_{q \in \mathbb{D}_{l-1}} S_l(d,q)} & \text{if } d \in \mathbb{D}_l - \mathbb{D}_{l-1} \text{ and } g \in \mathbb{D}_{l-1} \end{cases} \tag{6.11}$$

Thus, we can build the matrix $\mathbf{S}_{l-1}$ as

$$\mathbf{S}_{l-1} = \mathbf{W}_l^T \mathbf{S}_l \mathbf{W}_l. \tag{6.12}$$

$\mathbf{S}_{l-1}$ inherits the property of $\mathbf{S}_l$ by the interpolation matrix.

By repeating the above process, we choose one representative article for each topic. This algorithm is summarized in Algorithm 6.

Algorithm 6 Choosing Representative Articles via Weighted Aggregation and Max Pooling

---

Input:
    Tree $\mathbb{T}$ from hLDA, Articles: $\mathbb{D} = \{d_1, \ldots, d_n\}$, Article similarity matrix $\mathbf{S}_L = \mathbf{S}_{\text{comb}}$;
Output:
    The representative article for topics $\mathbb{T}\mathbb{D}$.
1: **for** level $l \leftarrow L, \ldots, 2$
2:   **for** each topic t corresponding path c at level l
3:     Score each article in $\mathbb{D}_{c,l}$ using Eq. 6.9
4:     Find the representative article $td_{c,l}$ for the topic t from $\mathbb{D}_{c,l}$ by max pooling (Eq. 6.10)
5:   **end**
6:   Generate the sets $\mathbb{D}_{l-1}$ and $\mathbb{D}_{c,l-1}$
7:   Calculate the matrix $\mathbf{W}_l$ based on Eq. 6.11
8:   Calculate $\mathbf{S}_{l-1}$ using Eq. 6.12
9: **end**

6.3.2.2 Representative Image Selection

Current web pages always contain multimodal information, such as text, image, and video. This work mainly focuses on news images. To give users a vivid and rich overview about their interested news, we summarize news images corresponding to a certain topic or subtopic, which is a complement of the above textual summarization.

Given the uncovered hierarchical topics, we can assemble news images included in certain news pages corresponding to each topic since news images are associated with news documents. From the assembled image set corresponding to one topic, a representative image is selected to visualize the textual information of the topic. In order to provide informative visual information to user, we also propose to deform the selected image to keep important object (e.g., news person) as much as possible. The details will be introduced as follows.

An event is composed of a connected series of sub-events with a common focus or purpose that happens in specific places during a given temporal period. The sub-event associated with more images is more important and more representative for the event. As a consequence, we cluster images belonging to the same topic into several groups and then choose one most representative image from the biggest group to describe the topic, which will be introduced in details as follows. First, images belonging to the same topic are clustered into several groups. Since news images belonging to the same sub-event are semantically similar and often visually similar, the near-duplicate detection algorithm is introduced to identify the semantically and visually similar group. For this purpose, the scale-rotation invariant pattern entropy (SR-PE) algorithm [34] is used in this work[7] to detect the very similar images and segment the corpus into several groups. SR-PE can evaluate complex patterns composed of near-duplicate images under unknown scale and rotation changes based on bag-of-visual word (BoW) scheme, which can enable the task of news topic tracking. In this practical framework, three components, i.e., bag-of-words representation, local keypoint matching, and SR-PE evaluation, are jointly exploited for the rapid detection of near-duplicates. Specially, near-duplicate (ND) pairs are first identified through the pattern entropy measure based on the observation that near-duplicate pairs share the duplication of regions and non-ND pairs often show random patterns. Besides the consideration of scaling and rotational effects, SR-PE utilizes mean-shift to cluster visual near-duplicate images. As a result, the corpus of images is segmented into several groups $\mathbb{G}_r, r = 1, 2, \ldots, m$, where m is the number of groups in total. For simplicity, a simple strategy is introduced in this work to identify the representative image for each topic. The biggest group $r^* = \arg\max_r |\mathbb{G}_r|$ is chosen to visually represent this topic, where $|\mathbb{G}_r|$ denotes the number of images within $\mathbb{G}_r$. For the selected group $\mathbb{G}_{r^*}$, the pairwise similarity is calculated using the Gaussian kernel and then the graph is constructed. Based on the graph, the degree of each image is calculated by adding all the similarities between this image and other images in the group. Finally, the image with the biggest score is selected by max pooling to be the representative image.

On the other hand, we should downsize the representative images with little information loss. Specifically, an image patch-based method is adopted to summarize each image, and the summary image should satisfy two properties: it should contain as much as possible visual information from the original image and should introduce as few as possible artifacts that were not in the original image. As we know, news images always contain the persons related to the news and people are always more important than other objects in the news. We should guarantee to change the human facial parts as little as possible. Consequently, we first make use of face detection method [20] to detect the facial parts. And then we introduce "importance weights" as

---

[7]Code is available at http://pami.xmu.edu.cn/~wlzhao/sotu.htm.

$$\omega_v = \begin{cases} 1.0 & \text{if } area(v_f) > 0.5 * area(v) \\ 0.4 & \text{otherwise} \end{cases} \tag{6.13}$$

where $area(v)$ denotes the area of patch v and v_f denotes the part of patch v corresponding to face. In experiments, the area is measured by the number of pixels. We introduce the importance weights into the objective function in [28]:

$$\min_T \frac{\sum_{v \subset O} \omega_v \cdot \min_{u \subset T} D(v, u)}{\sum_{v \subset O} \omega_v} + \frac{\sum_{u \subset T} \omega_{\hat{v}} \cdot \min_{v \subset O} D(u, v)}{\sum_{u \subset T} \omega_{\hat{v}}}. \tag{6.14}$$

Here, v and u are patches in the original image O and the target image T, respectively. $\hat{v} = \arg\min_{v \subset O} D(u, v)$ and $D(,)$ is a distance measure. We implement the gradual resizing procedure coarse-to-fine within a Gaussian pyramid, which can escape local minima and speeds up convergence. We present several examples of image downsizing in Fig. 6.4, which demonstrate that the utilized approach can achieve the expected goal.

6.3.2.3 Time-Bias Subtopic Linking

We have discovered the hierarchical tree and chosen one representative article and one news image for each topic. How to thread the topics as the presentation of their parent topic is a challenging and necessary problem. We formulate this problem as finding a spanning tree of a graph while considering the time coherence. A spanning tree is a subgraph of the original one, which is a tree that connects all the vertices together. Since the edge represents the similarity between subtopics, a spanning tree with larger weights may have more possibility to be proper. The best choice among

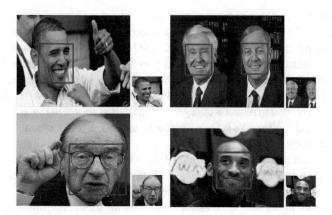

Fig. 6.4 The illustration of image downsizing. There are four groups: the original image with the detected face parts (*the left one*) and the downsized image (*the right one*)

all the spanning tree may be the one with the biggest weights, i.e., the maximum spanning tree (MST) [22], which is a spanning tree with maximum weight. It can be computed by negating the weights for each edge using the faster algorithms [4] with the complexity of $O(E)$, where E is the number of edges in the graph.

The time stamp is an important aspect for news. We should fuse the time information in the spanning process of MST. In this chapter, we propose a naive time-bias MST method. We rewrite the format of time as "YYYYMMDD", such as from "Sep. 12 2010" to "20100912", which is denoted as date. Then, as to news article d and g, we measure their similarity based on date, which is defined as

$$S_{\text{date}}(d, g) = 1 - \frac{|\text{date}(d) - \text{date}(g)|}{\sum_k |\text{date}(d) - \text{date}(k)|}. \qquad (6.15)$$

Then we linearly combine the date similarity and the similarity obtained by weighted aggregation in Sect. 6.3.2.1 as

$$S_{\text{MST}}(d, g) = \xi S_l(d, g) + (1 - \xi) S_{\text{date}}(d, g), \text{ for } d, g \in \mathbb{D}_{c,l-1}, \qquad (6.16)$$

where $\mathbb{D}_{c,l-1}$ is the set of representative articles of the topic at level l on path c, and d and g are the representative articles of its subtopics. In our experiments, we empirically set $\xi = 0.4$ to more rely on the time information.

Based on the weighted graph, we can abstract the spanning tree by incorporating the time information. For each topic, we utilize a time-bias MST to link and place all its subtopics properly.

6.3.3 User Interface Overview

In this section, we introduce the designed interface for multimedia news search and summarization. In our system, we present a summary view apart from a concise result list as shown by many news web services. Our interface contains two parts: the left part and the right part. We put the result list with the top three related news persons and top three related news articles for each item in the right part, which are mined by MPMF [11]. To provide readers a brief and rich view, we present the hierarchical topic structure related to reader's query in the left part as shown in Fig. 6.5. In the both parts, we present multimedia information: text and image information. We elaborate the summary view as follows.

As mentioned above, we adopt the hLDA model to explore the hierarchical topics. In our experiments, we set the depth of the tree to 3. The first level is the root node, the second level is corresponding to topic, and the third level is corresponding to subtopic. In the left view of the interface, we summarize the search results with above obtained hierarchical structure, where each blue rectangle frames the information belonging to a topic. Then we employ the proposed time-bias maximum spanning tree to link the subtopics from left to right. For each subtopic, we present

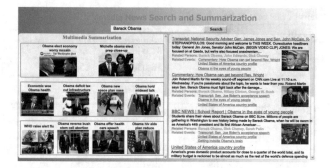

Fig. 6.5 The user interface of our designed system

the keywords of its representative article and the chosen representative image. Here we present an illustrative example of multimedia news summarization in search in Fig. 6.5. We adopt hLDA to explore the hidden topic structure among a modest number (up to 1000) of the top related news articles to the query "Barack Obama" [10]. The representative news article for each topic is identified by the approaches of tree-based article similarity, weighted aggregation, and max pooling. For each topic, the typical image is also chosen to complement the textual content to describe this topic. Finally, we utilize the time-bias MST to thread the subtopics of each topic.

Through the multimedia news summarization, we present the text summary and image summary in a hierarchical structure. Online news readers can browse news conveniently and access the desired information quickly and comprehensively.

6.4 Performance Evaluation

In this section, we introduce our news data set collected from multiple websites for the experimental verification. The objective of our experiments is to examine the effectiveness of our methods, which aim to provide online news readers a friendly, vivid, and compact interface. We fist explain the data set and the experimental settings in this section and then present experimental results by empirical justification.

6.4.1 Data Sets and Experimental Settings

We build a large-scale multimedia news data set collected from four news websites, including ABCNews.com,[8] BBC.co.uk,[9] CNN.com[10] and Google News. There are 135,308 news articles and 69,144 news images in total, whose distribution over

---

[8]http://abcnews.go.com.

[9]http://www.bbc.co.uk/news.

[10]http://edition.cnn.com.

Table 6.1 Details of our web news data set

Web site	ABC	BBC	CNN	Google	Total
#[articles]	47,163	11,073	41,649	35,423	135,308
#[images]	31,789	5309	16,636	15,410	69,144

Table 6.2 The graded score criterion

Degree of satisfaction	Score
Totally dissatisfied	1
A little bit satisfied	2
Satisfied	3
More satisfied	4
Very satisfied	5

these four websites is shown in Table 6.1. Considering that the person's name has the relative definitiveness and the meaning presented by one news event is usually broad, we mainly employ the person's name as query in our experiments for the convenience of experiment evaluation. It is worth noting that for our proposed approaches, there is no limited for the query, which can be persons' names and news events. We choose 180 personalities from multiple domains, such as politics, sports, business and so on, to conduct our experiments.

No well-defined ground-truth data set can be used to evaluate the performance of multimedia news summarization. Thus, we invite a group of 30 anonymous participants from two counties with a wide range of ages, to evaluate the news summarization and the interface. The group of participants consists of Ph. D. students, researchers and technical staff, who declared that they were proficient in English and always read news online. They were asked to freely choose queries and search news. As defined in Table 6.2, the participators can present five types of graded relevance according to their satisfactions about the results.

In addition, there are some parameters to be set in advance. For the parameters in hLDA, we set $\alpha = 50$ and $L = 3$ and will discuss the parameters η and γ. For each query, we choose the top 1000 related news articles for multimedia news summarization. Each participant is asked to randomly choose three persons' names from our data set to search. There are 70 queries in total selected from the 180 queries and we present these 70 queries in Table 6.3. Besides, queries are selected from the rest queries to tune the hyper-parameters in our methods.

6.4.2 Parameter Sensitiveness

In hLDA, there exists two important parameters η and γ, which affect the number of topics. Here, their impacts for our summarization task are studied. The corpus of related news articles to each query is used to discover topics and record the number of topics for each query. We average the total number of generated topics and shown results for different values of η and γ in Tables 6.4 and 6.5. It can be observed

Table 6.3 The query list used in the experiments

Andy Murray	Andy Roddick	Angela Merkel	Barack Obama
Bill Gates	Bobby Dall	Bret Michaels	C.C. Deville
Carl Lewis	Carlo Ancelotti	Charlie Sheen	Chen Kaige
Cheryl Cole	Colin Powell	Dara Torres	Debbie Rowe
Dwight Howard	Dwyane Wade	Elena Dementieva	Eli Roth
George Soros	George W. Bush	Gerhard Schroeder	Ian Crocker
James Blake	Janet Jackson	Jason Lezak	Jerry Springer
John Sculley	Ju Dou	Justine Henin	Karl Malone
Kill Bill	Landon Donovan	Larry Ellison	Lebron James
Li Kaifu	Ma Huateng	Mariah Carey	Martin Bashir
Michael Dell	Michael Johnson	Michael Phelps	Michelle Obama
Michelle Yeoh	Novak Djokovic	Paul Allen	Pete Sampras
Quincy Jones	Ray Ozzie	Rikki Rockett	Robert Rodriguez
Scottie Pippen	Serena Williams	Sharon Osbourne	Simon Cowell
Steve Ballmer	Steve Jobs	Steve Nash	Steve Wozniak
Toni Kukoc	Tracy Mcgrady	Tyson Gay	Usain Bolt
Victoria Beckham	Virginie Razzano	Wayne Rooney	Whitney Houston
William Hague	Wim Duisenberg		

Table 6.4 Average number of topics per query from hLDA for different η under $L = 3$ and $\gamma = 1.0$

η	0.5	1.0	2.0	5.0	10
#[topics]	187	41	23	7	4

Table 6.5 Average number of topics per query from hLDA for different γ under $L = 3$ and $\eta = 2.0$

γ	0.1	0.5	1.0	5.0	10
#[topics]	3	8	23	79	485

that small values of γ and large values of β suppress the number of topics. hLDA generates less topics with larger η and smaller γ, and more topics with smaller η and larger γ. When $\eta = 2.0$ and $\gamma = 1.0$, reasonable number of topics is generated and we set $\eta = 2.0$ and $\gamma = 1.0$ in the rest of the experiments.

Besides, the parameter ε balances the importance of similarities based on the textual information and the hierarchical tree. In these experiments, we tune it within the range of $\{0, 0.2, 0.4, 0.5, 0.6, 0.8, 1.0\}$. The performance in terms of participants' satisfactions by varying ε is presented in Table 6.6. When $\varepsilon = 0$ or $\varepsilon = 1$, users are not satisfied with the summarizations. The average score of participants' satisfactions achieves the best value when $\varepsilon = 0.5$. Thus, ε is set to 0.5 in our experiments.

Table 6.6 Average score of participants' satisfactions for different values of ε

ε	0	0.2	0.4	0.5	0.6	0.8	1.0
Average score	3.63	3.65	3.73	3.82	3.77	3.69	3.58

6.4.3   Summarization Evaluations

In this subsection, we evaluate the performance of multimedia news summarization and compare our approaches with other related methods. To evaluate the performance of news summarization, these participants are asked to give scores about the results according to Table 6.2. Each of them is asked to select three queries and determine their satisfactions with the returned results.

Experiment 1: On representative news article selection

To validate that our method is effective to discover the representative article for each topic, we compare our approach with the following methods:

- **LDA** [2]: LDA with different cluster numbers ($K = 5, 15, 50$). The article with the biggest score calculated by similar formula as Eq. 6.9 based on $\mathbf{S}^{text}$ is selected.
- **hLDA-t**: hLDA based on $\mathbf{S}^{text}$ to find representative news articles without weighted aggregation.
- **SUMMA** [6]: A hierarchical summarization system which summarizes multiple documents based on sentences.

We compare these methods in terms of the conciseness and comprehensiveness of their obtained summarization. Each participant gives the graded score for each approach. Figure 6.6 presents the average scores. Besides the above methods, other special cases of our approach, i.e., **hLDA-w** ($\varepsilon = 1$ in Eq. 6.3 in our method.) and **Tree** (Representative articles are selected without weighted aggregation in our method.), are also evaluated. The performance of hLDA-based approaches and SUMMA are superior to LDA, which indicates advantages of the hierarchical

Fig. 6.6 The comparative results for representative news selection. The average scores are shown for these approaches

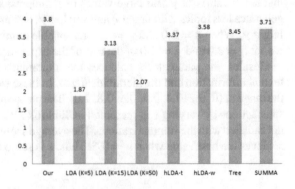

topics. Since LDA assigns the same topic number to all queries, it is not reasonable and cannot achieve good average performance. In addition, our method remarkably outperform hLDA-t, demonstrating the effectiveness of similarity based on the hierarchical tree and weighted aggregation. Users prefer our summarization results to SUMMA since our method can provide a more comprehensive result. In addition, the improved performance of our method over tree shows the importance and effectiveness of the proposed weighted aggregation. Without considering the tree-based similarity, hLDA-w is inferior to the proposed method. Thus, all aspects in our method for representative news article selection, i.e., text-based similarity, tree-based similarity and weighted aggregation, are helpful for our system.

We also conduct experiments to compare our approach with LDA ($K = 15$), which achieves the best performance among the LDA-based methods, and hLDA-t in terms of the summary reasonableness. In each pairwise comparison, participants are allowed to freely search with persons' names, and compare the returned summarized results. They can choose "better", "much better", and "comparable" options for the comparison of two ranking schemes. We quantize the results as follows. We assign score 1 to the worse ranking scheme and the other scheme is assigned a score 2, 3, 1 if it is better, much better and comparable to this one, respectively. Thus, there are 30 ratings for each comparison. The average rating scores and the standard deviation values are shown in Tables 6.7, 6.8 and 6.9. Since there will be disagreements among the evaluators, we perform a two-way analysis of variance (ANOVA) test [9] to statistically analyze the comparison and the results are also shown in the tables. From the results, it is observed that users obviously prefer our approach and the performance of our method statistically significantly outperforms others. The p values show that the difference of the two schemes is significant, and the difference of users is insignificant.

Table 6.7 The left part illustrates the average and standard deviation values converted from the user study on the comparison of our methods and LDA ($K = 15$) for representative news article selection. The right part shows the ANOVA test results

Our approach versus LDA ($K = 15$)		The factor of ranking scheme		The factor of users	
Our method	LDA ($K = 15$)	F-statistic	p value	F-statistic	p value
1.933 ± 0.449	1.100 ± 0.305	42.647	3.758×10^{-6}	0.209	1.000

Table 6.8 The left part illustrates the average and standard deviation values converted from the user study on the comparison of our methods and hLDA-t for representative news article selection. The right part illustrates the ANOVA test results

Our approach versus hLDA-t		The factor of ranking scheme		The factor of users	
Our method	hLDA-t	F-statistic	p value	F-statistic	p value
1.967 ± 0.615	1.200 ± 0.407	18.686	1.656×10^{-4}	0.152	1.000

Table 6.9 The left part illustrates the average and standard deviation values converted from the user study on the comparison of our methods and SUMMA. The right part illustrates the ANOVA test results

Our approach versus SUMMA		The factor of ranking scheme		The factor of users	
Our method	SUMMA	F-statistic	p value	F-statistic	p value
1.933 ± 0.640	1.233 ± 0.504	13.198	1.100×10^{-3}	0.191	1.000

Fig. 6.7 The average scores of our approach, naive selection, and random selection for representative image selection

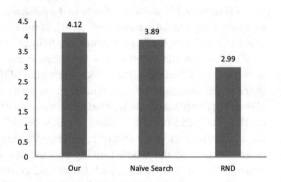

Experiment 2: On representative image selection

We conduct experiments to evaluate the performance of our approach to choose image for each topic. Our method is compared with the following two methods:

- NS (Naive selection): The image corresponding to the selected representative news article is chosen for one topic;
- RND (Random): A representative image is randomly selected from the corpus of images of one topic.

These methods are tested in terms of understandability of the selected image, that is, the selected image is helpful to understand the content of the topic. The comparative results are shown in Fig. 6.7. The superiority of our approach is obviously observed.

Similar to Experiment 1, we also compare our method with the other two approaches and perform ANOVA by conducting the same process. Tables 6.10 and 6.11 illustrate the mean and standard deviations of the rating scores as well as the ANOVA rest results. From the numbers in the tables we can see that the results of the representative image selection by our method is the best and the difference is statistically significant, which further confirms the effectiveness of our approach.

Experiment 3: On subtopic linking

The organization of topics is necessary for presenting the summarized results to users. The topic linking can be regarded as a ranking problem. To indicate the effectiveness of our proposed time-bias MST, it is compared with the method **TimeLink**, which links the subtopics of one topic purely based on the time information.

Table 6.10 The left part illustrates the average and standard deviation values converted from the user study on the comparison of our methods and Naive Selection for representative news image selection. The right part illustrates the ANOVA test results

Our approach versus NS		The factor of ranking scheme		The factor of users	
Our method	NS	F-statistic	p value	F-statistic	p value
1.867 ± 0.629	1.200 ± 0.407	14.500	6.723×10^{-4}	0.220	0.9999

Table 6.11 The left part illustrates the average and standard deviation values converted from the user study on the comparison of our methods and RND for representative news image selection. The right part illustrates the ANOVA test results

Our approach versus RND		The factor of ranking scheme		The factor of users	
Our method	RND	F-statistic	p value	F-statistic	p value
2.400 ± 0.455	1.133 ± 0.217	46.740	2.500×10^{-11}	0.250	0.999

Table 6.12 The left part illustrates the average and standard deviation values converted from the user study on the comparison of our methods and TimeLink for subtopic linking. The right part illustrates the ANOVA test results

Our approach versus TimeLink		The factor of ranking scheme		The factor of users	
Our method	TimeLink	F-statistic	p value	F-statistic	p value
1.970 ± 0.243	1.133 ± 0.195	33.263	3.02×10^{-6}	0.150	1.000

These participants are asked to give scores about the reasonableness of topic linking and averaged scores of our approach and TimeLink are 4.06 and 3.67 respectively. This indicates the effectiveness of our subtopic linking approach.

We conduct another user study with the same 30 participants and the process introduced in experiment 1 to compare these two linking schemes. The mean and standard deviations of the rating scores as well as the ANOVA test results are illustrated in Table 6.12. The results demonstrate the superiority of our approach over TimeLink. The ANOVA test shows the superiority is statistically significant and the difference of the evaluators is not significant.

6.4.4 Interface Evaluations

In our news retrieval system, we develop a new style interface as shown in Fig. 6.5. In this experiment, we evaluate the performance of our interface from a subjective view and compare it with other systems. While browsing results of the queries, each participant is asked to give scores according to Table 6.2 based on the following aspects:

- *Convenience*: The convenience of retrieval system is important for users to browse the results. Is it convenient to search and browse the news?
- *Efficiency*: Efficiency is a typical problem for retrieval system. Users cannot tolerate much time to wait for the results returned. How long do the systems cost to return results for each query?
- *Friendliness*: Users like web pages that make them comfortable. Do the users enjoy the interface? Does the interface seem comfortable?
- *Diversity*: Do the systems show users many kinds of information? Can they present users multi-view effectively?
- *Quick OverView*: News readers want to understand what they are interested in as quickly as possible. Do the systems provide news readers quick overviews?
- *Summary Effectiveness*: We should examine the summary's usefulness with respect to news retrieval. To what degree does it affect the effectiveness of news retrieval?

The average scores are presented in Fig. 6.8. It can be observed that compared with other news service websites, although our system costs a little more time to return the results to readers, it can provide readers multimedia information, more condensed view as well as a convenient and friendly interface. That is to say, users prefer the interface of our system and our system can present vivid and comprehensive information conveniently. Through the multimedia information, readers are provided a vivid overview about the returned results. Readers can quickly understand the information they require via the multimedia summarization in our system. Besides, the runtime is also compared. Unfortunately, it is not convenient to accurately obtain the average runtime for each query in the Timeline, Fastflip, and Correlator systems. Thus, we only present the runtime of our system and MMPNR. For each query, the average times of our system and MMPNR are 2.24 and 1.96s, respectively. It indicates that our system is practical. In fact, our system can be speeded up by further optimizing the software.

Fig. 6.8 The mean scores about the interfaces of several systems

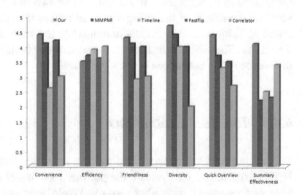

6.5 Discussions

In this chapter, we focus on designing an understanding-oriented multimedia news summarization system, in which the query-related news multimedia information is summarized to provide online news readers a brief and vivid browsing view. The element of "How" is enhanced by uncovering the latent topic structure to present an informative and complete news story including news origin, developing process, and its result about certain news subject.

The idea of exploring multimedia information and the "4W1H" elements actually opens up possibilities to a very interesting direction. Multimedia research under news search circumstances may understand not only text and image, but video and audio knowledge. A combination of all multimodal data may be better, which can provide news readers another aspect of information. On the other hand, the user is the essential factor of all the multimedia tasks. The goal of understanding-oriented multimedia tasks is to meet users' demand. Consequently, user's preference should be taken into account. People involve with the online multimedia information in a variety of ways, such as comments about a certain news document, and interaction with social websites. The understanding-oriented multimedia services should interact with user's behaviors. According to different users, different results should be provided. Taking news retrieval for example, users' behaviors in SinaWeibo and Google+ can be jointly analyzed for the news search service.

References

1. Blei, D.M., Griffiths, T.L., Jordan, M.I.: The nested Chinese restaurant process and bayesian nonparametric inference of topic hierarchical. J. ACM **57**(2), 1–30 (2010)
2. Blei, D.M., Ng, A.Y., Jordan, M.I.: Latent dirichlet allocation. J. Mach. Learn. Res. **3**(4–5), 993–1022 (2003)
3. Celikyilmaz, A., Hakkani-Yur, D.: A hybrid hierarchical model for multi-document summarization. In: Proceeding of Annual Meeting of the Association for Computational Linguistic, pp. 815–824 (2010)
4. Chazelle, B.: A minimum spanning tree algorithm with inverse-Ackermann type complexity. J. Assoc. Comput. Mach. **47**(6), 1028–1047 (2000)
5. Chen, Y., Zhang, B., Zhang, H.J.: Weighted aggregation based clustering algorithm for blog tag taxonomy construction. J. Chin. Comput. Syst. **30**(7), 1293–1297 (2009)
6. Soderland, J.C.S., Mausam, G.B.: Hierarchical summarization: scaling up multi-document summarization. In: Proceedings of Annual Meeting of the Association for Computational Linguistics, pp. 902–912 (2014)
7. Hofmann, T.: Probabilistic latent semantic indexing. In: Proceedings of ACM SIGIR Conference on Research and Development in Information Retrieval, pp. 50–57 (1999)
8. Jiao, B., Yang, L., Xu, J., Tian, Q., Wu, F.: Visually summarizing web pages through internal and external images. IEEE Trans. Multimed. **14**(6), 1673–1683 (2012)
9. King, B.M., Minium, E.M.: Statistical Reasoning in Psychology and Education. Wiley, New York (1999)
10. Lau, J.H., Baldwin, T., Newman, D.: On collocations and topic models. ACM Trans. Speech Lang. Process. **10**(3), 10 (2013)

11. Li, Z., Liu, J., Zhu, X., Lu, H.: Multi-modal multi-correlation person-centric news retrieval. In: Proceedings of ACM International Conference on Information and Knowledge Management, pp. 179–188 (2010)

12. Li, Z., Tang, J., Wang, X., Liu, J., Lu, H.: Multimedia news summarization in search. ACM Trans. Intell. Syst. Technol. **7**(3), 33:1–33:30 (2016)

13. Li, Z., Wang, M., Liu, J., Xu, C., Lu, H.: News contextualization with geographic and visual information. In: Proceedings of ACM International Conference on Multimedia, pp. 133–142 (2011)

14. Lin, J.: Divergence measures based on the Shannon entropy. IEEE Trans. Inf. Theory **37**(1), 145–151 (1991)

15. Mani, I., Bloedorn, E.: Multi-document summarization by graph search and matching. In: Proceedings of AAAI Conference on Artificial Intelligence, pp. 622–628. AAAI Press, Providence (1997)

16. Mani, I., Maybury, M.: Advances in Automatic Text Summarization. MIT Press, Cambridge (1999)

17. Manning, C., Schütze, H.: Foundations of Statistical Natural Language Processing. MIT Press, Cambridge (1999)

18. McKeown, K.R., Barzilay, R., Evans, D., Hatzivassiloglou, V., Klavans, J.L., Nenkova, A., Sable, C., Schiffman, B., Sigelman, S.: Tracking and summarizing news on a daily basis with Columbias newsblaster. In: Proceedings of Human Language Technology Conference, pp. 280–285 (2002)

19. Neto, J.L., Santos, A.D., Kaestner, C.A., Alexandre, N., Santos, D., A, C.A., Alex, K., Freitas, A.A., Parana, C.: Document clustering and text summarization. In: Proceedings of Internatgional Conference on Practical Applications of Knowledge Discovery and Data Mining, pp. 41–55 (2000)

20. Nilsson, M., Nordberg, J., Claesson, I.: Face detection using local smqt features and split up snow classifier. In: Proceedings of IEEE International Conference on Acoustics, Speech, and Signal Processing, pp. 589–592 (2007)

21. Paice, C.D.: Constructing literature abstracts by computer: techniques and prospects. Inf. Process. Manag. **26**(1), 171–186 (1990)

22. Pemmaraju, S., Skiena, S.: Computational Discrete Mathematics: Combinatorics and Graph Theory in Mathematica. Cambridge University Press, Cambridge (2003)

23. Radev, D.: A common theory of information fusion from multiple sources step one: cross-document structure. In: Proceedings of ACL SIGDIAL workshop on Discourse and Dialogue, pp. 74–83 (2000)

24. Radev, D., Otterbacher, J., Winkel, A., Blair-Goldensohn, S.: Newsinessence: summarizing online news topics. Commun. ACM **48**(10), 95–98 (2005)

25. Radev, D.R., Blair-Goldensohn, S., Zhang, Z., Raghavan, R.S.: Interactive, domain-independent identification and summarization of topically related news articles. In: Proceedings of European Conference on Research and Advanced Technology for Digital Libraries, pp. 225–238 (2001)

26. Radev, D.R., Fan, W.: Automatic summarization of search engine hit lists. In: Proceedings of ACL Workshop on Recent Advances in Natural Language Processing and Information Retrieval, pp. 99–109 (2000)

27. Radev, D.R., McKeown, K.R.: Generating natural language summaries from multiple on-line sources. Comput. Linguist. **24**(3), 469–500 (1999)

28. Simakov, D., Caspi, Y., Shechtman, E., Irani, M.: Summarizing visual data using bidirectional similarity. In: Proceedings of IEEE Conference on Computer Vision and Pattern Recognition, pp. 1–8 (2008)

29. Tran, G.B.: Structured summarization for news events. In: Proceedings of International Conference on World Wide Web, pp. 343–348 (2013)

30. Trieschnigg, D., Kraaij, W.: Tno hierarchical topic detection report at tdt2004. Topic Detection and Tracking Workshop (2004)

31. Trieschnigg, D., Kraaij, W.: Scalable hierarchical topic detection. In: Proceedings of ACM SIGIR Conference on Research and Development in Information Retrieval, pp. 655–656 (2005)
32. Tuan, T.A., Elbassuoni, S., Preda, N., Weikum, G.: Cate: Context-aware timeline for entity illustration. In: Proceedings of International Conference on World Wide Web, pp. 269–272 (2011)
33. Yan, R., Wan, X., Otterbacher, J., Kong, L., Li, X., Zhang, Y.: Evolutionary timeline summarization: a balanced optimization framework via iterative substitution. In: Proceedings of ACM International Conference on Research and development in Information Retrieval, pp. 745–754 (2011)
34. Zhao, W.L., Ngo, C.W.: Scale-rotation invariant pattern entropy for keypoint-based near-duplicate detection. IEEE Trans. Image Process. **18**(2), 412–423 (2009)

Chapter 7
Conclusion

Abstract Recent years have witnessed the rapid popularity of multimedia generation and social multimedia. Multimedia data have the big, social, and heterogeneous characters, which have posed challenges to multimedia content analysis and applications. In this book, we have introduced our research on understanding-oriented multimedia content analysis and applications. It involves with understanding-oriented multimedia data representation, personalized tag recommendation, and understanding-oriented multimedia news search and summarization. Understanding-oriented multimedia content analysis still has a long way to go. We will present several promising topics and prospects in the following.

7.1 Promising Topics

Toward the goal of multimedia content understanding, we have conducted exploratory work in understanding-oriented multimedia content analysis. Multimedia content analysis is a cross-discipline research area with significant application potentials. It involves with theoretical and technological findings from data mining, sociology, psychological theory, human–computer interaction, etc. Challenges as well as opportunities remain in both methodology innovation and practical application development.

Based on the methodological discussions and the investigation about recent developments, we foresee several research lines in the future work of multimedia content analysis and understanding.

- **Deep Integration of Heterogeneous Information**. Current multimedia data involve with many types of information, such as text, image, video and GPS, and user interactions, e.g., as user-provided tags, comments, groups, descriptions, owners. Besides, users are active in various social media networks. It is necessary to deeply integrate the heterogenous information for better understanding. Besides, how to effectively analyze the cross-network activities remains further investigation for understanding-oriented multimedia content analysis.
- **Big Multimedia Understanding**. Multimedia is increasingly becoming the "biggest big dat", which brings in new challenges. It may take much time to

Z. Li, *Understanding-Oriented Multimedia Content Analysis*, Springer Theses,
DOI 10.1007/978-981-10-3689-7_7

analyze the big multimedia data. And it is difficult to learn an effective and efficient model for big multimedia data analysis and understanding. Therefore, how to effectively and efficiently understand the big multimedia understanding still has a long way to go. High-throughput multimedia computing may be a research direction.

- **Social Multimedia Analysis**. Social multimedia data have been the major multimedia data, which introduce an important role, i.e., the user. Users conduct various activities in social media websites, which naturally indicate their preferences and can be used for user profile construction. Users' activities are helpful for many understanding-oriented applications, such as personal multimedia management and personal product recommendation. They also bring in benefits for traditional multimedia analysis and understanding.

7.2   The Prospects

Throughout the book, we have interpreted the characteristics of the multimedia data, and introduced our researches toward understanding-oriented multimedia content analysis, including understanding-oriented unsupervised feature selection, understanding-oriented feature representation, personalized tag recommendation, and understanding-oriented multimedia news services. We end this book with two more claims on the current multimedia data.

User is becoming an essential role. Currently, multimedia data are almost generated and consumed under social media circumstances. As an important role, user can connect the physical space, social space, and cyberspace. Cyber-Physical-Social (CPS) computing is attracting attention. User is the provider of multimedia data and also the ultimate information service target of multimedia applications. Information from multiple sources can be connected by the user. Cross-media information from physical and cyber spaces is associated by the involved users and the social interactions between users. If all the information is integrated according to the user, we can obtain a whole view about the desired target. Better understanding-oriented multimedia applications can be provided to users.

Unsupervised multimedia understanding is attractive. Deep learning has become a dominant technology for multimedia analysis, computer vision, and pattern recognition, due to its supervising performance. It needs a large-scale data set to train networks with multiple layers. The large-scale training data are very expensive. ImageNet is always used to pre-train the networks and then the pre-trained networks are fine-tuned. That is, it needs the supervision during the learning procedure, which is different for multimedia tasks, especially in the era of big data. Unsupervised multimedia understanding methods, especially the unsupervised deep learning models, are the main direction of future work.

Printed in the United States
By Bookmasters